Training for Transformation in Practice

Praise for this book

'This volume re-fires popular and community educators with vivid depictions of experiences and methods to inspire new approaches to transforming inequalities. It invites thought-provoking and creative introspection while challenging practices of power. It shows why Training for Transformation has sustained popular educators around the world for over 40 years.'

Shirley Walters, professor of adult and continuing education,
University of Western Cape, South Africa

'Reading these rich and diverse stories, I am invited to decentralize my Western, male and middle-class point of view. This book helps me to make an ethical and spiritual assessment of my work as an educator and academic. I will keep it close.'

Dr Dominiek Lootens, educator in pastoral care and counseling,
Caritas, Belgium, and lecturer in spiritual leadership and organizational
change, Philosophisch-Theologische Hochschule in Vallendar, Germany

'Training for Transformation is the most beautiful expression of development sector thinking I have ever encountered. It perfectly synthesizes principle and practice, and in so doing bypasses ideology. I believe that the enduring impact of Training for Transformation is because ordinary people recognize – and are inspired by – such a call to action.'

Daryl McLean, development practitioner, South Africa

'*Training for Transformation in Practice* brings together the vivid personal accounts of how a particular method and approach transforms lives. The method combines creatively the "psycho-social" method of Paulo Freire with theories of personal and interpersonal development. The outcome is empowerment and liberation for people.'

Dr Noel Bradley, Social Health Education Project,
Cork, Republic of Ireland

Training for Transformation in Practice

Edited by
Anne E. Hope and Sally J. Timmel

PRACTICAL ACTION
Publishing

Practical Action Publishing Ltd
The Schumacher Centre
Bourton on Dunsmore, Rugby,
Warwickshire CV23 9QZ, UK
www.practicalactionpublishing.org

ISBN 978-1-85339-831-5 Hardback
ISBN 978-1-85339-832-2 Paperback
ISBN 978-1-78044-831-2 Library Ebook
ISBN 978-1-78044-832-9 Ebook

A catalogue record for this book is available from the British Library.

The contributors have asserted their rights under the Copyright, Designs and
Patents Act 1988 to be identified as authors of their respective contributions.

Hope, A.E. and Timmel, S.J. (eds) (2014) *Training for Transformation in Practice*,
Rugby, UK: Practical Action Publishing <http://dx.doi.org/10.3362/9781780448312.000>.

Since 1974, Practical Action Publishing has published and disseminated books and
information in support of international development work throughout the world.
Practical Action Publishing is a trading name of Practical Action Publishing Ltd
(Company Reg. No. 1159018), the wholly owned publishing company of Practical
Action. Practical Action Publishing trades only in support of its parent charity
objectives and any profits are covenanted back to Practical Action
(Charity Reg. No. 247257, Group VAT Reg. No. 880 9924 76).

Cover photo by Ginoca Inês Neto, The Grail Centre
Cover design by Mercer Design
Typeset by Allzone Digital

Printed in India by Replika Press Pvt. Ltd

Contents

http://dx.doi.org/10.3362/9781780448312.000

Foreword

When *Training for Transformation* was first published, it generated a conversation between and among activists who were searching for tools through which to envision the future: a future that was non-sexist, non-racist, and free. The critical thinking that the books provoked ensured a rich conversation that exposed that there are no easy answers to the questions of transformation. This initiated a continuing learning process that allowed for a people to grow together and ask new questions.

This new book continues the journey towards transforming rather than to a transformed society. The stories in it illustrate how Training for Transformation has been adapted in India, Ireland, Rwanda, Papua-Indonesia and different countries in Africa, including my own home country, South Africa, and they all show us how challenging, flexible, and life-giving this approach can be. In widely different contexts and cultures, it has evoked strong creative leadership and deep commitment, sometimes bringing about major changes at both the cultural and legal levels. It encourages us on our own journeys and should be an inspiration to all those who are striving to enable marginalized communities to improve the quality of their own lives.

The Training for Transformation 'then and now' shows us that it is important to invest in a good journey rather than hurrying to arrive at the destination. Enjoy reading about the wonderful work that continues to emerge from Training for Transformation.

Phumzile Mlambo-Ngcuka, Executive Director of UN Women
Former Deputy President of South Africa

Preface

Training for Transformation is based on a philosophy of justice that seeks the common good. It has developed a very practical process enabling people to understand and take action in their world. As we look at our reality, and ask the 'but why?' questions, we come to see how many aspects of our situations are connected. For example, if lack of housing is the major concern, we discover how this is affected by economic structures, and these are linked to gender and the environment. Those concerns are all linked to power, and that challenges us to advocacy, and this affects our understanding of nonviolence. The connections continue like ripples moving on and on. Paulo Freire's methodology, which engages practitioners and participants to 'read our reality, and write our own history', becomes a lifelong journey. Our local, national, and global realities change all the time. Life itself – and our approaches to life – are not static. Routine solutions will not do.

Over the years, this work has grown to include many disciplines. Building on Freire's approach, Anne Hope and Sally Timmel incorporated a number of participatory education methods, social/economic analyses, organizational development, and spiritual commitment into a more holistic approach to community development. Since its inception 40 years ago, it has been put into practice in over 60 countries globally. Training for Transformation recognizes the importance of linking local and national initiatives to global civic movements. It is aimed at those concerned with the process of transforming societies.

In 2002, the work was developed into a one-year in-service diploma course, based on the four *Training for Transformation* manuals. Many recognize that the need for a new generation of ethical leadership is urgent, as our social, political, and economic realities become more complex. We believe that leadership is developed through praxis: cycles of action and reflection, which enable people to sustain their commitment to the common good, and to see that all of humankind 'are our neighbours'. Since 2002, the Training for Transformation course has trained more than 350 development trainers/organizers from 106 organizations and 18 countries.

In 2013, the staff of the Training for Transformation programme brought together 37 practitioners from 26 countries to reflect on the ways in which they had adapted this approach to transformation. This 'Think Well' (versus 'think tank') allowed space for 17 of the participants to write a chapter about how they had adapted the work in their own social and cultural context. (People who were not at the 'Think Well' but whose work is particularly interesting were also asked to contribute.) The other participants formed work groups to develop the impact assessment tools found at the end of this book.

This book is a down-to-earth account of trials and errors, traumas and triumphs. The chapters that follow show how this methodology is both a humbling and at the same time intensely creative process. These stories help to give educators inspiration in demanding circumstances and courage to step out of the conventional box to stimulate bursts of new energies, some of which may spread like wildfire.

CHAPTER 1
Introduction:
A history of Training for Transformation

Anne Hope and Sally Timmel

The Training for Transformation (TfT) philosophy and approach to community development grew out of a number of value systems and fields of study. Much of the original work was written by Anne Hope and Sally Timmel, who wrote clearly on the topics discussed. The reason the TfT books have been as popular as they have been might be that they were written in accessible English. In this brief history, we summarize: the content, or the 'why' and 'what' that form the basis of TfT; the historical context in which this approach was developed; how this approach was put into practice, both on a strategic level and practically on a local level by the authors; and how the learning from initial programmes was put into practice.

 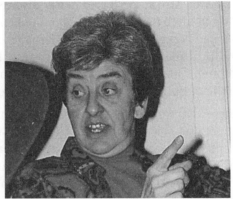

Keep your eyes on your destination and not where you stumbled.   *Nigerian proverb*

The roots of Training for Transformation: spiritual, intellectual, and experiential

The taproot of Training for Transformation's (TfT's) approach to development comes from the authors' own spiritual search. Anne Hope came from a South African urban background with rich international experience of Roman Catholic social teaching. Sally Timmel came from a small town in the United States, with her Lutheran Church formation extended by Protestant influences at college, the Peace Corps in Ethiopia, and the student YWCA.

Living out one's faith 'in the world', responding to the cries of those on the margins, drew both Anne and Sally to a common cause, and their bond within the International Grail cemented the partnership.

The Grail is an international ecumenical women's movement that began in 1921 in Holland. It was a strong Catholic women's movement in Europe before World War II but was driven underground by the Nazi regime. After the war, it transformed itself into an international Catholic women's movement responding to urgent human needs in over 25 countries. The Grail set up girls' schools, hospitals, clinics, training centres, and community development programmes with local women.

http://dx.doi.org/10.3362/9781780448312.001

In the 1960s, the Grail was involved in processes leading to the transformation of the Catholic church in Vatican II. Many theologians at that time were instrumental in opening up the Catholic church to active engagement in society and to dialogue with other Christian faiths. The Grail had been experimenting with different types of religious ritual, and now opened its membership to include other women, especially Protestant women, seeking a spiritual community. New programmes began.

Anne had been involved in the Grail since 1954. She taught for four years in a girls' high school in a rural village in Uganda and became involved in adult education. She was inspired by Julius Nyerere's vision of education for teenagers and adults, which had the potential to transform the lives of rural communities. She had strong bonds with members of the Grail in Portugal who had worked with Paulo Freire in communities of farmers and fishermen in Brazil and Portugal. She was convinced that his approach could be effective in Africa, and she began to adapt it with Steve Biko for training the leadership of the black South African Student Organisation (SASO).

Sources of inspiration

During our years in Kenya (1973 to 1980), we started the DELTA (Development Education and Leadership Teams in Action) programme there, became interested in the struggles of people throughout the countries of the South to gain political and economic independence and to overcome poverty. We read voraciously, including the new West African literature that was banned in South Africa. We based many discussions on the films of Ousmane Sembène, such as *Xala*, and on Souheil Ben-Barka's *A Thousand and One Hands* and Jean-Louis Bertucelli's *Ramparts of Clay*. We met Ngugi wa Thiong'o, a Kenyan, and worked with Ngugi wa Mirii, who produced Ngugi's political plays in the villages around Limuru. All facilitators attended a performance of Okot p'Bitek's play *Song of Lawino* at the university. It was one of the first literary works to challenge the cultural cost of the current model of development.

Julius Nyerere was president of Tanzania during this period and we continued to watch developments there. Nyerere was a creative thinker and a statesman. He recognized that the policies of dominant development organizations were failing to deal with problems and often made them worse, contributing to the impoverishment of the countries of the South. He was a clear thinker and developed an increasingly sharp analysis. He was constantly searching to find effective solutions, constantly thinking, constantly learning.

Unlike most development thinkers who were working in the offices of their organizations or in academia, Nyerere had the authority as president of Tanzania to put his ideas into practice. The disadvantage of this was that, if any of his ideas did not work, it was obvious, whereas most ineffective ideas remained hidden in the pages of books.

We read a lot about India and China, including Han Suyin's family history – *The Crippled Tree, A Mortal Flower*, and *Birdless Summer* – and her three-volume history of Mao Tse Tung and biography of Zhou Enlai. We were fascinated by William Hinton's account of the transformation of village life after 1949 in *Fanshen*, and by Joshua Horn's account of the transformation of village health services by the 'barefoot' doctors in *Away with All Pests*.

We followed Mahatma Gandhi's role in the early struggle against apartheid in South Africa and then the Salt March in India, which are still models for the world. We read Larry Collins and Dominique Lapierre's book, *Freedom at Midnight,* about the last years of the British Raj in India and the devastating violence in the Punjab and Bengal as India and Pakistan were separated from one another at independence. This brought to life the roles played by Gandhi, Nehru, Jinnah and Mountbatten. We discussed *The Jewel in the Crown* series, and E.M. Forster's *A Passage to India,* and used the *Gandhi* film as a starting point for group discussion. The presence of Xavier Manjooran, Johnny Khanna, and Vally de Sousa, three Indian Jesuits who spent months with the DELTA programme, meant that the Indian experience was included in the search for policies and practices that could contribute to the well-being of the poor. Perhaps most challenging of all were the insights of Walter Rodney in *How Europe Underdeveloped Africa* and Frantz Fanon in *The Wretched of the Earth* and *Black Skin, White Masks*. It became clear to us that South Africa was a microcosm of the wider world. What White South Africa was doing to Black South Africa was reflected on a larger scale in what the rich industrialized world was doing to the countries of the South.

Conviction that transformation is possible

With Paulo Freire coming from Brazil, and the Grail an international movement, the strongest external influence on the training programmes came from Latin America, especially Brazil – initially from Freire, but later from Ivan Illich and Dom Helder Camara. We frequently used a slide show, initiated by Cardinal Arns and Ana Flora Anderson, called *The Journey of a People*; this was about the changes the Basic Christian Communities had brought about in the archdiocese of São Paulo. Two films made by an Irish film company, Radharc, provided inspiration for the DELTA participants. One film, *New Day in Brazil,* was about Basic Christian Communities and showed lay people, nuns, and priests involved in the struggles of the poor. They risked their lives in the face of national state security dictatorships. The other film, *These Men are Dangerous,* was about the prophetic stand taken by bishops such as Dom Helder Camara and Bishop Casaldáliga in direct challenge to unjust government policies. Dom Helder Camara's challenge at the church's Vatican II Council in Rome to make 'an option for the poor' is still an inspiration to many. There was a poster around at the time with Dom Helder's smiling face, saying:

> When I give food to the poor,
> they call me a saint,
> but when I ask why the poor are poor,
> they call me a communist.

In many ways, it was Brazil and liberation theologians such as Gustavo Gutiérrez, Marcel Casters, Leonardo Boff, Jon Sobrino, and Ernesto Cardinale that kept alive the hope and conviction that transformation is possible, that 'the way things are is not the only way that they can be'.

The hope can be captured in the following quotation:

> Some people see things as they are, and they ask 'Why?'
> But others see them as they never yet have been, and they ask 'Why not?'

It is interesting that once again in 2012, Brazil has become a symbol of hope for all those who believe that a different world is possible. The city of Porto Alegre demonstrated how municipal leadership can transform a modern city into a humane environment for its citizens. It was the birthplace of the World Social Forum, which involves thousands of people from all over the world searching for alternative political, economic, and social structures. During his eight years as president of Brazil, Lula, a former trade unionist, introduced policies that have drawn 30 million people in his country out of poverty. Despite the protests, arising partly because the poor began to hope that 'life could be different', there is much we can learn from Brazil.

What forms Training for Transformation?

TfT is often associated with Paulo Freire's work. This Brazilian educator struck a chord in the minds of many practitioners in the fields of adult education and community development when his book, *Pedagogy of the Oppressed*, was published. Freire's work and life have been documented extensively. He studied law and found that the law was written for the wealthy and the powerful. He read extensively on the structures that set up local and global economies and systems of government. He was influenced by Antonio Gramsci and Frantz Fanon. Through trial and error, he developed an approach to adult education that, in Portuguese, is called 'conscientization'.

Freire's key principles of conscientization (or transformation) include the following:

- *The human vocation to transform our world* is based on the hope that it is possible to change our world into a more just society. Freire emphasized that the aim of education was radical transformation towards justice. Radical means going to the roots. To transform society, he suggests that we need to tap into deeper values of co-operation, justice, and concern for the common good. These values are at the base of almost all faiths, and it is a challenge to all of us to live out these values. This is why transformative education is essentially a spiritual process.

- *Education must be relevant*, based on generative themes that move a community to take action and claim their own power. Most education systems have been set up around what the elite in the society thought was relevant. But who decides what is relevant in a particular community or sector of our society? Freire recognized that emotions play a crucial role in transformation. By starting with the generative (or life-giving) themes of a community, people move from apathy to energy. Emotions are linked to motivation.

- *Dialogue* is crucial in every aspect of participatory learning, and in the whole process of transformation. For years, traditional educational, development, and public policies have relied on 'experts' or a 'person who knows'. The consultants, experts, and teachers come from their own context and limited experiences. On a great many issues, the so-called 'experts' have been wrong, with profound consequences. An example is that, from the 1990s to 2008, mainstream economists convinced most global leaders that they could rely on growth to create jobs that would trickle down to the poor. The economic recession that followed has led to greater global poverty and political upheavals. Freire's emphasis on dialogue recognized that both 'social' knowledge – that we all have – and 'scientific' knowledge – that 'experts' may have – need to be blended together to arrive at 'transformative' knowledge.

- Freire believed that *'problem-posing'* rather than *'banking'* education was needed to change the dynamics of learning. Traditional education strives to pour knowledge into the heads of the learners (who are seen as empty vessels). Freire called this 'banking' education and believed it needed to be turned upside down, starting with a common search for the causes of the problems that concern a community and helping them to search for solutions.

- The *cycle of reflection and action* (or praxis) is central. Freire believed in the ongoing process of community transformation. Nobody has all the answers to most problems, so facilitators and learners are involved in a common search. Classes are seen as 'learning circles', and programmes are 'learning organizations'. Sustainable change requires ongoing reflection and evaluation as events and circumstances change. New facts, more research, and ongoing dialogue with communities add to the knowledge within those communities.

- *No education is neutral.* This is a critical component of Freire's thinking. Does education 'domesticate' people to fit obediently into the roles required of them by the dominant culture, or does it enable them to claim their rights and responsibilities? To what extent do our programmes liberate people to be critical, creative, free, active, and responsible members of their society?

One of the key elements of this approach is to continually ask 'Why?' We saw how effectively this was used by David Werner in his book *Where There is No Doctor*. Werner showed how asking 'But why?', 'But why?', 'But why?' helped to unlock insights into the structures that hold people in poverty. Thelma Awori, one of the co-founders of TfT and later Deputy Director of UNIFEM (the United Nations Development Fund for Women) and Assistant Secretary-General and Director of the Africa Bureau of the UN Development Programme, translated this 'But why?' approach as 'What is the thing behind the thing, that is the thing?'

Freire developed this methodology working with the Movement for Basic Education in Brazil. This was a massive literacy programme with a new approach that enabled thousands of 'learners' to become activists. Using generative themes from communities and asking why their situation was as it was, and planning actions together, groups were mobilized to start thinking and acting for themselves. The literacy aspect of his work is fascinating in itself (for more on this, see his *Education for Critical Consciousness*, 1973).

Early in 1969 we heard that Paulo Freire was to spend part of the following year in Cambridge, Massachusetts. We had heard of his work of conscientization both through Colin Collins, a radical young Catholic priest who had already started trying to adapt his methodology with African Catholic teachers in South Africa, and also through Grail members who had been working with Freire in Brazil and Portugal.

Freire had been invited to Boston by a progressive group called International Development and Social Change, started by Denis Goulet and Jim Lamb. Jim's wife, Joann, was in the Grail and Anne had known her since the 1950s. We had read *Pedagogy of the Oppressed* and had been excited by it, so we were delighted when we were invited to join the study groups they were starting.

Inclusion and participatory methodologies

We met when we enrolled in the Adult Education Department at Boston University in 1969 and in the Human Relations Center. This centre had been started by Ken Benne, a warm, wise man who had turned leadership training upside down, by focusing not primarily on theory and content but on the process of interactions in a group. An understanding of these processes, and skill in working effectively with them, had been developed in the National Training Laboratories, to which the Boston Human Relations Center was directly connected. The Episcopal church had applied its methodology to the training of both clergy and laity to build open and loving Christian communities committed to justice and peace. This was the origin of the experiential courses initiated by Christian Education and Leadership Training (CELT) in South Africa.

Anne remembers Ken saying in one of his sessions, when the issue of sexism had come up after wrestling with racism: 'Once the women's movement really gets going, the cultural changes it will unleash will make all these other cultural changes look like child's play!' This was in 1969, the early days of what was later referred to as the second wave of feminism. It was astonishing for those times. We began to see a clear connection between the work of Freire and that of Ken Benne.

While we were at Boston University, a research project came out with the statistic: 'People remember roughly 20 per cent of what they have heard, 40 per cent of what they have both seen and heard, and 80 per cent of what they have discovered for themselves.' Of course, this varies in different situations, but, over the years in adult education, we have found this provides a reliable guideline for programme planning. Another useful insight from those days was that people believe statements they have made themselves, rather than those they have heard someone else say, so it is worth waiting for them to discover and express insights for themselves.

Linking content and process

Studying adult education and group process methods and becoming more engaged with social/ economic/political analysis with Freire, we eventually put these participatory and creative processes together. Freire's critiques were compelling and enlightening. However, his philosophy and practical methodology needed to be incorporated into programmes that used the insights about group processes, human relationships, and adult education principles and practice. Group leadership and group dynamics were tools to help a group move away from 'banking' education to participatory processes. This was essential if the work was to be effective.

The key principles of Freire, models of social/economic/political analysis from INODEP (the Ecumenical Institute for the Development of Peoples) in Paris, and the CELT group dynamics were the three main streams that formed the basis of the 'DELTA River', the training programme on the Christian concept of transformation that was developed for community leaders in Kenya. INODEP and extracts from *Our Best Kept Secret* (an exploration of Catholic social thought by Peter Henriot, Edward DeBerri, and Michael Schultheis), along with a number of other 'tributaries', became the basis of most of the work of DELTA in Kenya (Development Education and Leadership Teams in Action). In 1984, we published three handbooks on our methodology called *Training for Transformation*. These were revised in 1994 and a fourth book added. They have been translated into many different languages, and are standard texts in many different training programmes. More recently, the whole training process has been known as Training for Transformation.

This linking of content and process is the main difference between a 'facilitator' and an 'animator'. Freire called those who worked with literacy groups 'animators' because they were not neutral. If someone in the group thought, for example, that it was 'God's will' that they were poor, the animator would ask the group if everyone agreed. 'Is this really true?', he or she might ask, whereas a facilitator who acts in a neutral manner might say 'that's interesting'. Challenging a group to think more critically imposes a serious responsibility on group animators to think (and study) quite rigorously on the themes that the group will discuss. Perpetuating myths or stereotypes does not lead to a new level of consciousness. It can be disturbing to some, and that is why the discussion between all group members helps members to support and to challenge one another.

The power of connecting

'Connecting' is powerful, both connecting with other people who share the same concerns, and connecting one branch of knowledge to another. As well as the power of connecting with others in a larger current of transformation, there is the power of connecting concepts, ideas, and insights. This intellectual work can be part of the sustenance that nurtures a movement. New insights are often developed through making connections. We do not claim that TfT is entirely new, but we think that what has made it effective in groups and communities is the integration of social-political analysis, inclusive and participatory methods, and tapping into the commitment that arises from a deep spiritual rooting. This integration of theory and participatory processes is very down to earth and practical. One of the reasons why the books have been so widely used is that people feel very much empowered themselves when they are enabled to understand the connections between all the different sources and structures of power. The second reason is that quite difficult concepts have been expressed in very accessible language.

The context of the 1960s

It is heart-breaking to look back on the 1960s from the world in which we now live. The sense of hope regarding the future was vibrating all through the African continent and beyond. South Africa, where apartheid legislation was being systematically implemented, and where each new surge of commitment in the struggle for change was ruthlessly suppressed, was an exception. At that time, J.F. Kennedy had just been elected president of the United States, and we believed that it was possible to 'wipe ignorance, disease, hunger, and oppression off the face of the earth'. A broad-minded, loving pope, John XXIII, had been elected and was 'throwing open the windows of the Catholic church'. He had called all the bishops of the world together to meet in the Second Vatican Council, to rethink the role of the church in the light of the needs of the modern world. In Africa, one country after another was moving towards independence, confident that they would bring to the people a new experience of 'ubuntu'.[1]

Students, unions, and ordinary citizens on a global level were finding their voice and the silent generation became a distant memory. This surge of energy, the intellectual rejection of global warfare and discrimination, the rise of women's consciousness, all came together with an impact that generated great energy and creativity. As some said, 'Our eyes have been opened, and once opened, one cannot erase that new consciousness.'

The early practice

Practical and accessible methods

Two early practical programmes were developed, adapting Freire's work in Swaziland and South Africa. Because of anti-apartheid work in the USA, Sally was not allowed to enter South Africa. Ross Kidd at the University of Botswana, Lesotho and Swaziland arranged for Sally to work in the Department of Adult Education. At that time, UNESCO was implementing a national literacy campaign in Swaziland and we were asked to help with the development of the materials and to train the teachers.

We worked with the local literacy organization (Sebenta) and other local groups, going through the whole process, organizing listening surveys in different communities and finding the issues on which people had strong enough feelings to motivate them to action. The group chose their generative themes and linked them to a list of words that covered all the sounds in the Siswati language, from which all the words they wanted could be derived. Then we started to prepare posters and plays that presented important, but not explosive, issues in familiar contexts, along with discussion outlines that would enable groups to probe deeply into each problem, analyse the causes of the problem, and plan actions to solve them. We focused on actions that they could do themselves, not only on what they thought the government or the church ought to do.

Some of the groups started meeting regularly, once or twice a week. Teaching a literacy class can become fascinating work, particularly when using this method. As the group discusses and analyses all the issues that are important to them, they get to know one another well. Solidarity can grow between the members and give them the strength to take on tasks together that they would not have considered on their own. Often, a literacy group that has previously had little formal education becomes a key influence in its local community, just because it has discussed thoroughly the problems of the community and knows that group members will have support from one another.

There was already a budding interest in the application of Paulo Freire's work in literacy and in black theology in South Africa. In about June 1972, Steve Biko and Bokwe Mafuna came to Anne and said, 'SASO is planning to run a national literacy campaign all over the country during the long vacation at the end of this year. We have heard about this method of Paulo Freire's that combines reading and writing with conscientization, and we understand that you know about it. We would like you to teach it to us.'

'It isn't really something that can be taught,' Anne said. 'It involves a lot of research, preparing, and testing materials, trying them out with pilot groups, and then training facilitators in all the principles of this approach, before one can even begin such a campaign.'

'That's fine,' they said. 'That's exactly what we want to do, and we can do all that, if you are willing to work with us, to make sure we really do get the basic principles of the approach.'

This was an amazing request, and Anne was immensely flattered that they had asked her. This was the height of black consciousness, and these were two of the people at the heart of the whole movement. Steve already had huge influence among students at university and high school level, and Bokwe was working with emerging trade unions. The interest in black consciousness was moving up from students to older age groups. Although we did not know it at the time and we thought that Steve was still a medical student, his heart was already in political work.

Steve redefined 'blackness' as a cultural and political choice for all those who had been excluded from the privilege and power of apartheid. Indians and coloured people were drawn in and shared responsibility from the beginning. He didn't see 'black consciousness' as a separate liberation organization, but as a new way of looking at the world and at life that would build black solidarity and unity. He knew that solidarity and unity were of critical importance if the liberation struggle was to get anywhere. He had made it clear that blacks must no longer be dependent on whites. For him, the most important aspect of liberation was liberation of the mind and spirit.

Anne felt that it was not her that they were inviting, but Paulo Freire, whose life was deeply rooted in the third world struggle for justice and autonomy. SASO knew, as the South African government knew, that Freire's most famous book was called *Pedagogy of the Oppressed*, and they were fascinated with his challenge to indigenous people to 'read their own reality and write their own history'. They knew that writing their own history meant not only looking at the past, but also shaping the future.

Anne and Steve set up the programme for 15 people, with five core teams of three coming from each of the five major cities in South Africa, to explore the possibilities of Freire's approach and to prepare a set of materials that could be used in the literacy campaign. These teams would later be responsible for training as many students as they could recruit to run classes in their own areas, and for monitoring the whole process. The training was for one week every month over a four-month period. It was held at the Grail Centre in Johannesburg. The teams returned to their own cities for three weeks to carry out the different steps of the process.

Putting into practice the various stages of Freire's method immediately after the training gave us significant insight into linking practice with theory soon after a workshop. We recognized that it was very important to train teams rather than individuals, as the members of a team hold each other accountable in the work and can foster greater creativity.

The process that Steve and Anne had worked out together, of four one-week phases of training, became the basis of the DELTA training programme, which we developed further in Kenya in the 1970s. It continues to develop in the year-long TfT programmes that Ntombi Nyathi currently runs at Kleinmond in the Western Cape, South Africa, with teams from all over Africa and some Asian countries participating.

Sadly, the 1972–73 literacy campaign did not happen, because by Christmas many of the group had been arrested. This was not primarily because of the literacy campaign. They had been involved in a rally in support of FRELIMO (the Mozambique Liberation Front); this was the immediate cause, but several were questioned by the Special Branch about the workshops with Anne. It was becoming clear that Anne might soon be under house arrest or banned.

Anne's South African passport had been confiscated by the government but she discovered that her grandmother was born in Ireland, which allowed her to apply for Irish citizenship. After numerous discussions with colleagues in South Africa, Anne left the country in 1973 and travelled to Tanzania and Kenya, where she met various people within the churches. The development director for the Catholic Bishops in Kenya, Enda Byrne, encouraged Anne to come with Sally to begin the Freire work in diocesan development programmes that were emerging throughout Kenya.

At that time, the international president of the Grail was an Egyptian, Simone Tagher. She had been suggesting for some time that Anne should leave South Africa and continue the Freirean work with Sally somewhere else, and Kenya seemed promising.

Kenya

In 1973, almost all the development directors in the 15 dioceses of the Catholic church in Kenya were priests. Enda Byrne knew them all and helped us to get started on the project; he soon became a key member of our team. He was a whizz at raising money from the Catholic development funding agencies that were emerging in many European countries in response to the strong new emphasis of Vatican II. Under the influence of charismatic leaders such as Dom Helder Camara of Recife and Cardinal Arns of São Paulo in Brazil, and Archbishop Hurley of KwaZulu Natal in South Africa, the bishops had signed the schema of 'The Church in the Modern World', which stressed that the struggle for justice is an essential element of the gospel, a major way of responding to Jesus' command 'to love one's neighbour as oneself'. Wealthier Christian communities must find meaningful ways of living out the 'option for the poor', which Jesus expressed in his life and teaching.

Enda negotiated opportunities for us to work in six of the 15 dioceses, and he became an excellent trainer himself. Initially, general workshops were organized and open to anyone interested. These centred on the theme 'What do we mean by development?' After a few listening exercises and building together a list of 'norms of good communication', we introduced each discussion with a poster, a play, a clip from a film, or a simulation game. In Freire's terminology, these are called 'codes', posing a current problem or concern for the group to focus on. Then we divided the participants into groups of three to deal with a set of questions on the problems arising in their daily lives, the causes, and possible solutions. It was amazing how the discussions took off. It seemed as if people had never been asked for their opinions before, and they were only too anxious to give them in safe little groups of three, and later, as they gained confidence, in the larger group. Almost immediately invitations to hold more workshops started pouring in. Wherever energy erupted and people were prepared to work, we tried to follow it up.

After the first year there were requests for diocesan workshops from five areas. Each workshop was different and we began to recognize the enormous cultural differences between the various Kenyan tribes. They chose different ways to follow up the initial workshop. Some wanted to start women's clubs, others youth programmes. Machakos got into community-based health, Kitui started a literacy programme, and Eldoret, where we worked often with the East African Pastoral Centre, Gaba, used the methodology to develop a religious education programme. Another programme involved the local people in wildlife conservation and in lobbying to secure funds raised through tourism in nature reserves for local development. Food and agriculture were discussed in many of the different groups, as were childcare and education, gender issues, and marriage relationships.

No matter what a group started with, almost inevitably all these issues came up for discussion in due course, as they were basic life issues. And as the groups started to make decisions and take actions, power relationships began to surface, first in the church, then in local government, and later at the national political level.

Training of trainers

Two years after we had started work in Kenya, there were so many requests for workshops that we realized it was urgent to train local trainers. Using the model worked out in South Africa with Steve Biko and the SASO group, we organized a four-phase DELTA training programme. Initially, a team of four was invited from each of the seven dioceses in which we were now working. Several of the teams included development co-ordinators, many of whom were priests at that stage, and we had several Irish, Italian, and Kenyan nuns who became committed development workers. Each phase was held in a different diocese, and in each phase we worked out what each team had to do between phases (usually two months) in their own area.

The workshops were always five days from Sunday evening until Friday lunchtime. These proved such a stimulating and affirming experience for participants that they were honoured to be invited to join the training staff. All the training was conducted on a voluntary basis, and those volunteering expected no remuneration except the refunding of travel expenses, so we could keep the charges very low. Moreover, by this time most of the seven dioceses had obtained training funds from overseas funders, so they could subsidize their teams. Most of the workshops were held in school holidays so that teachers were free, but many government employees (mainly health, agricultural, social, and youth workers) were generously given time off, as the departments recognized that the training improved the quality of their work and their relationships. Many others happily used their leave to attend training programmes.

Enda Byrne, Sally Timmel and Anne Hope in Kenya at the first training of trainers in 1975

The flow of the four phases was as follows:

- Week one: developing a learning community, clarity on what is development, and facilitation skills.
- Week two: developing trust and core values of leadership with further facilitation skills.
- Week three: organizational development and how one's own leadership affects the development of an organization (including a survey of the needs of participants).
- Week four: social/economic analysis of their own area and the national context.

More details of the four-phases of the 'training of trainers' design can be found in Book 3 of *Training for Transformation*.

In 1985, Francis Mulwa in his master's dissertation asserted that the DELTA training had reached over 3 million people in Kenya through literacy, women, ranching, water, youth, parish, and development groups throughout the country.

Window

People enjoyed the workshops so much that there was never a shortage of trainers or participants, and countless small practical projects were emerging to deal with the problems discussed – onion gardens, bee projects, communal vegetable gardens, health campaigns, water projects, food stores, among others. As most of the development co-ordinators were men, they tended to send more men than women for training. They felt that most of the women did not have enough education to understand the issues discussed. It was true that women's level of formal education was lower, but we had realized, long before it was recognized in mainstream development thinking, that it was important to work more closely with women if authentic development was to take root in poor communities. Women were responsible for growing the food and for the young, the sick, and the old, so they were closer to many of the crucial daily needs and they were committed to meeting these needs. In South Africa and in most of the western world we think of farmers as men, but in Africa as a whole, between 50 per cent and 80 per cent of the food is produced by women. At the time, nearly all government and UN programmes were designed for men. It was essential to make it possible for the women to participate in decision-making.

We started a programme just for women, a three-week phased programme to help women gain the confidence to participate in the DELTA programme. It was called WINDOW (Women In the National Development Of Women) – rather a pretentious name, but the women loved it because it symbolized light and the opening up of new views onto the wider world.

Some of the most involved women in this group started to ask us about this mysterious group called the Grail to which we belonged, so we held a number of sessions sharing with them the Grail's vision and values, and the stories that inspired the search for the happiness and well-being of all people. This is symbolized in the Grail Cup of Blessing, representing the human in the divine and the divine in the human. A number of these women took part in a formation programme and became the core of the Kenyan Grail, which is still active and growing today.

Deeper training: an international DELTA and DELTA Plus

By 1977, there were about 35 experienced Kenyan trainers. That same year, we ran a two-month international training programme with teams of participants and staff from several other African countries, as well as from India, the UK, Ireland, Mexico, and Portugal. Three Indian Jesuits, Xavier Manjooran, Johnny Khanna, and Vally de Sousa, spent many months with us and then started the programme in Gujarat. Twenty-five years later, when we were invited to run a programme at Vishtar, an interfaith centre in Bangalore, they all came down to join us, and Xavier attended and helped with some of the TfT programmes currently being run at the Grail Centre in Kleinmond. He has written a chapter for this book.

There was always more, in the fields of both theory and practice, that we wanted to fit into the programme than there was time in the four-week phases, so we organized an advanced six-week programme for the group of 35 trainers who were carrying the responsibility for developing the programme. It turned out to be explosive.

Suddenly, the group reacted against white leadership in the church, which of course included some of us on the leadership team. We thought we had done everything possible to pass on our knowledge to those we were working with and share responsibility with them, but suddenly we were accused of domination, imposing western values, and withholding the secret source of our power and access to sources of funding. They assumed that we must be getting rich in the process, until Sally presented to the group one day a very detailed account of all the funding and all the expenditure, including our own allowances, which were the same as those of a Kenyan secondary school teacher. In fact, part of the anger was directed at the structures of the Catholic church as a whole. Unlike Uganda, where there had been a great number of African vocations to the priesthood and several African priests had become bishops, in Kenya at that time the majority of the priests and almost all of the bishops were white, mainly Irish and Italian. However, as experienced earlier in South Africa, the people who get the brunt of the anger regarding racial injustice are the ones closest, who are willing to listen.

The work of DELTA then expanded to Nigeria and Uganda, and the DELTA training team expanded and was called the Christian Development Education Service (CDES), a thoroughly international and ecumenical team that included Enda Byrne (Irish), Joseph Killer (Kenyan, Teso), Mary Bucharizi (Ugandan exile), Sister Becky Macugay (Philippine Maryknoll Sister), Jos Kronenberg (Dutch agronomist), and Adeline Mwau (Kenyan, Kamba).

A major evaluation of the whole programme led by Donal Dorr, Thelma Awori, and Kabiro Kinyanjui was organized. As Kenyans began to experience some of the difficulties of responsibility and leadership, they began to think that we should not exit too hastily.

Writing the Training for Transformation books

After the first two years of work in Kenya, we gathered together the hand-outs we had been using and bound them into two training manuals called the DELTA handbooks. These were typed on stencils and cyclostyled before each workshop. They were not for sale and we gave them only to people who had completed the training. We believed that the training was most effective when we combined the experiential workshops with well-tested materials that the participants could use in their own situations when they returned home. As they experienced some success with these, they gained confidence to prepare their own codes and discussion outlines in more direct response to local needs. By the time the stencils had been used about 2,000 times, they had become limp and full of holes, and the pressure mounted to have the books printed.

The two DELTA handbooks were rewritten in 1982 and published by Mambo Press in Zimbabwe as *Training for Transformation*. As the books were based on hand-outs used within workshops, all the processes had been thoroughly tested and were written in accessible English. Other than restructuring the books, the process of writing the new book was completed within three months. They have been, fully or partly, translated into several languages and are still widely used today by both development organizations and development departments in universities. A fourth book, dealing with environmental issues, gender, racism, culture, and governance, was published in 1995.

The Popular Education News newsletter from Toronto, Canada has described these books as follows:

> Few other popular education resources can match the comprehensiveness, systematic nature of the approach, and sheer volume of ideas and suggestions that make up [this resource]. A rich source for improving educational work for all communities seeking authentic development (May 2004, available at www.popednews.org).

The four handbooks are sold as a set and have sold more each year since 2000. As Phumzile Mlambo-Ngcuka (newly appointed UN Women Executive Director) says: 'Training for Transformation is as relevant today as it was [when it was initiated].'

Adapting Freire to the middle class

Freire's first book, *Pedagogy of the Oppressed*, which was published in English in the early 1970s, was a seminal work for most activists in the US. Although the translation was complex, the title itself pointed to class consciousness. At that time, the numerous Marxist study circles were the main context in which the Anti-Vietnam War or the Civil Rights Movements sought relevant guidelines to create a new society. Most of their work focused on those marginalized in society. In 1991, Daniel Yankelovich, a social researcher and public opinion analyst, published a book called *Coming to Public Judgment*. He explained the difference between public opinion and public judgement. He wrote that everyone has an opinion on almost any topic. However, to move to a different set of values, a country needs to come to 'public judgement' through thoughtful dialogue based on facts, not myths. He described this process as follows:

- awareness and naming the problem;
- analysing the problem;
- looking at alternative solutions;
- recognizing the trade-offs (ethical choices);
- wrestling with and coming to accept the trade-offs;
- building intellectual commitment to a solution;
- building emotional commitment to a solution.

What is fascinating about this process is that it is congruent with the approach used by Freire, but adds the crucial step of wrestling with the trade-offs when coming to a solution. This is the dilemma for the middle class is most societies. The questions for those of us who are middle class are: 'Do I opt for the common good or for my own narrow self-interest?'; 'Is my self-interest actually aligned with the common good?' He pointed out that the difference between the poor and the middle class is that the middle class has the possibility of making choices whereas the poor usually do not. An ethical education challenges them to make choices that are for the common good and not just in their own self-interest.

Another source for developing this process was the work of Sid Simon on values clarification. Simon had developed numerous tools for youth to sort out their values through 'forced choice' questionnaires followed by discussions. For example: 'If I were the head of the health department, would I support immunization programmes for 5 million children or open heart surgery for five elderly patients?' These are life and death issues and major ethical choices.

In the 1980s, the healthcare system in the US was in crisis. Over 40 million people had no medical insurance and public hospitals would not take new patients without cash upfront to cover costs. At the same time, over 60 per cent or 70 per cent of all medical costs were used to pay for treatment during the last six months of life. The medical system posed major ethical issues. Opinion polls showed that over 75 per cent of the public believed that the healthcare system needed major reforms, and new national legislation was introduced.

Sally and a team from faith-based communities in Washington, DC designed a tool with eight ethical choices. A full workshop was developed and implemented in nine states. Through this process (described more fully in Book 4 of *Training for Transformation*), over 30,000 people attended a workshop on ethical choices between 1993 and 1994 during the debate on healthcare reform. The results were stunning: over 64 per cent of those participating came to a consensus on healthcare reform that was geared to the common good and included healthcare cover for the 40 million people without it.

At the time, the congressional decision on healthcare reform was derailed by the private health insurance companies that poured millions of dollars into television ads based on fear. The 40 million people in the US who had no healthcare insurance had to wait another 20 years before President Obama managed to get through a modified healthcare reform bill passed by the US Congress.

Women's development training: DELTA in Cape Town

In 1992, as negotiations were being held between the old apartheid regime and the ANC in South Africa, it was becoming clear that women were still at a disadvantage regarding education and job opportunities. Anne therefore decided to start a DELTA training programme just for women. She gathered a team and they started a weekly programme that continued for 15 years in Cape Town and is still running in the Eastern Cape. Anne also taught courses with community leaders at the University of Cape Town and the University of the Western Cape. One of her students is now the director of UN Women. Among other codes in this programme, they used 'Star Power' to help participants understand the unfair advantages with which the rich start off, and 'Bafa Bafa', a simulation game on the clash of two cultures. This simulation helps to build intercultural understanding.

Confronting economic apartheid in South Africa

Another major theme in South Africa became clear as the negotiations for a new constitutional government were being developed. Petty apartheid was abolished and political power was about to be shared, but the prevailing economic structure of the 'haves' was kept in place. The consequence of this choice by the new government meant that the gap between rich and poor would continue to grow, with the rich continuing to hold the assets and profits from major industries and services.

'Fair Share' and the budget game

A team of four began looking at what kind of intervention could make some difference. At the time, the South African government was not greatly indebted because of international sanctions against the apartheid regime. The government budget was (and is) a great resource for the redistribution of wealth and the creation of jobs. Therefore, it was possible that trade-offs between national departmental budgets could be one means of giving priority to those living on the margins. The team named their initiative 'Fair Share'.

A simulation game (called 'the budget game') was developed as a one-day workshop where participants worked in small groups that represented various government ministries (health, education, transport, housing, job creation, and others). Three months of research had been completed and simplified into one-page summaries of the funds allocated to 10 departments dealing with the urgent issues of local communities. Different options for spending the funds available to each department were offered, and each group had to decide how the money would best be spent. Then each 'department' sent one member to a 'cabinet' meeting, where the real figures of the national budget were presented, and the representatives had to consider whether the amounts allocated to their department and to other departments were consistent with the common good of the nation. Of course, many groups decided that far too much was spent on defence or embassies abroad, and too little on education, health, water, and electricity.

These budget workshops were held over a four-year period and helped to build a stronger civil society response to the annual budget speech given in parliament. As trade unions, faith groups, women's organizations, and community groups had been engaged in budget workshops, their national organizations held three-day workshops during the time of the parliamentary budget speech. Press conferences with representatives from different sectors were able to point out aspects of the budget that did not respond to local needs, or show how the tax structure would increase the disparity between rich and poor.

'Fair Share' also worked with local municipalities. Workshops were held in specific towns and enabled ordinary citizens to analyse the budgets and understand the language used by officials. Workshops were then held to bring together elected councillors, officials, the business community, and grassroots groups. Fifty per cent of the participants were from the local community. Through a process of coming to a common vision and deciding on key priorities and accountability structures, new budget priorities would come to light.

Two telling statements came from officials. A leader on a provincial finance committee said that she had been to a number of gatherings where people knew more about the budget priorities than she did. When she asked how people knew this information, they said that it was through the budget workshops. She decided that she needed to do more homework in the future. In one municipality, an elected officer said that after the three-day common workshop, he thought the election of councillors should not be conducted by political parties but that members should be voted in directly by constituents. In this way, the municipality would be more responsive to the direct needs of the people it represented.

After several years and under different leadership, the 'Fair Share' project was moved to the University of the Western Cape. The focus became more academic, running courses for local officials on economics. The project started to tender for contracts with local government to bring local communities into the process. The budget game simulation was dropped from the curriculum, but many community leaders regretted this.

Partners in Ireland gathering in 2001

In 1980, Anne had staffed a number of TfT workshops with Father Donal Dorr in Ireland. Many priests who worked in Kenya and other countries were present. An organization called Partners grew from these workshops. It has organized numerous workshops adapting this methodology for different groups, and has published three excellent manuals: *Partners Companion to Training for Transformation* by Maureen Sheehy; *Reclaiming Economics: A Cooperative Inquiry*, a joint venture between Partners and Community Action Network; and *Partners Intercultural Companion to Training for Transformation* by Maureen Sheehy, Frank Naughton, and Collette O'Regan.

In 2001, Partners held a two-week gathering with over 60 participants from at least 25 countries who had been using the methods in different ways. This covered new insights that had emerged as the global situation had changed. During this gathering, a Rwandese woman expressed concern that she was unsure whether they had experienced all the elements of TfT fully. Participants felt that there was a need for a more advanced international course. Seven women got together at this conference and planned to seek funding that would enable people to come together on a one-year diploma course. This gathering was held at the Holy Ghost conference centre in Kimmage, Dublin, which offered courses in development studies (a diploma and a master's degree). The team approached the director of development studies and together they negotiated plans to start a partnership through which they could award diplomas to TfT students at Kleinmond in South Africa.

New beginnings

By 2002, funds had been secured through European church partners (MISEREOR, Trócaire, CAFOD, Canadian Development and Peace, and Cordaid) to launch a diploma course at the Grail Centre in Kleinmond. A core staff was recruited to design and implement a one-year diploma course in four phases: a two-month residential phase; four months back home to put into practice their learning with an experienced mentor; another two-month residential phase; and a concluding four-month

Sally Timmel, Thelma Awori and
Rebecca Macugay at the first Training
for Transformation diploma course, 2002

application period at home. The successful candidates would receive a diploma. This has worked successfully and, despite the economic recession, the model has grown in popularity.

During a short impact study completed in 2009, the need for a shorter course for busy directors of organizations was brought to the fore. In 2010, a certificate course was designed with a phase of residential training for three weeks, then three months practice back home, and a second residential phase followed by another three months practical application at home.

Both these models continue to be enriched with new material. New resource staff come to share their insights in the following modules: development studies, adult education methods, putting Freire into practice, community-building, ethical leadership, spirituality, gender, economics, local economic development, political economy, organizational development, and strategic planning. The residential phases also include weekly tutorials, and participants write a weekly paper on that week's module. Home phase reports are also part of the learning practice.

Neither the ongoing courses nor the expansion of work with new partners would have been accomplished without the strong leadership that has been provided over the years by Sister Becky Macugay, Ina Conradie, Carol Webb, and Ntombi Nyathi. Since 2010, new partnerships have been formed in Indonesia, Zambia, Sudan, Mozambique, and Angola. These have been possible thanks to the wise and strong guidance of Ntombi Nyathi, who has been the director and key trainer since 2010. The Christian Brothers have also been working very closely with TfT.

Think Wells

Since the 1970s, many practitioners have used the TfT books and have adapted the work and interventions to their own situation. Some adapted the work to engage local communities, others worked with women or youth, while others provided leadership courses. Some adapted the work in conflict situations, while others worked with government agencies. The core team working directly with the TfT diploma and certificate courses held in Kleinmond decided that gathering a variety of practitioners from time to time to 'think' and to share their insights would develop the work both locally and nationally, and improve the courses themselves. Instead of calling these gatherings 'think tanks', Rebecca Macugay suggested that they be called 'Think Wells' ('wells' being a more organic part of nature than 'tanks').

The facilitators realized that bringing together other facilitators for 10 days would require a very open and flexible design. Each Think Well has had a different theme, which have included the following:

- developing the diploma course content and target groups, and linking the course to the Development Studies Centre in Kimmage, Ireland;
- sharing designs and interventions that were creative and useful;

- popularizing knowledge with those in specific sector programmes;
- a 'new map of the world' reflecting the shifts in the geo-political reality and the major new roles played by China and India;
- the economic crisis and how it is affecting countries of the South;
- the transition to ecological sustainability;
- 'TfT in Practice', pulling together the adaptations of the work over a 40-year period and developing impact assessment tools consistent with the Freire methodology.

Some learning

Hindsight reveals that there were several elements of the TfT programme in Kenya, Zimbabwe, and South Africa that contributed to its effectiveness. These may be helpful to other programmes in the future. This list is not complete, and others can add to it from their own experience.

- *Timing.* This approach to development needs an 'open' space in the social/political context of a country. The initial work in Kenya began 10 years after independence when people began questioning why changes were not happening for the poor. They began to realize that nothing will change unless we get involved, as government cannot do everything. This intervention came at the right historical moment.
- *Spiritual base.* This refers to a spirituality of identification with the poor and the belief that transformation is possible and our work can make a difference. This developed and sustained deep levels of commitment. It is interesting to read David Korten's analysis that many of the most effective programmes to overcome poverty arise from a spiritual base, for example Grameen Bank, Mondragon Cooperative, and Base Christian Communities.[2]
- *Vision.* If the vision and mission of 'the work' (the intervention) are directed towards the common good, with a special focus on those on the margins of society, it is easier to keep programmes on track. Does the programme actually change the lives of those most in need? Are they able to work together on issues that impact the communities that they serve? Or are the programmes focused on 'training for training's sake' in order to chase donor funding? Has the training programme become a business to enrich those at the top? Again and again, we come back to the question: Whom do we serve?
- *Research and analysis.* Interventions to create change need to be based on real facts, or on the study of both the social/economic/political realities (nationally and globally) and also on cultural dynamics. Participants need to wrestle with cultural dynamics. Freire has some important insights in his writings on levels of consciousness. Social/economic/political analysis is important to interpret the local situation.
- *Problem-posing and new learning processes.* Training was never seen as complete and many programmes (phases) went on beyond the initial training. This was often linked to ongoing analysis, research, and finding facts that could enhance local efforts.
- *Meeting a recognized need.* Many individuals and communities have very immediate needs to which they will respond (e.g. literacy, youth programmes, saving and credit schemes, job training). These practical programmes were linked to workshops focused on deepening conscientization and a commitment to action for the common good.
- *Measure of success.* It is important to celebrate every small success. As communities and participants experienced a measure of success, their motivation was sustained. Groups that had seemed dead came to life as they started to deal with generative themes. This success bred further confidence and created a current that led more groups to join. Besides the ongoing training, biannual workshops led to cross-fertilization between geographic areas and ethnic groups, and sometimes to interfaith co-operation.
- *Identifying potential leadership.* How does one find future leadership that is open and curious about new ideas, demonstrates passion for the work, is flexible, listening, encouraging, and able to build teams and create unity in communities? One way is to have numerous

short-term workshops where leadership with these qualities can emerge. Afterwards, longer programmes might interest those who feel that this is their calling.

- *Strong structure.* It is critical to work with organizations that are strategic within a country. One can debate what constitutes 'strategic', but one way to look at this question is to ask which organizations have a commitment to the common good, are open to being a learning organization, are highly organized at the local, provincial, and national levels, and have a track record of accountability. Our experience in a number of countries is that faith-based organizations often fit these criteria well. However, this does not exclude working in alliance with secular organizations and it is important to build campaigns and extend the work to achieve real change.
- *Teamwork and team training.* In the TfT programme, participants were usually accepted for the training as teams and individuals were not expected to initiate things alone. This meant that they could reflect on their work, solve problems, adapt, and plan necessary changes together. Mentoring and coaching were carried out in teams, with many teams gathered together on a regular basis. This approach reinforced the idea that people learn from their peers, often more than from an outside 'expert'. This approach is also much more cost-effective.
- *Sustaining the extended leadership.* As well as regular gatherings to share new insights and problem-solve for teams engaged in this work, one can find people with a similar vision to nurture the team leadership. Our experience in Kenya showed that, although many people within the churches were not engaged in the direct work of training, they held a deep commitment to the vision of the overall programme. Leadership from someone with the ability to nurture and care for each individual was essential to ensure the greatest success in the work of a team.
- *Personal growth.* In these programmes and within the churches, people were not paid for training in their local context. They gave generous voluntary service because they felt they were gaining skills that truly helped their communities and they were growing themselves. The fact that the methodology demands adaptation to the local situation encourages creativity, and often motivates learning and long-term commitment. In the 2009 impact study, it was found that over 40 per cent of graduates from the diploma courses were given new and much greater responsibilities within their organizations.
- *Part of a current.* Ongoing commitment to the common good is difficult to sustain in isolated individuals. Feeling part of a wider effort is an important element for sustained motivation. In numerous experiences, participants have felt that they were part of a current that was bringing about some real transformation – on either the micro or the macro level.
- *Recruitment of participants.* As the major aim of TfT has been to strengthen civil society and help to level the playing field between ordinary citizens and governments, the recruitment of participants has mainly focused on trainers or organizers from non-governmental organizations and faith-based organizations. This type of leadership takes a lot of time, creativity, and energy. In hindsight, we recognized a gap in knowledge of the different models found in other countries and in new theories and practices emerging in this field of work. We should have engaged more committed university graduates in fields such as adult education, organizational development, economics, gender, and environment. In some ways, this gap has been filled in the TfT diploma and certificate courses with modules on these areas of work designed with extra resource people.
- *Research and development of new resources.* The testing of new participatory educational materials is often difficult to do when a programme is in great demand. It is important to set up specific times to test new participatory materials.

Conclusion

As the authors of this work, we know that this is only our perspective. Thousands of people have been adapting Paulo Freire's work throughout the world. Thousands of other adult educators and community development workers have been engaging communities in experiential and participatory practices. The TfT books themselves would never have emerged without the insights and work of the thousands of participants who were involved in the programmes.

The following chapters were written by a few of those practitioners who have committed themselves to the work of transforming our world into a more just and hospitable place where every woman, child, and man can reach their full potential. We hope that these examples and the work described will inspire and validate those engaged with people who seek a more just society.

Introduction to the chapters

The following chapters were written during a Think Well held at the Grail Centre in Kleinmond, South Africa in September 2013. This coincided with the 40th anniversary of the start of the TfT programme in Kenya in 1973 as well as the tenth anniversary of the diploma courses. The diploma (and certificate) courses are held at the Grail Centre and the centre is seen as the mothership for TfT. This was the sixth Think Well held; others had covered topics ranging from 'Popularizing knowledge' and 'Practitioners sharing their models' to 'A new map of the world: China and emerging markets' and 'The economic crisis and its effect on countries of the South'.

Thirty-seven people from 26 countries who have been adapting the TfT work attended this 10-day Think Well. Besides sharing their own experiences and learning from each other, the group divided itself into two sections for three days. One group met daily to write about their adaptation of TfT. This group took time to clarify what they would write, and focused on their theme, their title, subtitle, and sub-subtitle. This was a fun exercise because, as a group, we gave feedback to the writers about what would catch our own interest in their titles and themes. The writers often paired up to get individual feedback on their work during the days allotted to them.

The other group focused on developing an impact study guideline that would be consistent with the TfT philosophy and approach. This group worked in three subgroups preparing questions appropriate for the participants on the diploma and certificate courses; for the organizations that had sent the participants; and for the communities with whom they work. Those of us working with communities know that if we take the communities' concerns seriously (a bottom-up approach), the impact may take years to be felt. We are not constructing a building, but working with people whose lives are fraught with many dilemmas and difficulties. This gives us all an opportunity to learn with those with whom we work.

The impact study guidelines found in the last chapter of this book are questions. The group decided not to design plays, codes, or exercises to elicit responses because those need to vary according to the cultural context.

As editors of these chapters and the impact guidelines, we feel privileged to have come to know each person who has contributed. We also realize that there are hundreds of others within this field who have stories to tell of successes and challenges. It is our hope that this is the beginning of a conversation that can happen through the internet, on Facebook, or in any other media. We dream of this new world and, although we may not produce the perfect interventions, we know that the small part we play is of great value.

Enjoy these chapters. They inspired us and we hope they will be of value to you.

Notes

1   *Ubuntu* is the African concept of relating to all people and all circumstances in a deeply human and sympathetic way.

2   David Korten has written several important books on development and the causes of global poverty. One of them is *When Corporations Rule the World*. He worked for the World Bank in the Philippines for a number of years in the 1970s but then began to question the analysis of the 'Washington Consensus'. He is the founder of *YES!* magazine.

References

Berry, T. (1986) *The New Story: Life from a Planetary Perspective*, Langley, WA: Context Institute.

Biko, S. (1996) *I Write What I Like*, London: Bowerdean Publishing Company.

Camara, Dom H. (1971) *Spiral of Violence*, London: Sheed and Ward.

Camara, Dom H. (2005) *The Desert is Fertile*, Eugene, OR: Wipf and Stock Publishers.

Collins, L. and Lapierre, D. (1975) *Freedom at Midnight*, New York, NY: Simon & Schuster.

Fanon, F. (1967) *Black Skin, White Masks*, New York, NY: Grove Press.

Fanon, F. (1967) *The Wretched of the Earth*, London: Penguin Books.

Forster, E.M. (1924) *A Passage to India*, London: Edward Arnold.

Freire, P. (1973) *Education for Critical Consciousness*, New York, NY: Seabury Press.

Freire, P. (1973) *Pedagogy of the Oppressed*, London: Penguin Books.

Freire, P. (1978) *Pedagogy in Process: The Letters to Guinea-Bissau*, New York, NY: Seabury Press.

Freire, P. (1992) *Pedagogy of Hope: Reliving Pedagogy of the Oppressed*, New York, NY: Continuum.

Gramsci, A. (1991) *Prison Notebooks*, New York, NY: Columbia University Press.

Henriot, P.J., DeBerri, E.P. and Schultheis, M.J. (1988) *Catholic Social Teaching: Our Best Kept Secret*, Maryknoll, NY: Orbis Press.

Hope, A. and Timmel, S. (eds) (1995) *Training for Transformation: A Handbook for Community Workers*, Books 1–3, Rugby, UK: Practical Action Publishing.

Hope, A. and Timmel, S. (eds) (1999) *Training for Transformation: A Handbook for Community Workers*, Book 4, Rugby, UK: Practical Action Publishing.

Horn, J. (1969) *Away with All Pests: An English Surgeon in People's China, 1954–1969*, New York, NY: Monthly Review Press.

Korten, D. (1995) *When Corporations Rule the World*, London: Earthscan.

Ngugi wa Thiong'o (1977) *Petals of Blood*, London: Heinemann.

Nyerere, J. (1971) *Ujamaa: Essays on Socialism*, Oxford: Oxford University Press.

Rodney, W. (1972) *How Europe Underdeveloped Africa*, London: Bogle-L'Ouverture Publications.

Sheehy, M. (2001) *Partners Companion to Training for Transformation*, Dublin: Partners Training for Transformation.

Sheehy, M., Naughton, F. and O'Regan, C. (2007) *Partners Intercultural Companion to Training for Transformation*, Dublin: Partners Training for Transformation.

Simon, S.B., Howe, L.W. and Kirschenbaum, H. (1995) *Values Clarification*, New York, NY: Warner Books.

Suyin, H. (1965) *The Crippled Tree*, London: Jonathan Cape.

Suyin, H. (1966) *A Mortal Flower*, London: Jonathan Cape.

Suyin, H. (1968) *Birdless Summer*, London: Jonathan Cape.

Teilhard de Chardin, P. (1961) *The Phenomenon of Man*, New York, NY: Harper and Row.

Werner, D. (1978) *Where There is No doctor: A Village Health Care Handbook*, Palo Alto, CA: The Hesperian Foundation.

Yankelovich, D. (1991) *Coming to Public Judgment: Making Democracy Work in a Complex World*, Syracuse, NY: Syracuse University Press.

PART ONE
Moving a mountain starts with a small stone

Keywords: adapting education programmes to different circumstances; building movements; creativity; food security; gaining self-respect; human rights; innovation; lobbying parliamentarians; overcoming fear; perseverance; resisting mines; stopping genetically modified organisms; sustainable agriculture; winning over government officials

http://dx.doi.org/10.3362/9781780448312.002

CHAPTER 2
Creating uncomfortable spaces: speaking truth to power in South Africa

Nobuntu Mazeka

Nobuntu Mazeka helps to staff the Training for Transformation diploma course in Kleinmond. She works mainly for the Nelson Mandela Institute in the Eastern Cape, where she is the area co-ordinator of community education, creating tools that will improve literacy and numeracy levels. The Institute integrates TfT tools and methodologies to animate teachers, parents, and learners, to shape pedagogy in the classroom, and to build support structures that will contribute to justice through educational opportunities.

This chapter deals with building community power bases for two unique campaigns to confront government on issues that had become generative themes for rural communities in the poverty-stricken Eastern Cape. One dealt with the use of genetically modified seeds to replace indigenous food growing, and the other with stopping the mining of titanium on fertile agricultural land. They managed to establish dialogue with members of parliament, which led to laws requiring the labelling of all foods, and the organization of local farmers blocked the granting of permits to the mining company.

If you do not stand for something, you will fall for anything. *African proverb*

In 2005, the Nelson Mandela Institute at the University of Fort Hare invited me to attend a Training for Transformation (TfT) provincial introductory workshop in East London. At the time I was working in the field of human rights education as a paralegal fieldworker. My job entailed providing free legal advice, administering cases, and conducting human rights education. Together with my colleagues, we 'trained to death' and were convinced we knew exactly what we were doing. Although we tried to educate communities to fight and defend their rights, they kept coming back with similar problems and we kept doing the same thing. Contact with TfT came right at the point of insanity, when we lacked any logical plans about how to do things differently. I attended the one-week, information-packed training. It felt like a month, and that was the beginning of my journey, and of a rigorous paradigm shift in my world view.

Out of the training emerged new levels of consciousness, radical thinking, and motivation to try new tools and methodologies. According to Ken Wilber, everything we know is a holon, made up of different parts, and itself part of a greater whole. The understanding of the holon (showing how each individual person is part of a family, which is one of many institutions in the wider society, which are all part of the whole human community, which itself is part of the environment of the Earth) was for me one of the most meaningful tools used during TfT and became the starting point of my evolving consciousness. This idea speaks to me in many ways.

I became aware that I am who I am because of the people around me; that they influence and shape how I think, how I project myself, and how I relate to my surrounding environment. As we move from part to whole and back again in a dance of comprehension, we move in a circle of understanding, and come alive to meaning, to value, and to vision. I embarked on a journey – to influence my family, my colleagues at work, and our planning.

In February 2006, I enrolled on a diploma course that was intensive, challenging us intellectually, emotionally, and spiritually. The experiences I had and the processes I underwent shaped my ideology and opened a window into the mysteries of life in our world. The most fundamental insight I have drawn from the TfT process is the awareness of myself as a spiritual being, connected with nature and with those I am called to serve. I understood the essence of what community development is, how it should be done, by whom, with whom. The information I received was overwhelming because of the new revelations of reality, the demystification of the complex systems operating in our society, and how these systems lead to conflicts in people's lives and in the world at large, but I grew in levels of articulation, the ability to analyse, the ability to animate processes of engagement with people at any level – grassroots, nationally, regionally, and globally. All these are my most significant attributes and capacities, arising from my new consciousness.

These attributes had ripple effects not only in my work but also in my community. I went back with a small mouth, big ears, open eyes, and an open mind. I started listening to what makes people angry, what makes them happy, and what are their main issues. TfT has since become a philosophy for me to create uncomfortable spaces in which people at any level can start to engage in dialogue, in which ordinary people can learn to speak truth to power.

In our listening surveys, in rural areas of the Eastern Cape, two generative themes came through strongly:

- The first theme related to the introduction of a massive food programme by government. Community members were up in arms about who benefited from the scheme, as some people felt sidelined. Some were suspicious about why people were given packages of maize seeds, along with 'Roundups' (the Monsanto glyphosate-based herbicide), fertilizers, and lime for free, to use them in soil that is so rich in natural organic content. They see the massive food programme as a way of getting the soil addicted to inputs, thus destroying the livelihoods of people or putting them into a debt trap. They were given no answers about how long these packages would be handed out for free. Growing up in an area where working and living on the land form a major part of who we are, I decided to join the struggle as a small-scale farmer. The knowledge gained from the provincial workshops was sufficient for me to engage in this dialogue with the aim of promoting the rights of small-scale farmers to food security, and a clean and healthy environment. I tried to align the work that we do as an organization with the generative themes of the community.
- The second generative theme from surveys was the issuing, by government, of a mining licence for titanium on the sand dunes along the Wild Coast, without consulting the AmaDiba community, the owners of the land. Again, people were divided. Some wanted the mining as they were promised employment and shares, whereas others were totally against it due to its environmental impact on people's lives and livelihoods. These are the two most powerful issues, and adapting the Freirean approach of popular education has constantly brought wonderful 'aha!' moments to the communities with whom we work.

Dialogue on genetically modified food and mining case studies

Working with and in divided communities takes courage, especially if you are one of them (an insider). The big question is: how do you do what you have to do without being subjective? The biggest challenge in both cases was to light a fire that would raise the levels of consciousness of the people without promoting violence. The animation process, adapting TfT methodology, became an indispensable, humanizing pedagogy to solve conflicting issues in my community. In community meetings held at Komkhulu (traditional *imbizos*), I would be given a slot of three to four hours to facilitate discussion among the outraged men, women, and youth. I adapted Manfred Max-Neef's concept of fundamental human needs in relation to fundamental human rights. The codes[1] would raise questions about the type of needs we are trying to address when we get involved in massive food programmes, and what need we are trying to address when we allow mining in our communities. How do we organize around those needs? When organizing, how much and what do we compromise? Who decides how we should organize in order for us to satisfy our needs? People started engaging, asking questions, opening up, and making references to other development initiatives that did not have a positive impact on the lives of the people.

From the very first interaction, people's consciousness evolved, and the two chiefs whose villages were affected suggested another date for further deliberations. During the second, third and fourth deliberations, as the dialogue was reaching a climax, the Orange code, the Dynamic Model and the Arm code were all used to dig deeply into the root causes. Through these tools of analysis, the intentions of the government and Monsanto, as well as those of the mining company and its local cronies, were named and shamed. The impact of these two initiatives on the environment and people's livelihoods was discussed, as was who would bear the consequences, and what was the way forward.

In most of the discussions and dialogues, the information received from TfT played a major role in conscientizing the community. Case studies of farmers from Kwa Makhatini, here in South Africa, where a cotton plantation programme was first piloted, were shared during sessions. Case studies of the struggles of small-scale farmers in India, who were trapped in debt and committing suicide, were also shared. The purpose of sharing these case studies was not to scare those people who wanted the massive food programme, but to make comparisons and to widen our world view, and to show that food sovereignty and food security are global issues.

At this point the community was energized to act, yet it gave a chance to those who wanted to join the programme to go ahead, with the knowledge to make informed choices. As Ken Wilber (1995: 200) writes:

> The single greatest world transformation would simply be the embrace of global reasonableness and pluralistic tolerance. In other words the real problem is not exterior. The real problem is interior. The real problem is how to get people to transform from egocentric to socio-centric to world-centric consciousness, which is the only state that can grasp the global dimensions of the problem in the first place and thus the only stance that can freely, even eagerly embrace global solutions.

The TfT method assisted the community to use 'microscopic' lenses to deal with top-down approaches to development and to work as a collective in order to have a voice. We move from the egocentric (I) to the socio-centric (we) and the world-centric (we all). A resolution was taken to form committees to work closely with our organization to advocate a change in the way the authorities engage with local people on issues of development.

Tools of analysis to transform power

Coincidentally, at that moment in time, one of the committee members on the massive food programme came across an advert in a national newspaper. The advert was inviting interest groups to make submissions to the Agricultural Portfolio Committee in parliament on the Genetically Modified Organism (GMO) Amendment Bill. We set up a meeting with the community to talk about this opportunity and the small-scale farmers agreed to draft a submission, which was later approved by the committee and faxed to parliament. Three months down the line, we received a letter inviting us to make a presentation in front of the portfolio committee. We prepared our arguments and brought with us different maize varieties – the hybrid, the genetically modified and five traditional varieties. To present our analysis we used the 'Three-storey Building', which shows the economic, political, and cultural dimensions of a society,[2] to engage both the parliamentarians and the investors on the socio-cultural, socio-political, and economic issues, adding a fourth storey on the environmental impact of GMOs. Issues of consumers' rights to information were key. There was a disclaimer on the seeds' tags that liability ended with the 'end user', which we challenged. We also had the opportunity to forge networks with other partners, such as Biowatch and Africa Bio-safety. The bill was withdrawn and came back in 2011 with some clauses thrown out; food labelling, which was one of the main things we had argued for, was included. Now, at the time of writing, menus in major restaurants and food in major retailers in the country are labelled.

We also made contact with members of parliament who worked on our behalf when we opposed mining licensing. Funding was organized for exchange visits to Richards Bay Minerals, a sand mining operation. The AmaDiba Crisis Committee met with members of the community affected and visited the site on a fact-finding mission, which was part of the action plan. The findings were shocking. Communities had been stripped of their livelihoods. The avocado and papaya trees, which used to bear fruit that community members sold by the roadside, were sterile, no longer producing fruit. The soil had become less productive. Local people were promised jobs but only two people were employed, one as a caretaker and another as a cleaner. Houses were collapsing. Social cohesion was ruined as people were accusing each other of greed and blaming traditional leadership for accepting bribes and selling them out. Benefits were not being paid to the community as promised.

The second stage was to present a petition on the day the Minister for Minerals and Energy and the government delegation were declaring the licence. We forged a network with Sustaining the Wild Coast for media coverage. The minister was shocked to hear about the dubious processes undertaken by the investor to obtain the licence. The national department had been misled, the environmental impact assessments had been falsified, and the community had not been consulted. The community wants the area to be protected and declared a World Endemic Centre because of its very rich biodiversity. A commission of enquiry was appointed by the ministry and conducted hearings and made recommendations. The mining licence was then revoked and nullified.

Three members of the crisis committee attended the TfT certificate and diploma courses to deepen their knowledge on how to deal with struggles of social transformation. Their videos of this work are available on the internet under the title 'Too Great a Toll'. The struggle shifted to protest against the National Toll Road (known as the N2 toll road). However, we learned that structures such as bridges were to be funded by mining, so the toll road developments move at a snail's pace. The struggle in our area of Pondoland continues. TfT gives us the most relevant and powerful language one can use to speak truth to power. Aluta continua – the struggle continues.

Notes

1   A code is a very practical illustration of one of the problems about which the community has strong feelings and can be a poster, a short play, a story, or a film clip. Codes are used to initiate discussions. For further details of codes (including the specific codes referred to in this book), see *Training for Transformation*, Book 1, Chapters 2 and 3.

2   See *Training for Transformation*, Chapter 9 for further explanation.

References

Hope, A. and Timmel, S. (eds) (1995) *Training for Transformation: A Handbook for Community Workers*, Books 1–3, Rugby, UK: Practical Action Publishing.

Wilber, K. (1995) *Sex, Ecology, Spirituality*, Boston, MA: Shambala.

Wilber, K. (1997) *The Eye of Spirit: An Integral Vision for a World Gone Slightly Mad*, Boston, MA: Shambala.

CHAPTER 3

Fear transformed into power: experience with the Adivasis and the Dalits of Gujarat, India

Xavier Manjoorran

Xavier Manjoorran is an Indian Jesuit priest who has used the Training for Transformation approach ever since he participated in the International DELTA programme in Kenya in 1977. He works with the Dalit (formerly called 'untouchable') community and the Adivasi indigenous people in the state of Gujarat. In 2010 he used his sabbatical leave to participate in the TfT diploma course in Kleinmond, incarnating Freire's belief that we should all be both learners and teachers for the whole of our lives. He brought great wisdom and experience to the much younger group.

In this chapter he describes how, when he started work, both the Dalits and the Adivasis were severely discriminated against and too intimidated to challenge the persecution and humiliation they experienced. Gradually they became confident enough to take their cases to the supreme court, and to change certain laws. Xavier describes how this change took place. Unintentionally, he shows how much can be achieved when the TfT approach is used over a long period of time by a leader deeply committed to the well-being of his people.

If you want to walk fast, walk alone; if you want to walk far, walk with others.   *African proverb*

I am working among the Adivasis (indigenous people) of Gujarat, a state in the north-west of India. I also worked among the Dalits (previously known as the untouchables) of Gujarat for over 20 years. I was already working as a Jesuit priest in Gujarat among the youth of the Catholic community. I then participated in the International DELTA programme (this was the name for Training for Transformation or TfT in the early years) in Nairobi, Kenya.

Although I had been working for several years, my work was not focused nor had I much understanding of the Dalit community and its culture. DELTA gave me a direction and it made me understand how to work in a community. What touched me most was the approach of DELTA: that it is by knowing the community and understanding the felt needs of the group that we can work effectively. This was something that changed my work, and, ever since then, I have found that my work to enable the community has been transformed. I am convinced that this method is the answer to empowering a marginalized community.

The Dalit community of Gujarat and elsewhere was exploited and suppressed by the so-called higher castes. In the caste structure, the Dalits were considered outcasts and lived outside the official village. Their rights and dignity were violated, atrocities were committed against them by the caste people, and they had to accept this situation despite laws against such exploitation and discrimination. This community lived in fear and felt themselves to be inferior and helpless.

Our methodology

Fear, an inferiority complex, and a lack of unity and self-confidence were some of the characteristics demonstrated by this community. Through the DELTA/TfT methodology, our team tried to deal with these issues. One of the methods we used was to help the Dalits to accept their identity. For this we went into the caste structure and helped the members tell their story of exploitation and suppression. We asked the participants to prepare songs and drama to express their situation. This had a tremendous impact on the group; analysing caste and studying how it functions and how the oppressed community internalizes it and carries on caste hierarchy even when the oppressor is removed. Naming the problem and understanding it from historical and sociological perspectives helped the participants to challenge it and to raise their heads. This has brought a sense of freedom and courage to the community.

Community leaders killed but the community became powerful

As the Dalit community in the Bhal area of central Gujarat – a predominantly caste-ridden society – became aware of its rights and started asserting itself, the dominant class – called Darbars in Bhal – could not accept the change. They created tension between two Dalit communities: Vankars, who were in the process of awakening, and Valmikis, who did not join the process. Darbars supporting the Valmiki community attacked the Vankar community and killed four of its leaders. This spread great fear among the Vankar community, which had slowly become aware of its rights and dignity through our programmes. After this incident it was clear that they would not now continue with the programmes, and we thought it was the end of our transformative process.

But we continued to support the Vankar community and accompanied them in this situation; we did not leave them to themselves. That gave them faith in us. On the first anniversary of this incident, we gathered all the leaders and discussed with them how to commemorate it. We decided to organize a torch rally from the four corners of the area, carrying four torches representing the four leaders, and to take the rally through the villages of Bhal and to merge the flames into one torch at the place of the murder. People were afraid of the consequences, but after much discussion they decided to organize the rally. It took them three days to complete the rally, covering the entire area and going through the villages where the Darbars were strong. We were with them throughout to support them in case any untoward incident took place. More than 20,000 people took part and on the third day they all gathered at the place where the four leaders were buried. The programme ended with a song prepared and sung by one of the leaders while the four torches were merged. The Darbars did not dare come out of their houses. The confidence with which the Vankars undertook the rally and the sheer number that gathered made the Darbars very quiet. The Vankars felt the power of their unity and it was an affirmation of their courage.

This demonstration had such a powerful impact on the community that the Vankars lost their fear and started living courageously. The court case that was registered when the leaders were killed was fought bravely, and finally 14 leaders of the Darbar community were sentenced to life imprisonment by the highest court in the state, despite the Darbars having political and economic power. The judgment added to the confidence of the Vankars. Today, the Vankar community of Bhal is confident and they live with dignity. This has set a good example and given courage to other villages. The Vankars decided to forgive the Valmiki community, which had been used as a pawn by the Darbar community, and they decided to work together towards Dalit unity. Their fear was transformed into power.

Transformation through legal aid and legal education

TfT was used for legal education among the Dalits and Adivasis; this helped empower these communities through information, enabling them to become aware of their rights and to deal with the injustice and discrimination they face. We started this programme when one of the Dalits who was working as a clerk in the tax collection office (octroi) was pushed out of his job by the village chief without any reason. He approached us for help. We used this incident as a code to make the villagers reflect on the situation. Initially not all the community members were ready because the village chief was a powerful person, but the victim was ready to fight the case. We started with those who were ready. Within a very short time the village chief admitted his mistake and promised to reinstate the clerk and give him back pay. This has given tremendous confidence to the people in the village and the marginalized people of the area. With legal help they were able to teach the village chief a lesson and they have been able to get justice. This experience has helped the community and the Dalits of the area remain empowered because of the process.

The marginalized take centre stage

As I interacted with and accompanied Dalit students, I realized that unemployment was a problem for them. They felt helpless, disadvantaged, and without opportunities. I went round the rural communities, conducted meetings in the villages, and discussed their situation with them and what could be done to improve it. What came up was the need for job-oriented courses. In order to help the most disadvantaged, we decided to start an English course and training for secretarial work. The criteria for admission were not having studied English at school, being from rural and economically backward areas, and having no opportunity for further studies. Our choice was for those who were most disadvantaged and marginalized.

English was taught through a needs-based approach; grammar was not taught but people were encouraged to speak English in the way a child would start learning its mother tongue. The teaching of English was also an occasion for social awareness and social analysis. We asked the students to share with the group their experiences of exploitation. The group would translate their contributions into English, and then the English was corrected and used as a text for the whole group. This programme was successful on two counts: not only did all the students start speaking English, but all those who went through the course got jobs and formed a youth organization to help other young people. Today that organization is affiliated with both a national and an international youth organization and is doing a wonderful job of transforming the youth of the Dalit community.

Failure of a programme transforms the community

As I started working with the Adivasis, I realized that most people working among the Adivasi were outsiders – non-Adivasis. I thought of preparing a cadre of young educated Adivasi youth to work among their community. An 18-month programme was envisaged that was affiliated to a national centre under the Indian government's Department of Rural Development. We procured a small stipend for the trainees. During the course, we experienced a large number of dropouts. After conducting two programmes, the youth of the Adivasi community did not show much interest. The programme lacked participants and we had to discontinue it. Reflecting on and evaluating the programme, we realized that the indigenous community was still looking for its basic needs and families expected the educated youth to get jobs rather than enter community service.

Some of the trainees who completed our 18-month course enrolled in university degrees. One of them, Salu Moris, an Adivasi girl from the backward Bhil community, is studying for her doctorate. She is enthusiastic about her identity as an Adivasi and is pursuing her study of the women of her Bhil community. This year she has been selected to go to Canada to represent her university, a rare privilege. She may be the first Adivasi woman from Gujarat to go abroad.

Our team continued with our reflection and action process. With this experience of failure, and from listening to the youth, we realized that what the community wanted was something that would provide further opportunities for educated young people, support to find work and to establish themselves. We have now started a career development training programme with spoken English, computer skills, careers guidance, and personality development. The students are also given training on interview skills, how to manage competitive exams, and so on. We also dealt with the social issues, as we had done among the Dalits. The programme is going well. There is great enthusiasm among the youth and the community and we have had two years with 60 young people in each year. This programme is preparing the youth for social transformation by responding to their immediate and basic needs. The graduates of the first course have shown interest in their community, and we are confident that this programme will bring about a transformation in the community.

The power of a united community

I work with the indigenous community (Adivasis) of Gujarat, who form 15 per cent of the total population of the state of Gujarat. Indigenous people make up 8.2 per cent of India's population – about 85 million. The Adivasi community is the most exploited and marginalized group in India. The Adivasis can be fearful, afraid to face outsiders, much less a government official. Unable to face difficulties or tensions, they run away to the forest or give up easily. They will often keep silent and will not show any initiative or interest in anything, even in things that affect their lives directly. They can be apathetic and might not express themselves easily. Although they are the original inhabitants of the country, they have been driven out into forests and mountains. During British rule, several laws were passed that dispossessed the Adivasis of their land, forests, and natural resources. After independence, the government of India continued these policies. To make matters worse, the Department of Forests made a decision in 2002 to prevent the Adivasis from 'encroaching' on the forest. This meant that more than 10 million Adivasis were dispossessed of their livelihoods and turned into beggars overnight.

When we started the programme of community transformation through TfT methodology, Adivasis were facing displacement. The problem was too large to deal with on our own. We contacted other NGOs and local groups and started networking with them, initially to make the Adivasis aware

of the impending danger of eviction. We formed a network of 43 organizations in Gujarat called Adivasi Mahasabha and a national alliance called Campaign for Survival and Dignity with 11 states where the Adivasis were affected by the order of the Department of Forests.

We organized awareness programmes for rural communities with capacity-building for the leaders and the youth. We used drama groups which would perform dramas and folk dances regarding the rights of Adivasis and the need to fight for them. These drama-cultural groups would perform at night in different villages where 300 to 3,000 people gathered for every performance. This, together with leaflets with relevant information in simple language, was used to raise awareness. Through awareness and organization of grassroots communities – and advocacy and lobbying – we worked for national legislation to protect the Adivasis and to recognize their rights over forest and other natural resources.

This resulted in getting a bill passed in the parliament of India in favour of the Adivasis. This new legislation acknowledged the rights of the Adivasis and promised to undo the injustices done to them. Farmers were given up to 10 acres of land each and every village was given community rights over the forest around it. What was taken away from the Adivasis by the British has now been partly returned to the people by this legislation.

It is encouraging that the struggle was won through local people's efforts. Neither the national nor the local network organizations received any foreign money for this project. There was now a change in the mindset of the people. It challenged their dependency and brought out their resourcefulness. The struggle was the beginning of a transformation of the community.

Today more than 182,000 individual applications have been filed in Gujarat alone to get these rights. The whole process helped the Adivasis recognize their rights and their strength. In several cases they started challenging the forest officials and the police and even filed criminal cases against them for not following the new legislation. Implementation of the legislation is still under way.

TfT and my personal transformation

During the first DELTA programme, I did not realize that I had changed, but I went back to Gujarat a changed person. Being a priest means to me an openness to the reality around me. I am called to experience the earth as the incarnated Jesus did. I now understand that my work is to create a better world where people can become fully human. More recently, I have understood that I have increased my consciousness to include a greater connectedness to the universe. Previously, it had been *me* who was working; they were *my* ideas and my plans. I was enthusiastic about work *for* the people. Now I realize that working *with* people, giving them a central place, understanding their culture, aspirations, and needs, is more important in any particular project. When we work with people we are there as a person learning, reflecting, and challenging to bring out the best in them and to enable them to take decisions that will affect their lives and situations. We are like leaven, interacting with the people who are transforming themselves and their community. In this process, unlike the leaven, we too are transformed.

My capacity to observe, reflect, and understand has increased. I have developed the ability to challenge groups in a non-threatening way. I have begun to give importance to the process rather than the product. It has made me open to different realities – and has made me patient with situations and people who do not change easily. I have learned to work in a team. My religion has become a religion that unites rather than separates. My spirituality has become a call and challenge to be who I am and to become who I am meant to be. God, for me, has become an all-pervading God who gives hope and comfort and who leads me, irrespective of my response to his or her plans. Failure, though difficult to accept, has become a challenge for me to look for better options and to change my plans. I am aware that I am becoming, that I am being transformed, but the work is not yet complete. I can, with sincerity and humility, say: 'Be patient with me because God has not finished with me yet.'

CHAPTER 4

From the DELTA to an ocean of possibilities: the story of Partners Training for Transformation in Ireland

Maureen Sheehy

Maureen Sheehy *participated in the first DELTA course run by Father Donal Dorr and Anne Hope in Ireland in 1980. Since then she has played a key role in developing an effective and creative programme called Partners Training for Transformation. Partners has worked with a wide range of groups with diverse needs, in Europe and the USA as well as in Ireland. Partners always tries to respond to new challenges, inventing something fresh and creative to meet needs, not repeating a process just because it has worked in other situations. Maureen has facilitated many such programmes in intercultural communication, management, dealing with conflict, and creative facilitation. She has helped to write and edit the* Partners Companion to Training for Transformation *with many new exercises.*

This chapter outlines how Training for Transformation has been used and adapted in Ireland and how many of the exercises and processes created over the years by Partners have been written up and made available to others through their publications.

When the drumbeat changes, the dancers must adapt.   *Burkina Faso proverb*

Beginning at the end

Partners Training for Transformation in Ireland has journeyed far since our first workshop with Anne Hope in 1981. What began as a group of 36 people doing a course has today developed into a non-profit organization offering a wide range of courses, resources, and interventions.

When asked how Partners has adapted Training for Transformation (TfT), the answer is that we do it constantly, in all kinds of situations, and in many creative ways. We see TfT as both a course that we run with groups and a resource. As a resource, it is one of the foundational blocks from which we respond to new challenges. Over the years we have also drawn from many other resources, such as Mari Fitzduff's and John Paul Lederach's work on conflict, participatory learning approaches, dialogue, appreciative inquiry, process-oriented psychology, Clark's model of community, and Augusto Boal's theatre of the oppressed – to name but a few. In all our work, TfT is a constant, its values and process approach influence and underpin all that we do.

Combining consolidation, responsiveness, and innovation

In its overall planning and work, Partners endeavours to attend to three different but overlapping dimensions: consolidation, responsiveness, and innovation.

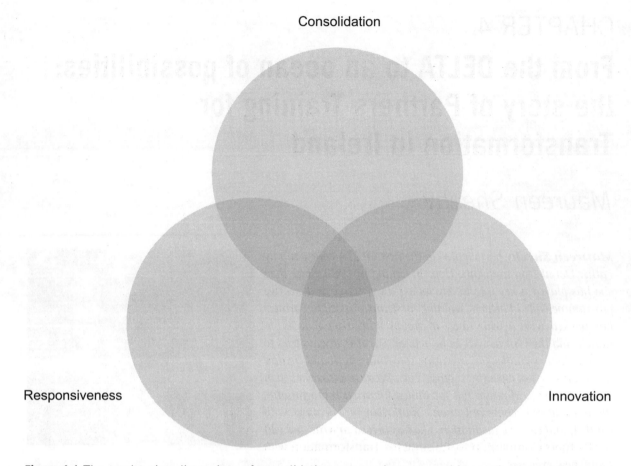

Figure 4.1 The overlapping dimensions of consolidation, responsiveness, and innovation

By **consolidation** we mean strengthening and building on the best of what we have always done, and this refers particularly to TfT. **Responsiveness** refers to the way we deal with requests from groups and communities as they invite us to provide new services or interventions. The third element is **innovation**. Partners seeks to be innovative and support innovation. Innovation generally involves seeing a need (which may be evident or unnoticed) and responding to it. But it may also be about seeing a new way of responding to a need, or indeed understanding or framing situations in new ways. It often carries risks because one is on new ground and the tried and trusted may not always work. It also carries risks because others may not perceive or acknowledge the need and may question the allocation of resources towards it.

What we do

Looking back over 32 years, one might ask:

- What kind of person does Partners engage with, or who uses its training and resources?
- What does it actually do today?

The kind of people that Partners attracted and engaged with, and who still use Partners' services, are people with high levels of commitment to social change. These can be members of local community groups with very different levels of education, paid and voluntary workers with local organizations, staff from local, regional, and national bodies, both statutory and non-governmental, and many others. What they all have in common is that they want society to be different. Many had searched for ways to do things differently and the approach they found in TfT resonated with something deep inside them. For many it was an 'aha!' moment when, together with others, they found a way to bring something they had dreamed of to life.

Partners in action

Today, Partners responds to many requests. Some are one-off pieces of work, but over the years several strong strands have emerged that usually are developed and improved on over several pieces of work. Much of our written resources have developed from these. Here are some examples:

- work with local community groups in both cities and rural areas;
- cross-border, cross-community work in the counties straddling the border of Northern and Southern Ireland;
- intercultural work;
- creative facilitation;
- reclaiming economics and making it accessible to non-economists;
- organizational development;
- specialized requests from particular groups.

Work with local community groups

Over the years, Partners has worked in every county in Ireland, both north and south of the border. One example of this is a community in West Dublin that Partners has supported and worked with since 1990. It began with a local group of women and two Partners facilitators, Fiodhna Callanan and Maureen Sheehy, doing a listening survey in the area. A local action group took the findings of the survey and based its community action on them. Two years later the facilitators returned and asked the women to listen again. Our contact with the group also led to three TfT workshops in the local area over the following 10 years. More recently, we have been invited to undertake intercultural work in the area for long-standing residents and newer residents who have emigrated to Ireland. People from the area have attended Partners courses, ongoing training, and nourishment days where they have had opportunities to meet other community activists from all over Ireland and beyond.

Cross-border, cross-community work

Partners has been involved in an enormous amount of cross-border work in the counties straddling the border, both before and after the peace settlement. TfT was an approach that lent itself to this kind of work and could be adapted to such things as reconciliation and dialogue. At present, one facilitator, Jacqui Gage, is involved in a third programme of conversations with migrants and Irish people. There have been workshops for Catholics and Protestants together and for Protestants from both sides of the border, and a course was held in Omagh quite soon after a tragic bombing that killed 29 people. People came together to get to know and understand each other and to work together for peace and justice for all.

Intercultural work

The work mentioned in the last paragraph in the north and south of Ireland is part of this work, but a new chapter in Irish history and in the life of Partners began in the mid-1990s when Ireland became, for the first time in modern history, an attractive destination for migrants from many places, but particularly from Eastern Europe, Africa, and Asia. Partners saw a need emerging but we did not have many resources to respond at first. We researched, learned, and innovated, and then, very significantly, got great help from Veronique Schoeffel, a very experienced intercultural trainer and a TfT practitioner from Switzerland, who guided us to think through what we needed to do and then pointed us towards useful resources. As we engaged more in this work, we began to record the processes and exercises. Our publication *Partners Intercultural Companion to Training for Transformation* (2007) is a direct result of this work and has been extensively used by individuals and groups both inside and beyond Ireland.

Creative facilitation

Over many years, people admired the way we worked and wanted to know how they could take a similar approach to their own work, and thus a new course was born – creative facilitation. This has run now for about 10 years and is attended by people from all walks of life. Also, we sometimes specifically run it for groups from a particular community, profession, or institute. One example was our work over nine years with the national body of Adult Education Guidance Counsellors. They wanted us to write a book for them; instead, we accompanied them as they developed a collection of relevant resources for their work with adults.

Reclaiming economics

Again, in this area a publication grew from an inquiry engaged in by Partners in conjunction with facilitators from Community Action Network (CAN). As training organizations, both groups had struggled with economic concepts and thinking, and in trying to help others grapple with the same subject. The joint group met over several months with sub-groups researching and experimenting with different processes. This resulted in a final product, *Reclaiming Economics: A Cooperative Inquiry* (2005), which described the process and outcome of what had been done.

Organizational development

For many years, Partners has been invited to work with organizations as they develop their own internal systems and structures. This can involve looking at participation in the group and how staff work together, what stage an organization is at, its vision, mission, and values, what networks it relates to, or what projects and activities it is engaged in. Partners designs what it does according to the needs of the particular group. Another publication emerged from this work when in 2010 two Partners facilitators, Jacqui Gage and Frank Naughton, working in conjunction with The Integration Centre in Ireland, developed and wrote *From Seeds to Trees: A Resource for Organisational Development*. (This publication is available to all and can be freely downloaded from the internet.)

Specialized requests

As well as mainly working with local community groups, Partners has also been invited to work with groups that have specific missions. Looking back at the variety of these groups has a kaleidoscopic feel to it – to name just a few, the Irish Wheelchair Association, members of the Travelling community (a minority group in Ireland), universities in Ireland and Scotland, the Anglican bishops of Wales, Concern America (a development agency in California), intercultural work with hospital staff and educational bodies, including the vocational education sector, and lots more.

Partners publications

Our publications reflect the evolution of our ongoing work and engagements. They are a practical example of consolidating, responding, and innovating. A guiding principle was to write simply so that the resources we were producing could be used by local community activists, even if they did not have a lot of formal education. And our attitude was that, if we don't have it or can't find it elsewhere, we will put our heads and imaginations together and invent it!

Publications to date

- *Partners' Companion to Training for Transformation* (2001): Our first publication was a collection of exercises and processes that had been developed by many facilitators over several years in conjunction with the original TfT handbooks by Anne Hope and Sally Timmel.
- *A Gathering at the Oasis: A Report on the Millennium Project* (2003)**:** This recounted the event held in Dublin in 2001 when TfT practitioners from 26 countries gathered in Dublin to share our experiences and learning.
- *Reclaiming Economics: A Cooperative Inquiry* (2005): This publication grew out of the combined work of two organizations, Partners and Community Action Network (CAN).
- *Partners Intercultural Companion to Training for Transformation* (2007): This is a collection of exercises and processes to use in intercultural work.
- *Rekindling the Fire* (2007): Tony O'Grady of Partners took the lead role in the production of a resource document from the Eastern Region Network of the Community Development Programme in Ireland.
- *From Seeds to Trees: A Resource for Organisational Development* (2010): As mentioned above, this was a joint production with The Integration Centre in Ireland.

Many of the processes we have developed are available in the books listed above, while many of Partners' resources, exercises, processes, and hand-outs are available to download. We are also presently writing up our creative facilitation work.[1]

How it all began

In 1981, the first TfT workshop took place in Ireland with Anne Hope and Father Donal Dorr as the leading facilitators. Half the participants had worked or were working in Asia, Africa, and South America; others worked in Ireland. They were people involved in a wide variety of activities including healthcare, education, pastoral work, and development work. A major concern of the participants based in Ireland was the growing marginalization of large sections of Irish society. They were seeking an approach to working in and with groups who were suffering the worst effects of deficient economic, social, and political structures and policies.

While several of the participants had read or studied the writings of Paolo Freire, many admitted that this was the first time they had seen his theory being put into practice in a way that was readily accessible and practical in terms of their work. The workshop proved to be a seminal experience for many involved. The challenge to truly listen for the 'generative themes' of those they worked with and to pose questions rather than give answers was for many their greatest learning. Two more workshops followed in 1982.

Setting up a core group

A group of people who had participated in these first three workshops and were mainly based in Dublin continued to meet regularly to exchange ideas and discuss work that they were trying to do using an approach that gave due attention to process. Their meetings became a very significant place of ongoing learning, support, and friendship. This led in 1984 to some forming a core group and setting themselves the task of continuing to run the two-week summer TfT workshop. They believed that at that time in Ireland it was something uniquely new and that there was no other similar 'process-type' training available for those working in all kinds of community situations. From 1984 to 1989, this group ran one or two national workshops each year.

A significant change in those attending the workshops occurred during the 1980s. At first there had been a mix of people from Ireland and of Irish people working overseas. Later, the participants on the courses were increasingly people from local communities or those working in voluntary or paid capacities in local groups and communities in Ireland. As these participants returned to their home-based projects, the voluntary core group began to get more and more requests to deliver the training to local community groups and organizations. The inaccessibility of the 12-day residential training for many people required that workshops be organized on a more flexible basis. So day, night, and weekend courses, which were later to become the norm, began to happen.

Partners established as an organization

Throughout the 1980s, Partners was an entirely voluntary organization, but, when demand for workshops greatly outstripped its capacity to respond, the voluntary core group decided to set up a limited company with charitable status. This happened in 1990, and two full-time workers were employed to develop the organization and to respond to the growing number of requests for courses.

By the mid-1990s, Partners was a prominent organization in the world of community development and community education in Ireland. As well as responding to training requests from locally based communities and organizations, Partners was for several years also under contract to run courses with the Department of Social, Community and Family Affairs, the International Fund for Ireland-sponsored Community Leadership Programme, and the Programme for Peace and Reconciliation. All of this work was with groups disadvantaged for various reasons.

During that same period, as an independent agency, Partners continued other work in Ireland and engaged in a significant and growing amount of work in Britain.

Partners also participated in a Grundtvig European Partnership Project for 2002–05. Practitioners working in formal and non-formal adult education sectors from organizations in seven countries – Norway, Denmark, Slovakia, England, Greece, Lithuania and Ireland – met twice yearly. The aim 'was to use the shared knowledge and understanding obtained through the practice-based workshops to act as a catalyst for stimulating discussions and debate on multicultural education within their institutions'. This was a very beneficial experience for Partners, and we believe we also contributed to the learning of others who participated.

Over the years, Partners has developed close working relationships with a wide range of individuals and organizations on the Irish scene – both north and south – as well as in Britain and Europe. At the same time, Partners has maintained links with a range of TfT practitioners and other organizations in the southern hemisphere and in the United States. These links allow for an interflow of innovative ideas and practices.

Partners approach and methodology

Partners' work is characterized by a number of features:

- Integral to the work is a group learning process whereby a temporary/learning community is created. This community-building function of the learning is a key characteristic.
- A variety of learning methods is used – discussion, art, simulation, role playing, drama, reflection, personal sharing, small group work, large group work, input, etc.
- The intention of the learning is to build confidence, competence, and commitment in participants as they engage in the creation of a society marked by equality, respect, and participation, and a particular concern with addressing the circumstances of marginalized communities.
- The content of the learning is primarily shaped by the expressed needs of the participants. Hence, Partners does not have a fixed template applied uniformly in every situation. Rather,

each piece is of a bespoke nature, tailored to the particular needs of the group involved, and it is in this constant design work that the creativity of our workers is best displayed.

- The learning has a problem-posing nature based on the belief that participants know their own needs and have the resources to address them.

What might Partners have done differently?

As we look back over 32 years of TfT in Ireland, we are for the most part happy with much of our work. We believe that when there were difficulties we reflected on them afterwards and learned from those situations. With hindsight, were we to do it all again, these are some of the things we might have done differently:

- In the early years we could have recorded and written up the new exercises and processes we developed. We tended to create and move on and often forgot worthwhile pieces of work. In recent years this is something we have improved on; by the end of 2013 many resources will be available on a new website.
- With hindsight, it would have been wiser to have refused to take on some pieces of work. This would mainly have been with groups who really wanted us to 'fix' people, although that was not how the project was presented to us initially. We became wiser as the years went on, asking more appropriate questions of anyone who was inviting us to do some work. This has led us to turn down some pieces of work, when we believe our core values about working with people and our methodologies do not match the request. This is a difficult choice to make at times when financial resources are low, but we believe it is important to do it to maintain the integrity of Partners.
- While over the years our emphasis has been on training and learning, we did not give an equal amount of time or energy to advocacy or networking. We put our energy into responding to immediate training needs, sourcing and developing new resources, and, while participating in some networking, we did not build strategic alliances that might have been of benefit in the long term.

So, 32 years on from that first workshop, we are grateful that Anne Hope, when exiled from her native South Africa, was able to get an Irish passport and in turn repaid the land of her grandmother by coming and sharing Africa's wonderful treasure of TfT with us.

Note

1   Resources are available at www.trainingfortransformation.ie, or books can be ordered from partners1@eircom.net.

PART TWO
Seeking the self

Keywords: circle conversations; community book writing; environmental awareness; masculinity; nature; peace-building; the rights of the child; the rights of the girl child; story-telling; self-esteem; wilderness experiences; young girls

http://dx.doi.org/10.3362/9781780448312.003

CHAPTER 5
What on earth are you doing? Girls using TfT to become visible in South Africa

Marilyn Aitken

Marilyn Aitken is the one of the founders of the Women's Leadership and Training Programme (WLTP). Before that she was the Justice and Peace co-ordinator for the Southern African Catholic Bishops' Conference. Now she works with women and girls in KwaZulu-Natal. She prepared the two excellent WLTP manuals, called Emthanjeni (At the wellspring), *applying the Training for Transformation methodology to programmes with young women. In the WLTP training, girls and young women are exposed to a wide range of experiences that build their capacity for holistic leadership. The experiences are categorized under seven themes: leadership and life skills; strategic gender analysis; culture and heritage; earth and environment; economic literacy; women's health; and ethics and morality.*

In this chapter she describes how TfT encouraged teenage girls to become visible, especially in relation to earth issues. It also stresses the need for all of us to observe 11 October as the United Nations Day of the Girl Child.

Footprints in the sands of time are not made by sitting down.   *Liberian proverb*

It is October 2013. A group of Zulu girls and a few boys meet regularly to discuss their new sightings of birds. Girl: 'I saw a beautiful bird yesterday in a tree near my house. It was blue-grey and had a black ring around its neck. It was making a cooing sound. What is its name?' Boy: 'That's a turtle dove. Before I joined this bird club my friends and I used to kill doves with our slings, roast them over an open fire, and eat the meat while we were herding cattle.' Another boy: 'Yes, we did that too. We also raided their nests for eggs.' Girl: 'You can show us where these nests are so that we can get their GPS co-ordinates and send the information by email to the ornithologists who are doing research on birds' nests and eggs.' Girl: 'I am so excited about this new world that is opening up for us. It's much better than staying at home sweeping, washing clothes, and cooking. I am glad we now have bird books, binoculars, and the birdcall package to help us become good birders. I am going to put the turtle dove on my Facebook page. My friends will think I am crazy, but I hope that one day they will also discover how exciting birds are.' Another girl: 'The cuckoos are due back from East Africa any day now. Has anyone heard them calling?'

Flashback to 1979. Anne Hope, Sally Timmel, Thelma Awori, and Jeremias Carvalho are facilitating a Grail workshop in Portugal. I am enthralled by what I am experiencing as Paulo Freire's theories become incarnated. All that has gone before in my life suddenly finds a new gestalt (framework). That 'aha!' experience revolutionized my life. Back in South Africa, I used my position in the Justice and Peace Commission to organize DELTA staff members in Kenya to run two workshops in Maseru, Lesotho, for South African Justice and Peace groups and for a Lesotho NGO called Transformation. Why Lesotho? Anne and Sally were banned from South Africa, and Kenyans would not have been granted visas. That was the beginning of many phased workshops from 1980 to 1984, in which South Africans and Kenyans (Josphat Mulyungi, Joseph Ikalur, Stephen Kyonda, Raymond Mnene, Wambui Muthoni, and Dominic Mwasaro), together with Enda Byrne and Donal Dorr, grappled with theological, economic, cultural, and political analyses, presented by experts such as Filip Fanchette (Mauritian), Theo Kneifel (German), Donal Dorr (Irish), Chris Langefelt (South African), and Prexy Nesbitt (American). The struggle against apartheid was reaching crisis levels and many of the workshop participants were involved in that struggle against oppression. The workshops were very exciting: the songs we sang were militant and the faith-sharing filled us with hope for our liberation. And the *codes* ... ! They are imprinted on my memory more than 30 years later. Since that time, I see 'codes' in many situations.

I was conscientized to question why there were so few women doing social justice work. The dream of a close friend, Emilia Charbonneau, became the 'code' that galvanized me into action. 'I was standing near a river. On the opposite bank were women holding out their hands to me. Tears rolled down their cheeks as they implored me to come and work with them.' In March 1985, the Women's Leadership and Training Programme (WLTP) was born.

First period of work with girls and young women, 1986–98

In 1986, the nationwide school boycott against the oppressive education system became the catalyst for a programme with girls. Lindi Mabaso, the 13-year-old daughter of Zodwa Mabaso, a WLTP staff member, brought her friends to meet us. They requested a workshop because they were tired of having nothing to do. That workshop for 30 teenage girls was the beginning of workshops for girls from the Johannesburg townships every long school holiday. We then answered requests from people in far-flung areas and trained core groups of young women to establish centres for girls in 12 locations in six provinces. One of these young women, Sibongile Mtungwa from Centocow, is now the director of WLTP.

My listening (and observing) survey took many years

A clause of my Justice and Peace job description read 'promoting the integrity of creation'. However, the immediate and pressing demands of the very anthropocentric liberation struggle gave me no time to explore the meaning of those words. Working with WLTP in the last decade of the twentieth century and over the past 13 years has helped me understand how important 'integrity of creation' is for the survival of the human species. The Teilhard de Chardin books I had read in 1969 began to make more sense after attending workshops on earth wisdom run by Hanna Remke, Emilia Charbonneau, and Miriam McGillis in the 1990s, and reading Thomas Berry's books. I am still working hard to discover my identity as a creature journeying and interacting with many other creatures and elements in the universe.

Natural phenomena are important in traditional family and religious rituals. For example, a deceased family member's spirit can be fetched from her grave in the city using the branch of a sacred tree. She is brought home to join her ancestors in the rural area. The girls we worked with had never previously been in a protected area because apartheid laws had excluded their families from game reserves. Unlike their grandparents, they had no spiritual connections to mountains, rivers, the sea, or indigenous forests. I once asked some girls to name the trees they knew. They answered 'peach, plum and orange'. Not one indigenous tree was mentioned. Many rural people who visit Durban to shop and stay with relatives do not bother to spend time by the nearby Indian Ocean.

People relate to weather almost as though it is an enemy. They complain bitterly that 'it's bad' (meaning it is raining) or 'it's too hot', 'too windy', or 'too cold'. They live against nature. In our Johannesburg office I observed my young colleagues coming to work in miniskirts in the middle of winter with temperatures of 2 degrees Celsius. They hugged the heaters or fires, kept the windows closed, and often did not open the curtains to let in natural light and warmth.

I found that girls had no understanding of the importance of the soil. To them gardening was something that old people did. It was definitely not for educated, 'cool' girls. The city girls knew nothing of the relationship between seeds, soil, sun, air, and water and the beetroots and cabbages they bought in supermarkets.

Then there is what Thomas Berry calls the 'technological trance', the preoccupation with mobile phones and social media, which excludes not only nature but also the people nearby. During my survey period, I met Annelies Henstra, a Dutch environmental lawyer, who is working with the IUCN (International Union for the Conservation of Nature) to lobby for the inclusion of the right of children to be immersed in nature in the UN's Convention on the Rights of the Child. My survey confirmed that, among girls, there was no understanding of the umbilical connection between humans and natural phenomena.

The challenge was how to make an unfelt need a generative theme

In 1996, I used a very risky code – a three-day trip to the uKhahlamba Drakensberg Wilderness in KwaZulu-Natal for 30 of the Johannesburg girls who had never before been immersed in nature. On the second day of the trip, we tackled the long 11-kilometre walk along the Tugela River Gorge towards its source. The more athletic girls set a cracking pace. The overweight girls kept up with them for the first 5 kilometres and then began to tire, groan, and complain loudly. I feared a revolt, but they gathered their energy to reach the end of the gorge, where we sat on the rocks and ate lunch. Many swam in the rocky pools below the waterfall. They somehow managed the 11-kilometre return walk.

At the end of the three days, we evaluated the variety of walks and activities, including self-catering. I was amazed and thrilled when all 30 girls chose the gorge walk as the highlight. It confirmed what theologians Albert Nolan and Donal Dorr have said: when people are exposed to the natural environment, they begin to connect with a milieu deeply hidden in their past consciousness. I was encouraged to continue with the work.

In 1999, I moved from Johannesburg to live in KwaZulu-Natal near the uKhahlamba Drakensberg Park (UDP), a very beautiful World Heritage Site area bordering Lesotho. My house is close to a rural settlement of 800 people. I discovered that no one in that village had ever been to the mountains of the UDP, which they could see from their homes. Our workshops from then on included a day in the UDP with a long walk along the Pholela River and a very steep climb to view the San/ Bushman rock art in a sandstone cave gallery. The Zulu youth echoed the earlier enthusiasm of the Johannesburg girls for the wilderness.

The earth and environment is now one of the seven themes in our programme with girls. They have attended UN meetings and have been noticed. Four girls were at the fifteenth Climate Change Conference of Parties (COP) in Copenhagen in 2009; four girls travelled alone to Nagoya, Japan, to the COP 10 of the UN Convention on Biological Diversity; and 40 girls and WLTP staff attended the UN's seventeenth Climate Change COP in Durban in 2011. One of these girls, Anelisa Shamase, gave the keynote address at the International Conference of Youth (680 participants) that preceded COP 17, and three of the girls were selected to be interfaith ambassadors before and during that conference.

Anelisa, who is studying environmental management and politics, said:

> I grew up in the city and there was literally no connection between me and the environment. I have attended three COPs where I have been with thousands of people coming together out of concern for the earth and the growing loss of biological species. That made me more aware that what we had learned in WLTP workshops was very serious. I now have a different approach to the environment and a new relationship with the tree outside my window that I see when I draw the curtains in the morning.

WLTP girls, together with a few boys from their brother project, Inhlabamkhosi (the Trailblazers), attended a recent meeting in which the head of Ezemvelo KZN Wildlife met with the Underberg

community. After Dr Bandile Mkhize's presentation, it was announced that he would leave after a short time, to get some sleep before an early plane trip. The WLTP girls were the first to ask questions and they continued to engage him for more than an hour and a half. His public relations officer, Richard Compton, told me afterwards that the girls had made that meeting the most interesting of all the meetings he had organized for Dr Mkhize. He wants to make a film of the work the girls do.

Work with young men and women, 1999–2006

From 1999 until 2006, WLTP entered a new phase of including young men on our staff and in our work. Young people were being buried almost every weekend in the rural areas of KwaZulu-Natal, so training HIV and AIDS education teams was a priority. Other projects were related to culture, heritage, and tourism, as well as gender work and environmental education. The agendas of the young men and their bad behaviour began to sap our energy, and we closed the projects at the end of 2006.

Making amends to girls

We regret losing our focus on girls during WLTP's seven-year detour at the beginning of the 21st century. In 2007, we reverted to working with girls only, aged 9 to 18, with five Grail staff members. Now, in 2013, we have an intergenerational staff, aged 19 to 75, having been joined by five of the young women we began working with in 2007.

The themes we developed in the previous phase provided some of the content of the new Emthonjeni (Come to the Wellspring) programme. A key element was ethics and morality, to address the 'WaBenzi' syndrome that has dominated South African culture since the dawn of democracy (the WaBenzi are those who drive Mercedes-Benzes and are preoccupied with wealth). In our workshops in the 1980s, the Kenyans had analysed this phenomenon in their own society. We were sad when our new rulers became WaBenzis, modelling materialism and the scramble for status symbols, the internalized values of the ruling class they replaced (Ngugi wa Thiong'o, 1986).

In South Africa, many women have suffered at the hands of the patriarchy. Without any way to analyse their internalized oppression, they pass it on from generation to generation through their interactions with their daughters. Girls crave love and affirmation from their mothers, but what they receive is negative criticism. Women in the community and family members call girls 'makoti' (young bride) from a very early age and many girls move into this cultural mode of being the household domestic worker – a young woman who waits on her brothers and father, and nannies her younger siblings. Girls' many household chores prevent them from being involved in activities and decision-making on girls' issues.

Through their literal interpretation of the creation story in Genesis Chapter 2, churches also reinforce the belief that girls are the inferior daughters of Eve, the evil woman. By promoting a different understanding of the process of creation, WLTP tries to counteract the negative cultural messages given to girls. By relating the first creation story in Genesis Chapter 1 to the scientific evolutionary story, girls grasp that they are important creatures who are connected to many other creatures in the web of life. Their self-esteem grows.

A number of WLTP girls have attended hearings of the UN Commission on the Status of Women (CSW), where they discovered that abuse of girls and young women is a worldwide phenomenon. CSW addresses women's and girls' oppression and honours girls who have done outstanding work with their peers. As a result of CSW's work, the UN has declared 11 October the International Day of the Girl Child. August in South Africa is celebrated as Women's Month, but girls and young women are largely excluded from the events held to empower and celebrate women. So this year, WLTP will celebrate the Girl Child in a small way on 11 October in the three areas where we work. At the same time, we will lobby the South African CSW to create a public holiday on 11 October because girls deserve to be celebrated!

Why birds?

This is a question we are frequently asked.

Birding is an easy, fun way for young people to enter into the web of life. Birds, since the days when dying canaries warned British coal miners of lethal gases, are an indicator species. They warn human beings of impending danger. The many bird species that are on the brink of extinction are alerting the human species to the dangers of global warming and climate change and the factors causing these phenomena. South Africa is the custodian of the third largest number of animal and plant species after Brazil and Indonesia. Of these species, birds are the most beautiful, the most visible, the most mobile, and the most eloquent. They are faces of the creator. They do not recognize political boundaries, have many different habitats, and some fly very far. The cuckoos migrate between East Africa and South Africa. The red-chested cuckoo, the Phez'komkhono, starts calling persistently early or later in October, monitoring the timing of the spring rains. According to Zulu people, it is saying, 'Raise your forearms. It's time to start planting.'

An amazing small bird, the Amur falcon, flies 10,000 kilometres twice a year, linking northern China with South Africa. The Amurs arrive in December and sit on our telephone lines during the day, looking out for a meal. They roost in their thousands in a few tall trees until March, when they head back to China to breed, via Zimbabwe, Mozambique, Tanzania, Kenya, Somalia, India, and Afghanistan. A major disaster befell 120,000 of these Amur falcons on their last migration south: they were caught in nets in Nagaland in north-east India. Conservationists in the area have taken major steps to work with the local people to stop the slaughter of these birds in the future. In this case, birds are telling us how urgent it is to close the gap between rich and poor.

WLTP girls are involved in work to conserve a number of critically endangered bird species while also educating people about ways to reduce their carbon footprints.

Learning for the future development of this approach

- Don't be afraid to go where angels fear to tread.
- Use innovative codes.
- It is possible to raise awareness even when the need is not felt by your target group.

- Follow your heart and study the new fields opening up (my certificate course in environmental education in 2006 was a further 'aha!' experience).
- Until girls are empowered, it is better to work separately with boys and girls. We initiated a boys' training programme in 2009 for that purpose and collaborate frequently in projects such as actions against gender violence and birding
- Intergenerational work is mutually very enriching, challenging, and energizing.
- Girls can be seen and heard even in meetings where the majority of people are as old as their grandparents and of a different racial group.
- Don't listen to those in the environmental field who say that it is not possible for historically disadvantaged youth to become good conservationists.
- It is crucial to 'decolonize the minds' of those who cannot see the relevance of earth issues, so that all creatures will continue to thrive for many generations to come.

References

Berry, T. (1986) *The New Story: Life from a Planetary Perspective*, Langley, WA: Context Institute.

Ngugi wa Thiong'o (1977) *Petals of Blood*, London: Heinemann.

Ngugi wa Thiong'o (1986) *Decolonising the Mind: The Politics of Language in African Literature*, London: James Currey.

Teilhard de Chardin, P. (1961) *The Phenomenon of Man,* New York, NY: Harper and Row.

Teilhard de Chardin, P. (1965) *Building the Earth*, Wilkes-Barre, PA: Dimension Books.

Teilhard de Chardin, P. (1965) *The Divine Milieu*, New York, NY: Harper and Row.

CHAPTER 6
Unshackling my heart: when masculinities become equalinities – a South African story

Mike Abrams

Mike Abrams works primarily with boys and men in community development in Cape Town and the small towns in the Southern Cape of South Africa. Acutely conscious of the effects of apartheid, and more recently of massive unemployment, on the self-image and self-confidence of boys and young men, he has done pioneering work helping them to build a new understanding of masculinity, finding their own potential and new hope for their future lives. Mike has also facilitated the gender module in the Training for Transformation diploma course in Kleinmond. He utilizes transformative education in all aspects of his work, especially community development.

In this moving chapter he shares how he works with men using conversation circles and wilderness areas as contexts in which men can discover who they really are and how they could relate in a more fulfilling way to other men and to women.

Every elephant has to carry its own trunk.   *Zimbabwean proverb*

Imagine if you will, in your mind's eye, thousands of men queuing to vote for the very first time. The dawn of democracy in South Africa and a chance to put years of oppression and horribleness behind us, building equality and peace between our people. Flip the switch and travel forward with me to 2013 and feel the pain and groans of our nation suffering under a tsunami of interpersonal violence between men and women, men and children, and men and men.

What we never understood in that moment of new power was that oppression overwhelms the emotional and physical resources of people and communities. Three hundred and fifty years of conflict over resources, power, and control had scarred the nature of our society. Brutality and violence, revenge and shame, loss and dispossession, repeated over and over again, across generations, have ripped apart the psychological skin of individuals and communities leaving human bonds fragile, people dislocated, and communities in trauma. The effects of this trauma linger on and on and on. We thought we could wash the history of brutal oppression away with the Truth and Reconciliation Commission, 'Mandela magic', and the 'miracle of the Rainbow Nation'. What we did not realize at that time was that the thousands of men who queued that day to vote were carrying inside them hearts deeply scarred by this legacy. How naive a newly free nation can be, and how difficult is the transition from war to peace and democracy.

Traditionally indigenous men's role was to be the external link between family and community – the hunter, protector, and provider. The material basis for this was a nomadic and/or pastoralist existence in which land was communally owned and thus access to land and, therefore, wealth open to all men. This conferred ranking and status, meaning and purpose, which were the foundation blocks of male identity. Colonial land theft, forced and migrant labour, and influx control systems destroyed these social and economic relationships, separating men from their families and their land. Men learned to live in societies of men where control was exercised through coercion, normalizing violence as a way of life and creating a new sense of masculinity, a scarred and wounded sense of identity.

This was true of those of slave heritage as well, and also of men of the oppressor group who emerged into the new South Africa with scarred and wounded identities from years of conflict.

The new democratic government did little to address war-torn forms of masculine identity. There were no campaigns to help men scarred by generations of war and dispossession to rediscover new identities based on peace and democracy and to find an equal place in their families. The lack of a national understanding of the impact of war on masculinity allowed for these skewed identities to become normalized and legitimized and transferred from generation to generation. The unemployment visited on us by globalization and the sense of betrayal of the promises made by our liberation movements have extended these scars into deep feelings of rage and anger that seem to burn out of control.

However, the story I want to share with you is not one of pain and loss, of violence and control, of racism and mundane brutality. This story has been told many times. I want to share with you a story of hope and passion, a story of men unshackling their hearts to overcome the legacies of oppression; a story in which a group of men found a key to the chains binding our hearts, creating new masculine identities based on equality and peace – equilinities, a masculine identity based on equality.

The first part of the story begins in the late 1980s amidst the states of emergency and the struggle against apartheid. At that time I was working for the South African Domestic Workers' Union, desperately seeking approaches to use in educating workers. I was given a photocopy of a book smuggled into the country and passed from hand to hand by a guy called Paulo Freire, *Pedagogy of the Oppressed*. To be frank, at that point I did not even understand what pedagogy was. What a book! Difficult to read and make sense of, but jam-packed with ideas that exploded my heart and began to give me a framework to work with. I struggled along, trying to implement these ideas, until in the early 1990s I came across *Training for Transformation* (TfT). At last a series that made Freire practical and understandable, full of techniques we could immediately implement. The last strand came from discovering the work of Augusto Boal, an application of Freirean theory to theatre and therapy. Boal's work ensures that, through the use of drama, participants are actively engaged in deep learning using body, heart, and soul. His use of theatre techniques in therapeutic processes provided me with practical ways of engaging people to become responsible for their own healing.

These philosophies and the experience of popular education transformed me. They soon became a way of life, deepening my own consciousness and enabling me to develop a practice that is holistic, fun, and transformative.

My work with men started in 2000 as part of a group of community development workers[1] facilitating a programme in a poor suburb of Cape Town. We quickly began to realize that the violence and dislocation plaguing the neighbourhood were caused by men and young boys, while the renewal programmes were driven by women. A scarred division of labour, to say the least. The women often scoffed at men and felt that they were mostly a lazy bunch only interested in drinking and being violent. So we began a conversation with men on street corners, in schools, and in shebeens. We asked what was going on for them. Why were they resisting change and liberation? What would get them involved in reconstruction and development?

The answers shocked us. Men began telling stories of pain and anger. Stories of how unemployment and being unable to provide for their families were crushing their spirits. Stories of the hurt and rage caused by forced removals. Stories of how living under apartheid had robbed them of their dignity and ability to speak up and act. Stories of how alcohol and drugs helped to fill the inner emptiness and overcome the pain. Men told us of how they would like to have better relationships with the women in their families, but somehow they were unable to speak to them about what was going on inside them, skewing the meaning and purpose of life. Stories of men's hearts bound so tightly that the only emotions they could feel were anger, frustration, and loneliness.

These stories began a journey that has lasted till the present, as we have grappled with understanding how oppression and social trauma can overwhelm individual men and communities as a whole.

It has also led us to develop tools for providing men with a space to debrief and rediscover who they are, and in so doing create new masculine identities for themselves. Absolutely central to this was our understanding of popular education and the work of Paulo Freire and TfT.

Freire's work calls on us to develop a critical consciousness about who we are and how the world is, and to engage in action to transform these realities. This philosophy also directs us to start with where people are, and allow them to journey to where they need to be. What we felt was missing for the men to enable them to make this journey was an emotional literacy that would allow expression of their deeper feelings – a personal clearing of the emotional path and a releasing of new energies to discover a different self. In the first years of our work we developed two key tools to provide a platform for men to engage in a process of creating a new language and a new sense of power.

The first tool we developed we called 'circle talk'. It was a chance for men to get together regularly in their own communities and engage in a process of consciousness-raising, a space for movement in which individuals could relate to one another in a different way that would encourage a new level of communicating and thinking, a space within which participants could begin to see their potential, a common healing space, a thinking space, a problem-solving space, in which individuals could discover their passion and a new sense of purpose, inspiring each other to break the chains around their hearts. Our belief was that inspiration creates hope, hope generates energy, and energy produces power. The more inspired we are, the more hopeful we are, the more energetic we are, and the more power we produce. As we began to experiment with the characteristics of this 'circle space' we learned that inspiration, hope, energy, and power are inseparable – they flow from one to the other. This process embodies the mind, body, and spirit. The work of Augusto Boal was also helpful in that it assisted us in understanding the phenomenon of 'circle talk', and how it allowed us to move between action and reflection in a simultaneous moment. A participant could stand up and act out a story from his past, and we could discuss and understand it and provide him with an opportunity to 'rehearse for reality' by trying out new ways of being.

However, for men to 'open up' and tell their stories it meant that we, as facilitators, had to find the right questions and themes. The learning we had gained from the use of codes in TfT helped us to develop these themes. Over the first three years, participants developed codes and questions that were relevant to their own situations. Topics such as: what message did you receive from your father about being a man? What is fathering? What is father hunger? How are these related to the history of your community? How can you 'fix it' with your father? With your community? How are your relationships in your family? In your community? Why do you always feel lonely? Competitive?

These themes were then tried out among men of different communities and cultures, allowing us to begin to develop manuals and train facilitators to extend our reach beyond the initial group of five men. However, codes and themes that lit the fire of discussion and reflection were not enough. Men wanted to come to our circles and de-stress, have fun, and enjoy themselves. This led us to introduce games and play as a way of reconnecting to our inner child, assisting with understanding the journey from childhood to manhood, and recognizing what was lost in this process. We also used visual arts and music for men to discover their ability to be creative human beings.

Whenever I describe these circles, my listeners become excited with the possibilities inherent in them for challenging and overcoming existing forms of power and woundedness. However, we discovered that the circles were not enough for self-realization. Men had been deeply wounded and the continuing unemployment and social dislocation were feeding this. Circles helped but did not allow us to go deep enough into the histories and stories of each man, uncovering the sources of wounding and seeking new ways of going forward.

To circle talks, we added the idea of a 'wild space', a collective and personal space that would peel away the layers of emotional hurt experienced by men, allowing a new consciousness to develop. This led us to experiment with the indigenous tradition of 'going to the mountain' to seek clarity and direction in one's life. Over time, the 'wild at heart' wilderness experience was developed as a healing space. Participants are taken from towns and cities into a mountainous area that is free of houses, people, and other forms of development. The wilderness is an un-boundaried, uncontained space and is very evocative; consequently, in the process, staff and participants need to be carefully contained while allowing the elements/nature to engage the individual in a process of inner and outer exploration and healing.

The wilderness component was designed as a form of interactive theatre in which the individual man and the group are offered an opportunity to enter into the hearts of their lives, discover the source of their pain, release that pain, and begin the journey of seeking new sources of their power. Facilitators play many roles in this process as participants are led on a journey that includes overnight solo time, storytelling, fire dances, rituals, and cleansing ceremonies. We found that the reconnecting of men to nature, to their essential state, was an extremely powerful tool for healing. To assist us in the design of this 'wild space', we drew on the drama therapy techniques of Augusto Boal and on Freire's philosophy of experiential learning. Having come through the 'wild at heart' process, men are more able to see their lives and social context more clearly, enabling them to make the link between individual experience, oppression, and social dislocation.

Over the last 10 years, we have had many success stories of men who have engaged in circle talk and wild spaces and have changed the nature of their relationships and engagement in the world. These range from drug merchants and youths in the juvenile justice system to couples and families developing healthier forms of relating to each other. We have developed manuals, trained facilitators, and begun circles in towns and villages across the Western Cape region. One such example is from the district of Cape Agulhas, situated on the southernmost tip of Africa. Over the last five years a circle of men has developed that is known as Boys2Men. This group of nine male facilitators has a regular programme of workshops, camps (wild spaces), and indigenous games. Events such as Father's Day offer counselling and engagement in other social development activities in the community. The group is completely voluntary with support coming from the local municipality in the form of access to venues, stationery and photocopying, transport, and food for events and workshops. Recently, the group has begun a series of dialogues between men and women in partnership with a local women's organization. The dialogues are focused on men and women sharing understandings and perceptions of each other, and seeking a common understanding of how to be and do together.

So the story sounds wonderful, and yet here we are in 2013 under a tsunami of male violence and a crisis of masculine identity, which reminds us of how little we have achieved. While we have small victories on an individual and group level, the situation has grown worse, not better. In some respects our own failures lie at the heart of this. While we have changed lives, we have failed so far to engage the wider society to generalize our understanding and learning. Besides outside funding proposals and the odd article, we have not managed to write much about what we are doing or train nearly enough facilitators to reach a tipping point, even within our own communities and province. The shortage of funds and support from men in leadership positions serves as an enormous obstacle. In addition, conflicts over approach and objectives continue to plague the wider grouping of organizations working in this area. As non-governmental organizations, we are struggling with differences over our broader vision of creating spaces for men's healing, which is what we are doing, or initiating a men's movement. As men develop the emotional literacy to talk about their oppression, trauma, and experiences, and as we learn as a nation that men can also be harassed and violated, we are beginning to argue that men's and women's experiences are equal. This has the unintended effect of masking the true nature of the patriarchal system, through which men are always in an objective position of greater power.

Through our experiences we have also learned that any intervention with men must contain five key elements, which we call the spice of life:

- *Social:* How we relate to ourselves, to people, to groups, and to the world.
- *Psychological:* How we think about ourselves, and others, and situations.
- *Intellectual:* How we engage with exploring, questioning, reasoning, and reflecting.
- *Cultural:* How we develop a sense of history, community, and togetherness.
- *Emotional:* How we feel about ourselves, our families, and other people, and how we nurture the spiritual inside ourselves.

Perhaps an even more fundamental learning has been that men need to work with men. If we want to travel deep into the heart of a man, provide confessional moments, and create new sources of power, this process must be facilitated by men. This seems to be because the presence of women facilitators inhibits men from making this deeper journey as they feel judged and found guilty before the journey begins. In addition, we have learned that the facilitators doing this work often need lots of support as they work through their own issues and develop the skills necessary to facilitate the spaces men need to overcome the chains binding their hearts. Leading healing journeys, whether in communities or wild spaces, requires skill and deep self-awareness and an individual 'toughness' of character that prevents other people's pain from destabilizing the facilitator. Leaders of these processes need constant debriefing and support to ensure their own emotional and psychological well-being.

The journey of unshackling our hearts has begun, nurtured by the work of Freire, Boal, and TfT, and by the enormous spirit and desire for change shown by unnamed South Africans from all parts of our province. The journey will continue despite the obstacles, for 'a journey of a thousand kilometres always begins with the first step'. Aluta continua!

Notes

1   This group included Des Van Niekerk, Nic Fine, Solly Marlowe, Nolan Abrahams, Anthony Daniels, Lionel Arnolds, and Mariette Griessel. Thanks to all, I hope the chapter reflects your amazing insights and companionship on this journey. The chapter also details the work of Hands On Collective and Hearts of Men.

References

Freire, P. (1973) *Education for Critical Consciousness*, New York, NY: Seabury Press.
Freire, P. (1973) *Pedagogy of the Oppressed*, London: Penguin Books.
Freire, P. (1992) *Pedagogy of Hope: Reliving Pedagogy of the Oppressed*, New York, NY: Continuum.

CHAPTER 7

Even the smallest bird can sing from the tallest tree: community publishing for transformation

Kathy Bond-Stewart

Kathy Bond-Stewart *began community publishing with Chris Hodzi in a development ministry in 1986, and about two years later they were joined by Ntombi Nyathi and later Lucia Manyuchi. In 1995, the four founded Africa Community Publishing and Development Trust. Over the years they have held storytelling workshops in every corner of the country, and discussions with rural communities on crucial issues concerning the participants. These include civic education, peace-building, local government, poverty reduction, gender equity, and children's rights. Training for Transformation has been used to develop leadership in their own and other organizations.*

This chapter describes how they have adapted TfT by adding book production and distribution of community books and poster codes. In the process, important capacity-building has taken place, and constructive communication and relationships have been built across the divides of politics, roles, gender, and age.

A precious jewel may be found in a ragged bag.   *African proverb*

Community publishing has developed amidst the hopes and problems of post-independence Zimbabwe as a way of overcoming destructive power relations and the exclusion of impoverished rural communities, women, youth, and children from media and public life. I attended Training for Transformation (TfT) in 1983. Although I had learned Paulo Freire's methodology in Portugal, the clear practical guidelines on the use of codes and symbols, socioeconomic analysis, understanding groups, social movements, and spirituality were very helpful. From 1986 to 1994 in Zimbabwe, Ntombi Nyathi, Lucia Manyuchi, artist Chris Hodzi, and myself blended TfT with the collective production and distribution of books in order to design training and training materials for 7,000 village community workers. Community-based books were chosen as a tool for change because of Zimbabweans' passion for reading and writing.

Practice

Community publishing is an internally driven process of change, rooted in the wisdom, creativity, and solidarity of communities, combined with relevant information. The process of community publishing includes community-based research, publishing, education, and organizing. The process is as important as the products – the books and picture codes – and both are used for capacity enhancement and advocacy. The phrase 'Even the smallest bird can sing from the tallest tree' (which is also the title of the book) expresses the essence of community publishing. Each person, at any age, no matter how difficult the circumstances, has something special to contribute to the world. Once given recognition, encouragement and support, the smallest, those whom society has forgotten or excluded, including children, can become very creative, influential, and significant in transforming their situation.

Over the years, community publishing was further developed and applied to poverty reduction, democratic development, gender equity, good local governance, peace-building, and children's rights. The main shifts as community publishing developed were:

- leaving a development ministry and becoming an independent trust, Africa Community Publishing and Development (ACPD), in 1995;
- focusing on local governance in rural districts;
- balancing problem-posing with confidence-building;
- from 2008, after violent elections, prioritizing the reduction of all forms of violence through building constructive communication and relationships across the divides of politics, roles, gender, and age;
- scaling up by increasing print runs (from 1,000 to 3,000 books, to 10,000 to 30,000 books, followed by reprints), distributing books nationally through more than 70 non-governmental and governmental agencies, and increasing coverage of workshops to about 100 wards;
- recognizing the family as the key site for social change;
- from 2010, setting up children and youth book teams and publishing young voices in all aspects of community publishing.

Impact

In an area with a history of intense violence, police and local leaders estimated that ACPD's peace-building programme had reduced both organized and domestic violence by 75 percent. A previously violent man testified:

> Before I used to beat my wife, ill treat my kids and brutalize communities on any grounds, but because of the peace-building workshops from ACPD I am now a real husband, father, and man of the people.

Illustration by Anxious Katuruza

A woman from the same province said:

> The books have helped us come up with our own solutions. Most of us women had no voices in the community but now we can contribute to the decisions on local government and development. Our local leaders and men actually listen to us now. Every view is valued.

ACPD designed a creative process, called 'What about us?', to enable 4,000 children from 10 provinces to participate in constitution-making. This was done in co-operation with Childline, Justice for Children, UNICEF and the Ministry of Constitutional and Parliamentary Affairs. The young campaigners achieved 80 per cent of what they had advocated for in the children's rights section of the new constitution. A core group of young poets and artists have continued to contribute their views on all sections of the constitution in ACPD's constitutional awareness materials entitled Our Country, Our Home. They are very active in promoting a culture of constitutionalism. These young writers, artists, and researchers have also contributed new insights into children's experience of dealing with violence, in the book entitled *Singing to the Lions*. A young poet and junior facilitator who was previously out of school writes:

> Before I met ACPD when I was 16, I was like a lost sheep wandering in the jungle, with low self-esteem and conforming to everything imposed ... I was like a doll, docilely meeting societal expectations no matter how ridiculous they were. However, now, through community publishing, I have a strong voice backed by massive confidence ... I can now challenge and question all forms of injustice and abuse ... I am proud to be a lion singer, for my sweet melody makes a difference in my community and society.

Illustration by Anxious Katuruza

What could have been done differently?

- The haste with which civil society organizations advocated for constitutional reform 15 years ago actually slowed down the process of a transition to a peaceful and democratic society.
- The organizational basis of ACPD programmes should have been developed simultaneously with the rapidly growing community publishing and capacity-building programme.

Lessons

Over 27 years, we have learned the following lessons:

- The production of books and posters rooted in community creativity enables females and males, young and old, to develop confidence, critical consciousness, and organizational skills, influence public opinion positively, and explore practical, democratic alternatives.
- The books and posters are a cost-effective way of communicating important messages and transferring effective development methods across rural and urban Zimbabwe and linking the local to the national spheres (and, in future, through the internet, to international readers).
- For new ideas and methods to be internalized, on a large scale, they need to be integrated within local governance and linked to national governance.
- Through using positive forms of power to challenge negative power, creative subtle ways of communicating and constructive relationships, it is possible to reduce violence, break through many barriers, and open up democratic spaces.
- Diversity is fruitful and stimulating, blending children, youth, and adults, female and male, rural and urban, from different backgrounds in workshops and publications.
- Children in Zimbabwe, as in most African countries, are a silenced majority, but their intelligence, creativity, courage, compassion, and resilience are among the best sources of hope.

Changing lives

Community publishing, an offshoot of TfT, can make a difference to the lives of previously marginalized people and contribute to their happiness. As a child and a woman commented:

> When I discovered community publishing I was the happiest person and about to touch the sky because I knew I could use my talent for writing and drawing to change people's lives – Bright Pencil

> The books help us to live together peacefully and have happiness and abundance – Lizzy Chipo Marusha

PART THREE
Healing the wounds of war

Keywords: empowerment from below; follow-up and support; healing conflict; intercultural; interfaith; networking; overcoming historical enmity; peace-building in the Balkans; people with disabilities in campaigns; phased training; rebuilding communities; redress; reparations; restitution

http://dx.doi.org/10.3362/9781780448312.004

CHAPTER 8
Unity and peace-building after conflict in Rwanda

Chriseree Niyonsenga

Chriseree Niyonsenga is from Rwanda. She was working for the Irish Catholic funding agency Trócaire when Sister Colette Corvin introduced her to the Training for Transformation *handbooks. Together they tried using some of the codes in their work of rebuilding trust in local communities after the trauma of the genocide. It proved so effective that they set up a programme of TfT courses. In 1998 Trócaire closed its community development department in Rwanda, but Chriseree and three others who had been using the TfT methodology decided that it was essential to continue this type of training. They founded their own training organization, which they called Association pour le Développement et la Transformation Sociale (ADTS). Over the years, they have built a solid series of training programmes, starting with introductory courses, then holding the four basic phases of training as they were developed in Kenya. They have added more advanced training for those using the method, and the people trained have worked in many effective ways to rebuild trust and peace in communities after the genocide. This is the story of their work in conflict resolution and relationship-building in Rwanda.*

It is not where you are but what you do there that matters.　　*Rwandese proverb*

I want to talk about the background of the Training for Transformation (TfT) approach in my own work life in Rwanda. I worked for an international organization (Trócaire) from Ireland as a social worker from September 1994. During that time, the activities were focused on emergency programmes to assist internal refugees (with food, kitchen materials, and medicine, particularly in the camps). This period was characterized by suspicion among people from different ethnic groups and from different historical backgrounds, especially as a consequence of the genocide. People had almost lost the value of life, because death, violence, fear, and other sorts of terrible emotions had taken a big toll on Rwandan life.

In 1996, Trócaire moved from emergency relief to development to help people plan for life in the future. According to the reformulation of Trócaire's mission, I found myself in the Community Development Department. At the beginning, our work was focused on the integration of genocide survivors from different camps, both inside and outside the country, in their respective communities in Nyaruguru district. It was a challenge to help them from the trauma of genocide to feeling comfortable in the community, where they were surrounded by people who they thought had killed their relatives. We were all traumatized by what we had been through.

I was with Sister Colette Corvin from Ireland in the Community Development Department. She told me that she knew a training approach called DELTA that came from the philosophy of a Brazilian, Paulo Freire, and that could be used at this difficult moment. She had the three TfT books and gave them to me, asking me to read them carefully and come back with my insights.

After I had read the books, we tried to select codes that could be used with our target groups in the community. Our selected codes were River of My Life (Journey of My Life), Win–Lose, Broken

Squares, Arm code, Animals code, and Johari's Window, and we used the principles of DELTA training. We brought together the survivors and other people in the community in Nyaruguru district for the first training session. In that session, participants discussed all these different codes, analysed them, and related them to their life situation. After this training, trainees committed to change their view of their neighbours. They decided to forgive and start a new life. In the villages where there were trainees, I saw how people started to understand each other, to work at common activities in order to build their relationships, and to help each other without discriminating. The trained people testified how DELTA training helped them in their personal life and in the community. From the experience of the first training sessions, we learned that DELTA training can play a major role in changing our mindset, from internal and civic conflicts to a spirit of co-operation in the work of healing ourselves and peace-building for the future.

That is why, when Trócaire closed the Community Development Department in 1998, three colleagues and I decided to start our own organization that would continue this important work in our country. It is called Association pour le Développement et la Transformation Sociale (ADTS) and was created with the goal of radical transformation of the human society through the TfT approach. From that time, as committed members of ADTS, we have struggled to gain skills in TfT/DELTA training. Through our experience of both the four phases of DELTA training in Kenya and the TfT diploma course, as well as further reading, we have felt empowered to adapt and further develop the four phases to meet local needs with a range of different emphases.

What has been done

Focusing our vision for using the TfT approach

We thought about the direction of our TfT work so that we had a clear vision of what we wanted to achieve. After thinking, we came to a common understanding that we want to build a society where members live peacefully and have the capacity for mutual understanding and a co-operative spirit.

We were able to clarify our specific objectives:

- enable people to develop mutual understanding and stimulate a culture of critical thinking;
- encourage and promote self-reliance and free expression;
- enable people to analyse their situation in life, identify the problems they face, analyse the root causes of those problems, find solutions themselves, and implement together potential solutions to their problems;
- enable people to meet their real needs and become responsible for their living;
- help the promotion of social justice and conflict management.

Facilitation of TfT training in phases

Different TfT training is conducted for different categories of groups (community members, organizational staff, and local government structures). All of this training is divided into the following phases.

Surveying generative themes. This precedes any intervention. Its main objective is to get to know the people undertaking the training, their strengths and weaknesses, their opportunities and threats.

The four basic phases. These phases are considered a base for any activity related to social transformation. Each phase lasts five days and the phases are separated by one or two months dedicated to translating into action what was discussed in the previous phase. This helps participants analyse their context – from personal to communal. After the four phases of training, a new orientation is developed by trainees to begin a process of change as individuals, in their places of work, and in the community. The participants are equipped with facilitation skills and group management techniques, and a number of potential trainers are selected at the end of the four phases to attend a 'training for trainers' session. Among the exercises used is the River of My Life. It helps trainees explore their lives and find similarities across the different ethnic groups and among people with different historical backgrounds. This leads trainees to acknowledge that solidarity and support are the solutions to problems people are facing.

Accompanying trainers in action. After the four phases of training, various field visits are undertaken with the aim of equipping the trainers with the required experience in conducting their TfT activities. This helped us to go into the community. Different community members were active in conflict resolution, especially in the *gacaca* court (a traditional court equipped to help people resolve problems relating to genocide). The trainers are still active in promoting unity, social justice, and peace-building.

Trainer recycling sessions. Recycling is reserved for the trainers who are improving their organizations and communities after the fourth phase. The aim of the recycling sessions is to equip the trainers with new knowledge, information, and skills, and repair the challenges faced during their practice of the TfT approach.

Specific training programmes. These training sessions are planned to resolve specific problems. The majority are focused on leadership and communication, conflict management, gender-based violence, domestic violence, and women's economic empowerment.

Follow-up and evaluation. Follow-up and evaluation are done after the beneficiaries have had enough time to implement the plans put in place after the four fundamental phases. It is a time to reflect on our work and give new orientation.

Material production. Different materials or modules are adapted in order to make them accessible. In our case, these materials are in our local language. My organization has been able to build an office, with the support of Trócaire. This has some facilities and over time has hosted training sessions. We still need to find the resources to build accommodation facilities so that trainees can stay under one roof during the training period.

TfT training impact

Trainers have played a major role in facilitating conflict resolution among community members and neighbours. Training provided an opportunity to share and strengthen commitment in order to build unity among community members. The trainers are active in their respective communities, working for unity, reconciliation, and peace-building. In some areas, they have initiated dialogue among community members, determined priorities together, and acted to improve their own lives. In other areas, widows of the genocide are now working together with other women in rural associations facilitating reconciliation. A number of people have been released from prison due to the influence of the trainers; this was the result of social justice awareness, created among people from both sides of the genocide, perpetrators and victims, all of whom were active afterwards in claiming the rights of people in prison (after overcoming their fear and trauma) or in denouncing human rights abuses (after recognizing that what they had done – perhaps accusing someone falsely – was unjust). The people are empowered by sharing ideas and information, so that they can take the initiative, solve problems, and improve their lives. People are motivated by being held accountable for the outcomes of their actions and they contribute to their own life satisfaction. So far, the lives of many people have been changed and improved.

One of the trainers participated in all four phases of TfT training organized by ADTS for representatives of the community. After the training, he committed himself to putting his efforts into peace-building work. He started his work at the village level with the creation of a space for dialogue in his village. He started to help the people with conflicts in his community. The result of this good work was many transformed people who also became engaged in promoting unity and reconciliation among the community members. With his experiences, he felt confident and he began to help mutual understanding of their neighbours. At the sector level, he is now the president of *abunzi* [a traditional court]. He is also one of the *a bavugarikijyana* [opinion leaders] in his community.

My organization (ADTS) was invited by other organizations to train their field workers or partners in the TfT approach. So far, 10 organizations in Rwanda have integrated the TfT approach into all of their projects.

CHAPTER 9

From the weight of a stone to that of a dry leaf: how the 'me' became part of the 'we' in post-conflict Liberia

Dorothy Toomann

Dorothy Kwennah Toomann is the Executive Director of the Development Education Network in Liberia (DEN-L), which works in close co-operation with many other NGOs on issues of governance, gender, peace-building, advocacy, and literacy. When she attended the Training for Transformation diploma course she had already started work on peace-building in co-operation with other NGOs. She has used TfT to meet capacity needs in various organizations, and to promote women's empowerment, sustained dialogue, and local enterprise development. Her chapter tells how they have been rebuilding communities after the distrust resulting from the civil war in Liberia.

The road to freedom is full of thorns and fire, yet happy is the one who follows it.   *African proverb*

It was in October 1998, after the first few events of the Liberian civil war, that I was exposed to the approach of popular education at the Catholic Women's Training Centre in Gbarnga City, Central Liberia. A total of 40 women from three women's organizations (Women in Action for Rehabilitation and Development (WARD); Liberia Women Action Group; and St Martin's Women's Programme), all involved in home economics and skills training activities, were gathered in the training room of the St Martin's Women's Programme to discuss the causes of their limited participation in public life and to develop strategies to enhance that participation. The workshop was organized by a group now called Development Education Network in Liberia (DEN-L), an offshoot of the Jesuit Refugee Service (JRS) programme led by the late Sister Miriam Therese O'Brien SSL. JRS provided humanitarian assistance to internally displaced persons and Liberian refugees in Ivory Coast and Guinea, as well as DELTA training. DEN-L is a national organization involved in providing training in development, democratic participation, and equality.

For a housewife developing skills in household management (home arts), the workshop provided a unique space for women, including myself, to discuss and articulate our challenges and aspirations – and we began strategizing to improve our situation. For me, it was the space created 'to hear and be heard with strong links to joint action' that glued me to the work of popular education through Training for Transformation. I could see that the TfT approach had the potential for growth beyond the level of the household.

I had been brought on board in 1999 as an adult literacy facilitator in training to support the action plans of the women, and DEN-L provided me with capacity-building opportunities, not only to increase my ability to share information on popular education but also to create the space for me to 'learn by doing'. This new learning was complemented by well-organized, unique family interventions; for example, caring for my three little children at the time I was studying abroad.

Ending the war, building the peace

It is almost impossible to sustain or maintain a training programme or organization in violent conflict. As a training institution established during the Liberian civil crisis, DEN-L was faced with this reality, including the death of two staff members, displacement, and the looting of its head office. In order to ensure an end to the bloody civil war in the country, the organization worked with other partners to advocate for nonviolence. DEN-L worked with the Women in Peace Building Network (a programme of the West African Peace Building Network) to organize across the interfaith and intercultural divide, as well as across the divide of literacy and illiteracy to advocate among women for an end to the civil war.

Providing spaces for reflective-action processes, training, and relief assistance, as well as for staff members' active involvement in nonviolent action, DEN-L provided unique support to the Women of Liberia Mass Action. It helped it to deal with some of the internal challenges of the group, increased its capacity to decentralize its advocacy approach, and helped it to become a peace-building agent at the community level. The intervention of DEN-L was also supported by Irish Aid and Trócaire.

DEN-L works with many community-based groups as well as with international organizations in the country. It has also worked with partners such as the Minister of Gender and Development, UN Women, Open Society Initiative for West Africa and Africare, to support the capacity-building of women's institutions including the Kpaai District Women's Association, the Rural Women's Organization of Liberia, and the Association of Women in Cross-Border Trade. Many women in these organizations are now conscious of their rights and responsibilities, and are engaged in peace-building and development.

Tying broken community bonds

Violent civil wars leave behind wounds that are difficult to mend. DEN-L is one of the key organizations in Liberia supporting communities in healing broken community bonds. Quardu Gbondi is the newest of seven districts in Lofa county and over the years has been inhabited by the Lorma and Mandingo ethnic groups. The post-war peace-building story of this community is one of many examples of the organization's work in Liberia. Prior to the civil war, ethnic groups co-existed, intermarrying and sharing social and economic activities – regardless of their religious beliefs. During the civil war, according to people in the district, each ethnic group committed atrocities, destroying property and looting the sacred places of the other group. As a result, the people in the community could not speak to each other – their interethnic bitterness deepened the broken relationship between the Mandingo and Lorma tribal groups.

DEN-L's innovative use of TfT with sustained dialogue processes, supported by Pax Christi and later by the Inter-Church Organization for Development Cooperation, helped the Lorma and Mandingo tribal groups in the district to meet (intra- and inter-culturally), reflect, discuss, and analyse their history. Trust was so eroded that DEN-L was asked by the local people to arrange separate catering during the initial phases of the process. However, the Lorma and Mandingo in the area identified what helped and what hindered their co-existence, and together they developed practical ways to address their concerns for the common good. Guided by DEN-L, the men, women, and youth of the districts worked closely together to address their challenges and to mend the broken bonds of their community.

Today, the Lorma and Mandingo tribal groups in Quardu Gbondi district in Lofa county feel secure enough to participate in intercultural ceremonies and community development activities. They now work together to deal with any conflicts that arise, through dialogue. Although the peace-building process was a success, DEN-L was challenged by the desire for a 'quick fix' at the national level – with limited resources.

Conclusions

DEN-L was established during the civil crisis and worked in post-war Liberia. It has the unique experience of surviving the war and promoting popular education in the country. After a week-long gender and leadership training programme in Bong county, a 75-year-old rural woman challenged her colleagues to face their realities with boldness, with the words: 'Change the weight of this massive stone to the weight of a dry leaf.' In order to ensure positive social change, people and institutions need to respond to this challenge. If we liken the weight of oppression, injustice, and violence our world is experiencing today to the weight of a massive stone, people and organizations involved in popular education need to make every effort 'to change that weight into that of a dry leaf'. It may not be achieved in our time, but every effort towards it is important.

CHAPTER 10

Victim to victor: justice, reparation, redress, and restitution in post-apartheid South Africa

Noma-Russia Bonase

Noma-Russia Bonase *is a provincial co-ordinator with Khulumani, a grassroots organization for the victims and survivors of apartheid injustice in South Africa. It was formed in the 1990s to empower those affected to 'Speak Out' at the Truth and Reconciliation Commission, and it continues to train its members to advocate for the rights of those who remain poor and under-privileged. Through Training for Transformation, Noma-Russia learned that education should be an active learning process. One can use codes to address the sense of voicelessness and powerlessness, both psychological and economic. She believes strongly in working in the mother tongue, respecting a community's own culture, and using a variety of different art forms to encourage awareness, communication, and thinking out of the box about globalization, colonization, imperialism, and capitalism. Noma-Russia went first to Limpopo and then to the Eastern Cape to work with the widows of the Marikana massacre. She also helped to make a video about her work.*

In this chapter she tells how since the 1994 elections in South Africa, Khulumani has continued to work with those who remain marginalized, including the widows of the dispossessed.

> **A little hidden, even a difficult path, may be the one that leads to the highway.**   *Kenyan proverb*

I am Noma-Russia Bonase. I discovered the Training for Transformation programme in 2009 through the Khulumani Support Group Organization.

Khulumani (Speak Out) is a membership-based organization of 85,000 victims and survivors of gross human rights violations during the apartheid era and post-apartheid. It was established in 1995 by victims and survivors to enable us to speak out during the Truth and Reconciliation Commission (TRC) processes, and after the TRC, as governors in South Africa. Having moved from victims to victors, we still need to fight for justice, reparation, redress, restitution, and restoration of human dignity, peace, unity, and transformation, in order to prevent a recurrence of the previous injustices.

Three women founded Khulumani, one of whom, Sylvia Jele-Mlangeni, came up with the idea of bringing victims and survivors together to speak about their exclusion and non-recognition in TRC processes from the inception of the Commission.

Before TfT I was a Khulumani provincial leader and facilitator in the Gauteng province of the East Rand region (today called Ekurhuleni). There was constant political violence there from 1989 to 1999 and the involvement of many soldiers from different countries (including the South African Defence Force (SADF) and the notorious 32 Battalion) as well as United Nations soldiers, many of whom added to human rights violations by killing, torturing, and raping residents, in particular women and girls. I used to conduct meetings and facilitate workshops and I identified projects for members. It was not, however, a productive time, as members expected miracles.

I was struck right at the beginning by the TfT application form. As I was filling it in and answering questions, putting down my ideas, explaining my understanding and knowledge of transformation, I felt great hope and excitement. I said to myself: 'Yes. This is the kind of training that will be good for me and my organization, and also for my community. It needs to transform its understanding of itself from victim to victor.' I felt welcomed by the comfortable spaces created by the facilitators, and by the animators of discussion, sharing, and dialogue. I was impressed by their listening skills, the ways of building trust, and the whole methodology. I appreciated how they managed to respect and draw out the knowledge and experiences of participants.

The critical elements that changed me, my work, and my organization were the practical methods of care, healing, motivation, and empowerment. While I was on the TfT course, I received the painful news of my husband Mandla's sudden death, which clouded my heart, but the people I met during the TfT training encouraged me to come back after the funeral and complete my training. The importance of TfT was acknowledged by both my family and my husband's family. After holding discussions, they came to the conclusion that they had to allow me to finish my TfT studies. The last words of my husband were: 'Do not stop her in her work, which will bring change to you and your community, and bring fruits to your children.'

That experience became my tool for healing processes that I used with different forums, starting with individuals, and again recently after the Marikana massacre of 16 August 2012. To give a little background, my commitment to healing processes of transformation came through my own difficulties, and also from being a victim and survivor of gross human rights violations together with my family during apartheid. While I was still in my mother's womb at eight months, she was raped by a white South African policeman on the west side of Johannesburg, but I survived. In 1993 I lost my brother, who was killed by SADF soldiers. I found him under a pile of corpses with black polish on his face during the political violence in East Rand. My name has an underground meaning of 'no more oppression', Noma-Russia.

In TfT I developed a critical consciousness and awareness and learned methods of popular education. We looked at global analysis and the theories of Paulo Freire, and we discussed the Dynamic Model and all the codes in Book 3, and in all the TfT books. After I went through this programme, I used it in our organizational work. It helped us to see the importance of our work, and confirmed that we should stick to our mission, values, and vision of transforming victims to victors through the process of reparation, redress, restitution, and justice.

All this is the reason why I took a life commitment to work for transformation, which led me to come up with this theme for one of the chapters in this book, 'victim to victor'. I am calling for the involvement of all groups in society, from grassroots to higher-level structures, to engage in dialogue about the following:

- the unfinished business of the TRC;
- the big gap of inequality;
- a wounded society still bleeding and in tears.

Unfinished business of the Commission

The South African government established the TRC in 1995 after the ANC had won the 1994 elections. To me, the TRC was about trust-building and reconnecting. According to my understanding, it was decided in the absence of victims that the perpetrators were expected to tell what really happened, and to receive amnesty. That was one of the reasons for the formation of Khulumani Support Group, to go to the TRC to speak out. There we presented case studies drawn up by the Khulumani Support Group with regards to this unfinished business of the TRC.

In 2012, Khulumani members in all provinces undertook case studies, using TfT methods and codes, to gather information. The findings of the case studies showed that women's issues of sexual violence and harassment were not taken into consideration or thought of as a criminal act against humanity. Recommendations made during the TRC were not implemented by the

South African government. A one-off reparation of 30,000 rand to each victim was decided by the government. Victims and survivors were not consulted or involved in coming up with such a small amount, a mere gesture.

Big gap of inequality

South African society is witnessing the growth of the gap between rich and poor. Again, we are calling for measures to close the gap of socioeconomic injustice, as people are facing poverty and unemployment at grassroots levels.

Wounded society still bleeding and in tears

This theme came from the national art-healing workshop, which we did in 2013. It included our reactions to the Marikana massacre of 44 Lonmin mine workers in August 2012 by South African police. The miners were fighting for an increase in wages and other labour-related matters. It was a wake-up call for us to see the unresolved issues of apartheid government being ignored by our democratic government. This is causing instability in our country. We connect this strike with that of the Sasol workers who were killed by apartheid police while striking for wage increases in 1987, and we remember other matters not attended to by the TRC. With the Marikana massacre and today's Commission of Enquiry, I do not see a clear outcome. I have a sense that victims and survivors and their families are not treated as citizens or people of value on the basis of their humanity. Injustice continues to erupt in our nation, despite the fact that victims are willing to change their lives. Sadly, the effect is diluted because the ones who are seen as heroes and heroines are those who run away from connecting.

The above experience left us with no choice but to commit ourselves to the idea of helping victims to become victors, by looking for and engaging with reparation, redress, and restitution processes for healing our society.

Reparation, redress, and restitution is a process of restoring human dignity, where victims and survivors find ways of rebuilding their lives, of building peace and unity, and of sharing historical memories, wisdom, knowledge, and experience. Through transformation processes they become victors and prevent repetition. We have made a video of the Sasolburg strikes and the Marikana massacre; the production of this video was an important learning process.

I managed to get some remarkable results from the establishment of forums by Khulumani members themselves in 2010; an example is the *gogos* (grandmothers) and *mamas* (mothers) forum, which consists of 60 Khulumani members who came up with sustainable projects. Their motto is 'moving forward together'. They completed a sexuality workshop ('Celebrating the Wisdom of Older Women') and became sexuality educators in 2011–12. Body-Ubuntu was facilitated by myself and by Ruth Loubser (video available), and in Khulumani we have more than two TfT graduates. However, we have failed to develop combined sessions or workshops with each other in our local regions to strengthen our work.

Conclusion

In conclusion, I would like to put forward some suggestions:

- Production (of art, videos, etc.) can be an active learning process (education through production). It addresses voicelessness and powerlessness (psychological and economic).
- Art-making (of all forms) is a way to access participants' knowledge and understanding. It builds confidence and strengthens voices and moves towards healing. It helps people to

think 'out of the box' by creating their own language (visual or audio images based on their own experiences and interpretations).

- Use people's own culture – not imposed culture. Use the mother language for discussion and the cultural forms people are most familiar with (toyi-toying and hymns, for instance). Adapt these to the immediate issues for advocacy and communication to build a sense of community.
- Use creativity to challenge power structures. Motivations and codes should identify and challenge issues of power, especially around gender, race, poverty, and class. Use their own culture to motivate people; often there are clear lines of cultural resistance in their own culture that can be built upon.

CHAPTER 11

Extending DELTA's philosophy and approach to the post-communist and post-conflict Balkans

Enda Byrne

Enda Byrne made the DELTA programme in Kenya possible by persuading bishops and priests that it was necessary, and raising the money for it from Catholic funding agencies in many European countries. For 40 years he has been one of the most deeply committed trainers, promoters, and organizers of the programme, starting new initiatives in Madagascar, Liberia, and the Balkans, and supporting its development in many other places. He is currently the co-ordinator of DELTA in the Balkans.

In this chapter he shows how he has adapted the Training for Transformation philosophy and approach to the post-communist, post-conflict situations in Bosnia-Herzegovina, Kosovo, Macedonia, and Montenegro. DELTA courses are used to build interethnic and interfaith co-operation for peace-building in Bosnia. His team runs four phased and community action programmes for local religious leaders of different faiths, together with their close lay leaders. They also run special interfaith programmes for women and youth.

Judge each day, not by the harvest, but by the seeds you plant.   *Guinean proverb*

The historical animosities that existed between the very different Slav, Turk, and Albanian peoples in Yugoslavia were magnified during World War II when military brutalities and concentration camps killed hundreds of thousands of people. After the war, Tito's brand of communism was ruthlessly imposed and all discussion of the war's atrocities was rigidly suppressed.

The vicious civil wars that followed the break-up of the former Yugoslavia at the end of the Cold War in the 1990s were in fact a continuation of the historical ethnic feuding in the region. These civil wars, in turn, produced a legacy of bitterness, suspicion, and hatred, as well as deep emotional and psychological wounds, which remain largely unhealed and unresolved today and continue to fester just beneath the surface.

Seven new countries emerged from the disintegration of Yugoslavia – Bosnia-Herzegovina, Croatia, Kosovo, Macedonia, Montenegro, Serbia, and Slovenia. In 2001, I was asked by Renovabis, the German Catholic bishops' organization in support of reconstruction and development in the former communist countries of Eastern Europe and the USSR, to undertake a mission to Kosovo to explore possibilities of training in DELTA's participatory approach to human and community development.

Let me begin with a story, 'Voting for human rights and peace in Bosnia-Herzegovina'.

Nada Mihajlovic and Ifeta Imamovic will never forget the vicious killing of immediate family and local community members that changed their lives forever 18 years ago. Nada lives in Kravica, a Serb town, and Ifeta in Konjevic Polje, a Muslim village just a few kilometres away. Contact between their villages was non-existent – in English, 'balkanized' means 'divided into small, totally separate areas'– until they were swept up in the civil wars of the 1990s and a spiral of mutual barbarous ethnic killings.

Nada and Ifeta are co-ordinators of two women's NGOs, Maja Kravica and Jadar Konjevic Polje, in their villages. They met for the first time on a DELTA four-phase training programme in the region in 2009. Speaking about the situation in their villages and of the hopes and concerns of the women in their associations, they found many common problems and challenges. People were tired of looking back at the past, of the manipulation of ethnic divisions by politicians, of the hatred and resentment that kept people closed in their memories and in their communities, as well as their fear of a recurrence of ethnic violence in the future.

The NGOs asked DELTA to co-operate with them to plan and run a community awareness programme during the 2010 Bosnian general election campaign. They wanted to question the policies and messages of division and hatred used by the mainly nationalist and ethnically based political parties and candidates for election purposes. They also wanted to show that people from different ethnicities and faiths could work together for a common purpose and for the common good.

Twenty-four volunteers from the three main ethnic/faith communities were brought together by the NGOs to participate in the project. In Bosnia, where ethnicity and religion are almost synonymous, almost all Serbs profess the Orthodox faith, Bosniaks are Muslims, and Croats are Catholic.

The volunteers, who were mainly women and youth, as well as a few men from the two villages, took part in three long-weekend training workshops run by the DELTA team to prepare and plan the awareness programme. For three months before the elections, the volunteers:

- engaged over 6,000 people in conversation surveys during the campaign;
- distributed 1,600 brochures focused on human and political rights that they had designed during the training – it is estimated that about 4,500 people read the brochures;
- held discussions with 18 candidates from different political parties in the area;
- contacted and distributed brochures to 16 regional and national NGOs;
- mobilized local media (radios and papers) in favour of the campaign.

Major changes were experienced by the volunteers themselves meeting and working together with people from other communities for the first time in their lives. They had come to the programme with the same prejudices and fears common in their families and villages. In an evaluation workshop to conclude the project, the volunteers emphasized how they had changed:

I changed my prejudices about people from other faiths and ethnic communities. I have new friends and built trust with people from other communities.

I realize that we need to communicate more with others to solve our problems together in groups.

Working with others helped to soften my pain and to feel free and confident to discuss problems that we share. I am ready for more of this kind of co-operation.

I enjoyed the friendship in the group and the work that we did together for the community.

I was very sad to see that the main opposition to the project came from within my own family.

The project organizing team learned that change and transformation can take place in Bosnia when people from different backgrounds work on something together with a common purpose to make their lives different.

Evolution of DELTA's work in the Balkans

Since 2002, DELTA's programme in the Balkans evolved in four stages.

Stage 1

Between 2002 and 2004, DELTA worked exclusively in Kosovo where senior staff members from 20 NGOs and civil society organizations (CSOs) were trained in four-phase programmes. Priority was given to local bodies and organizations. Key partnerships were developed with faith-based (mainly Catholic) NGOs.

Stage 2

Following such positive results from this earlier work, an extensive programme of meetings with 147 community-focused NGOs and CSOs in four other countries was undertaken which resulted in running DELTA-Rainbow four-phase regional training programmes each year from 2006 to 2009.

These programmes were focused specifically on NGOs already working for interethnic dialogue and co-operation in their own countries. The main elements of the training were based on dialogue and trust-building, including intercultural analysis, building open identities, stereotypes and prejudices, uses and abuses of history, and human dignity and human rights, as well as group work skills to learn how to deal with these themes in participatory ways with groups and communities. While the results were positive in terms of reflecting on these vital themes, it was clear that longer and more intensive training was necessary to use them effectively in delicate interethnic situations.

These programmes were successful in extending DELTA's methods and participatory philosophy and in provoking small local community initiatives; in building cross-border links and co-operation in the region; and in identifying key organizations with which DELTA later developed close working partnerships. However, the extensive travel in the region and the costs, both for the participants and for the DELTA team in following up the inter-phase fieldwork, were not sustainable and these regional training programmes were concluded in 2009.

Stage 3

In order to root DELTA's approach more effectively within the work of carefully selected partners, DELTA decided to focus on intensive co-operation with a small number of key organizations in Kosovo, Macedonia, and Bosnia-Herzegovina. These key partnerships resulted in joint projects that were successfully carried out by DELTA. Some examples of these are described below.

'Democracy for All', in partnership with an NGO called HandiKos in Kosovo, was an outstanding success. DELTA trained about 130 people with physical disabilities in an intensive eight-month programme prior to the 2004 Kosovo general elections. The aim was to enable people with disabilities (PwD) to rediscover their human dignity and to participate actively during the election campaign. In the course of three training phases, materials were prepared that were used by small groups of PwD to challenge the political parties and candidates. HandiKos selected 120 PwD from 24 municipalities in the country who were engaged for the seven-month project.

One of them, Artan, takes up the story:

> We came to the first three-day residential workshop with mixed feelings, excitement, apprehension, even anxiety – would we be up to the task? The informal atmosphere, the humour, the sense of purpose soon encouraged me to try to raise up my twisted and contorted Thalidomide body in my broken wheelchair. For the first time ever, we were being asked our opinions, about our society, our country, about ourselves – people seemed to think it was funny

when I told them that my trendy hairstyle made me the sexiest of all those present! But there was work to be done. We learned about a listening survey; we designed questions to guide our 'conversations' with other PwD in the fieldwork before the phase two workshop; we practised the questions in pairs, learning to listen with our eyes and hearts, as well as our ears; we revised some questions and planned our listening survey to work in pairs from the same municipality. But most of all we learned that we are people with human dignity and human rights, that we don't have to be just beggars entirely dependent on others – and that we share a large part of the responsibility for shaping our own future. We were soon on our way ... bursting with enthusiasm. The fieldwork required us to identify other PwD in our area and to engage them individually in a guided 'conversation' or interview. People were so keen to talk it was difficult to finish the questions in two hours. Each interview took five to six hours including travel, as well as recording the answers, but I managed to do 33 by starting at 6 o'clock each morning. Three weeks later the second training workshop was buzzing with excitement – and stories, so many stories, of people's fieldwork experiences. We reviewed the listening survey process and made some adjustments to improve the next round of interviews. The major task was to analyse about 300 of more than 3,000 completed questionnaires to distil the main points. After the workshop, HandiKos and DELTA used these as the basis for writing the *PwD Agenda 2004* for dialogue with politicians and the political parties. I completed 36 more interviews during the second round – many PwD contacted me when they heard about the project but I had no time to meet them all. By the time we came for the third and final workshop in September, a total of 7,075 interviews had been done – the most comprehensive survey of PwD ever undertaken in Kosovo. Three attractively produced glossy versions of the *PwD Agenda 2004* in Albanian, Serbian, and English were ready for the final workshop. We were so proud that all the ideas in the *Agenda* came from ourselves, the 120 PwD workers in the project and the 7,000 interviews. It spoke of our struggle to be recognized as people with human dignity and equal rights as citizens. From these values, it moved to the changes in attitudes and behaviour towards us that we demanded from all levels in Kosovo society. The training focused on how to use the *Agenda* during the election campaign with other PwD, with politicians and their parties, with the media, and with the wider community. We had already worked so hard – to be told that the real work starts now! The *PwD Agenda 2004* was the most important resource produced by the project and 6,538 copies were distributed to the five categories listed above. We held a total of 191 meetings with political parties and candidates. The project received over 400 references in the Kosovo media and the prime minister at the time, a retired surgeon, remarked that this was the most professional campaign of all those undertaken before the elections. It is not easy to quantify the overall impact of the project, but two things are certain: many thousands of people now look with new eyes at PwD in Kosovo; and, most importantly, those of us who worked so hard on this project and the 7,075 PwD interviewed will never be the same again.

When asked if they were happy with this and who was going to change this mentality, the participants realized that:

- they were the ones interested in changing the situation;
- the situation would change if they started to change themselves from a 'beggar's' to a 'lord's' mentality. Beggars are humble, have no voice and receive what others decide to give them, while lords are proud people who know and demand their rights.

The results of the programme proved how much people had changed and the respect they commanded by being 'lords'. The participants spent about 12,000 hours listening and talking, for the first time, with PwD in the villages. Over 9,000 PwD took part in the project.

Another programme was initiated called 'Women Together for Peace in Kosovo-Mitrovica'. This had four training phases run in conjunction with a multi-ethnic NGO called Community Building Mitrovica. They realized their aim of establishing an association for five local multi-ethnic women's NGOs to work together to address common problems, and the association is still working today.

In Macedonia, an interethnic dialogue in high schools was initiated to build multi-ethnic students' associations for dialogue and co-operation in public secondary schools, where deep tensions existed between Macedonian and Albanian students. The project was approved by Macedonia's Ministry of Education and implemented by DELTA over an 18-month period in close co-operation with Common Values, an NGO in Skopje. A three-phase training programme for teachers from three large schools selected by the ministry was followed by a three-phase student leadership training programme. The project generated much enthusiasm among those students who took part in the training alongside some teachers.

Stage 4

It was increasingly obvious that Bosnia-Herzegovina was the country that remained most severely affected after the Yugoslav wars. In 2009 to 2010, DELTA decided to concentrate more efforts on the country and the following programmes were carried out in co-operation with groups of local NGOs.

DELTA-Rainbow in Eastern Bosnia. This was a four-phase training programme mainly with women's NGOs from Srebrenica, Bratunac, Kravica, and Konjevic Polje, towns that were deeply affected during the war. The aim was to integrate interethnic dialogue and co-operation into the NGOs' community development programmes. The story at the beginning of this chapter, 'Voting for human rights and peace in Bosnia-Herzegovina', grew out of this regional training programme in eastern Bosnia.

Women Together for Peace. The 'DELTA-Rainbow in Eastern Bosnia' project was inspirational for the NGOs that took part. Together with two other women's NGOs in Srebrenica, they are now working with DELTA to design a project called 'Women Together for Peace', to develop a multi-ethnic consortium of local NGOs. Their objective combines two aims: to continue working on an interethnic basis, and to train and support small groups of local women working together on small-scale economic or social initiatives.

DELTA-Rainbow in North-Western Bosnia. A similar programme in a different part of Bosnia was also a four-phase regional training programme with teachers' NGOs in areas that suffered severely from the atrocities during the wars of the early 1990s. This programme was focused on building skills for interethnic dialogue and co-operation into the work of teachers and their professional organizations.

DELTA's inter-religious and interethnic initiatives in Bosnia-Herzegovina

Another initiative in 2011 brought together Caritas and the corresponding national Orthodox, Islamic, and Jewish welfare organizations in Bosnia. One purpose was to explore the possibility of organizing a joint training programme for these four bodies. At the conclusion of the workshop, it was decided that the programme be part of the Inter-religious Council (IRC).

In the course of discussions with the IRC, it was agreed to develop local IRC chapters in four key towns in northern and western parts of the country. A programme of research and a series of meetings took place in the four towns with local religious leaders of the three major faiths – Serbian Orthodox and Catholic priests, and imams – and a four-phase programme was agreed for the religious leaders, together with women and youth from the three faith communities. This in turn led to a range of small interfaith activities in each of the four towns, the first time the faith communities co-operated in this way. The organization has continued working with the four chapters and is busy developing new chapters in other towns.

Our work now has focused on developing a similar programme in the deeply divided southern region of Herzegovina. Most senior faith leaders responded positively to this initiative and, at a local level, priests and imams, as well as their faith community members, have warmly supported the project. In a country where faith and ethnicity are synonymous, this programme, as with that of the IRC in the north, represents unique opportunities to bring members of the three main communities together in a non-threatening, constructive programme of dialogue and co-operation.

In addition to the above, DELTA has run successful workshops with students in the two separate, and ethnically divided, state universities in Mostar. Plans are under way to run a phased programme, 'Intercultural Communication for Human Development', and to bring together student leaders from both universities.

Reflections on post-communist characteristics in the Western Balkans

This overview of DELTA's work in the Balkans would not be complete without a comment on some characteristics of post-communist societies in the Western Balkans. Firstly, many of the former communist political leaders seem to have undergone remarkable 'ideological conversions': many remain in power as ardent free-market capitalists and 'democrats'. The reality is that they simply transferred corrupt political leadership styles and strategies from one system to another. These corrupt patterns of leadership at the top filter down to the wider society, where they affect the poor most of all.

Secondly, the communist system has conditioned many people to live in fear of the state; top-down decisions are normally unquestioned and people have learned not to take the initiative. A different kind of legacy from the totalitarian period is that unjust and repressive laws in the past have often produced a culture of disrespect for today's democratically enacted laws.

Thirdly, there is no tradition of independent civil society organizations, as these were not tolerated under communism. Consequently, NGOs and other civil society bodies are not considered as having important roles to play in the development of a modern democratic society. Government bodies at all levels tend to view NGOs and CSOs either as rivals or as interfering amateurs, and the idea of forming working partnerships with NGOs or of making resources available to support their work is not part of the agenda.

Fourthly, faith bodies that were suppressed during the communist era learned to survive by keeping a low profile and focusing exclusively on traditional spiritual activities. Consequently, some faith leaders do not consider that they have any role to play in the social, educational, or health fields, while some others remain closely aligned to political leaders and structures. In addition, some faiths were isolated from progressive theological developments and influences in the wider world during the communist period and consequently view their roles from a traditional and limited perspective.

Finally, DELTA's involvement in promoting interfaith co-operation has clearly shown that many limitations and restrictions in relation to social engagement on the part of some faith leaders are either self-imposed or remain as vestiges of the former communist era.

PART FOUR
Listening into dialogue

Keywords: changing approaches of evangelization; changing habits and patterns; constructive feedback; deep dialogue; deep listening; ecology; listening; nonviolence; relationship with the earth; restoring dignity; speaking truth in love

http://dx.doi.org/10.3362/9781780448312.005

CHAPTER 12
Missionary conversations in Kenya

Daniel Martin

Dr Daniel Martin *came into contact with Training for Transformation as a young missionary priest in Kenya in the early 1970s. In a remote rural parish in Ukambani, he started to use dramatized versions of the gospel stories as codes to help his parishioners get to the heart of the Christian message and find its relevance in their own lives. This began to open up new insights for him into the local culture. He wrote his PhD with Thomas Berry (author of* The New Story*). Later he worked with the United Nations Environment Programme and helped to produce the 'Earth Charter'. He has continued to work in leadership training both in the USA and with the Green Belt Movement of Wangari Maathai in Kenya, focusing on the importance of in-depth dialogue for authentic*

transformation to take place. This chapter tells the story of the different stages of his adaptation of TfT in Kenya.

With yourself, use your head; with others, use your heart. *African proverb*

My initial experience of Training for Transformation (TfT) with Anne Hope and Sally Timmel was in the early 1970s in Kenya where I was a young missionary priest, influenced by the new thinking on mission developed by the Second Vatican Council of the Catholic church (1962–65). The essence of this new thinking was an openness to the value and validity of other religious and cultural forms in contrast to the traditional insistence on the exclusive nature of the church, expressed in the Latin phrase *extra ecclesiam nulla salus* ('outside the church there is no salvation'). It was this shift, along with a focus on the humanitarian aspects of missionary work (education, healthcare, community development), that, in a sense, created a readiness for the TfT programme, whose focus on engagement and empowerment of people in their own lives and challenges offered a method for translating the new thinking on mission into action. For a short period during that decade this creative marriage flourished, but soon enough it came up against the reactionary response of the still dominant paradigm to the changes that were perceived (rightly) as a threat to the status quo. Unfortunately, the dominant paradigm prevailed by closing the lid on what it saw as a 'Pandora's box' and attempting to return to the old ways. In later years, I found myself adding the 'art of dialogue' to the method in ways that I felt allowed the movement of change to continue, however slowly, rather than fester like a sore or simply explode, to paraphrase the poet Langston Hughes.

Practice

I was already somewhat familiar with Paulo Freire, whose thinking on 'conscientization' was an inspiration to Anne and Sally, but it was their suggestion that this kind of thinking could be a useful tool for working with and shaping the energies of the changes that we were experiencing in the world of Catholic mission that fired my imagination.

The TfT programme helped concretize our developing thinking about mission in Kenya by marrying it with Freire's practical method of community development, and thereby gave us new missionaries a focus for our good intentions and a potential strategy for our efforts, along with a practical application of the Christian perspective. For me, this translated initially into an attempt to put the weekly preaching/teaching of the Christian message that was a central part of the priest-led mass and the catechist-led services into a TfT format. And so, using the gospel message as a springboard or theme, I would focus on an issue that my somewhat informal community analysis (over tea or beer, or chatting around a fire in the evenings) had surfaced, in a way that would engage people in actions that would address the issue.

This approach developed through a number of stages. The first, I can recall, involved introducing Freire's model, which happened under a thorn tree in a remote place in northern Kitui called Kandwia – one of the many churches of the parish of Kimangao, where I worked at the time. In this initial experiment I collaborated with a young teacher who would later be a big part of TfT in Kenya: Josephat Mulyungi. We learned a lot that day under the thorn tree, but specifically an appreciation of different ways of learning and the need to be truly local. Freire's method involved engaging people in the issues of their lives through what he called a 'code': in his case a picture that would catalyse a group conversation about an important community issue. We had drawn a picture that described, quite clearly we thought, the challenge of water, which was a clear community issue – specifically, women and children having to walk long distances and carry heavy containers of water from the river to their homes. To our surprise, the participants in the gathering did not seem to be at all catalysed by the picture. We were able, nonetheless, to get a conversation going but realized something had to change in the way we 'encoded' the issue to be addressed.

Afterwards, we each continued in our own way with the new method; this was when the second stage of my TfT-informed missionary approach unfolded. While my thinking about mission and cultural autonomy had developed a little through my reading and our conversations in the seminary, I had no clear idea of an alternative missionary approach to the traditional one of proselytizing and forming Christian communities that were essentially western, except that it had to be different; not Irish, but local in some way. So, my initial missionary method had quickly become something like 'Wow, is that the way you do it?' What this meant in practice was that, since I was not going to be an imposer of an outside 'one size fits all' model, and since I really had not discovered what might be a more appropriate approach, I had decided I would be a visitor and, hopefully in time, a friend.

Thus began my visiting and listening programme – my informal community analysis, if you like – of walking around homes and gardens, which were often great distances apart, in the hot and dry semi-desert of northern Kitui. At the end of a day of walking and talking, a group would gather in a home where we would have a religious celebration – some rather loose version of the Catholic mass: 'loose' because it included everyone who wished to share in it, baptized or not; and 'loose' too because, over time, it took on its own local form that integrated traditional customs, such as *mutaa* (a plant used for blessing), and was celebrated in a back and forth chant and response mode that reflected local Kamba ritual.

One particular element that became increasingly central to this stage of the emerging method was the discovery of the power of local proverbs. We have our own western proverbs – 'look before you leap', for example – but they do not carry the power that the local (Kamba) proverbs did, certainly in those days. To come up with the appropriate proverb in a debate in Kitui was to clinch an argument. Proverbs such as '*kyaa kimwe kiiuaa ndaa*' – literally, 'one finger can never kill a flea' – were expressions of a deep collective wisdom born of often hard life experience, in this case that we need each other – all of us – to tackle difficult problems. So, an important part of this second stage was finding proverbs that touched on the critical aspects of life – birth and death, community, and so on, aspects of life that the Christian message also addressed, albeit from its own framework (sacramental theology) and perspective (western – moral – assumptions).

Every week I would design the mass or service to include local wisdom as well as local customs, perhaps – at least this appears to be the case in retrospect – because of an instinctive appreciation of the critical nature of empowering people, or, more simply, pointing out what was already there but no longer seen by them for whatever reason. The 'whatever reason' actually covers a multitude of colonial practices that were directed at subduing and controlling a people by convincing them that their ways – their language, their native wisdom, their agricultural practices, their institutions – were inferior to those of their colonial masters.

The third stage of this somewhat organic application of the TfT method came as a result of trying to figure out an alternative 'code' to the picture technique, which clearly didn't have the expected impact. It happened accidentally, in fact, when I was invited to see a local elementary school's rendition of the Christian nativity scene, where I was amused at the way the kids literally made up their own version of the event, with their various additions and adaptations. But it also hit me that this was something that seemed to come naturally to people here, many of whom were not literate: to act, to improvise, to play out a situation in such a way. Sometime later I was leading a mass and found my by now customary discomfort about the foreign nature of the experience building up, specifically around having readings from the Bible that seemed so remote from their lives, when it hit me. There surely had to be a better way of sharing these stories than reading out the often stilted language of the Bible. So, instead of choosing readers for this often awkward and clearly unexciting process, I invited a handful of the congregation to take the Bible story – it happened to be the story of the Good Samaritan (someone set upon by robbers and left at the side of the road, where a priest and a wealthy person both passed by without stopping, then finally a Samaritan, a traditional enemy of the people of that neighbourhood, stopped and helped the victim) – and asked them to act it out. It took them all of three minutes to prepare a five-minute play and the result was amazing: everyone got the message immediately, everyone saw the issue and understood the causes, everyone could relate the story to real-life situations in their own community, and everyone had an opinion on what they could do about such things. All of these are, of course, the essence of the questions used in the TfT programme for engaging people in addressing their own problems rather than waiting for someone else – government, the wealthy, or the church – to do this for them.

Stage three, then, consisted of developing 'local codes' that would effectively catalyse a conversation around an issue, and then integrating them into the schedule for mass readings which was mandated (for me) by church authority. Obviously, some readings were easier to 'en-code' than others: parables, especially agriculture-based parables, were straightforward in this rural world; and stories about events in the life of Jesus were also readily adapted into 'play-codes'. Of course, some were not so easy, like those that recounted what were essentially speeches attributed to Jesus, such as the Sermon on the Mount, or conversations between Jesus and others about who he was or what his message was about. But something new had begun that felt right.

In summary, what had emerged out of my attempts to apply the TfT method to our developing missionary thinking was this: the contribution of another perspective – for example the Christian message – could be valuable, but only if it allowed people to absorb it and apply it in their own way.

What followed after that was really an elaboration of these realizations or principles. This happened through the development of a simple handbook that used the schedule of Bible readings for the weekly mass or catechist-led service and offered guidelines for the process of presentation (through a play), an exploration through the TfT questions (What do you see happening? Why does it happen? etc.), and a community 'discovery' of how to respond that was inspired by Christian wisdom but built on local wisdom, and was reflected in an appropriate Kamba proverb. Everything else – all the other parts of the mass or service that essentially celebrated and reinforced our interconnectedness – were built around this elaboration of 'Wow, is that the way you do it?'

Impact

As I look back on those years, I can see that the TfT method truly became the essential thread of my entire missionary approach during those exciting, halcyon days of my youthful priesthood that helped me break down the false dichotomies that I felt hindered missionary work: between sacred and secular (or ordinary) for example; or between multiple responses to the Christian message that could all be valid. It also helped me understand the true role of leadership (missionary work is a form of leadership, however arbitrary) as the facilitation of an innate capacity in every living system, both individual and collective, to live its own life.

In 1978, I was asked to go to Rome for further studies in theology. Before I left, the Bishop convened all of us priests to discuss this TfT-informed missionary approach that had begun to gain some traction in other parishes. There was genuine excitement about the possibilities of what some of us referred to as 'giving it back to the people'. 'It' referred to the emerging Christian church. I recall getting an insight into the magnitude of the challenge of this 'giving it back' in something the Bishop said as part of his words of appreciation for some of my, and our, efforts: 'But, you know, Rome will never approve this …'.

The implication was that Rome could make our lives in Kitui impossible by withdrawing the financial support that made them possible. Clearly, the local people were not able to (financially) support our presence and work. I can also recall my own reaction, which in euphemistic terms suggested that Rome should not interfere in the private affairs of a local community. But one of the deeper challenges of change had surfaced.

In fact, the challenge had become much more than that by the time I returned to Kitui in 1981. John Paul II, who had been elected pope while I was in Rome, was the Catholic church's equivalent of Ronald Reagan in US politics or Margaret Thatcher in the UK. All three represented the dominant culture's reaction to the changes that threatened the position of those who held power. Each, in their own way, proclaimed a return to former glory and stability, which, in times of uncertainty, is a very attractive proposition. On my return to Kenya, I experienced first-hand the trickle-down effects of this reaction: a tightening of church control and an insistence on compliance with traditional thinking and practices. A government crackdown that followed an attempted coup in Kenya the year after my return resulted in the closing down of the church's national office for social development and a clear directive from church leadership to missionaries like me to keep a low profile in terms of community development. Effectively, this meant a return to an older missionary method and a stepping back from the TfT approach.

My response was to begin a personal campaign for the 'strategic withdrawal of missionaries'. In conversations and articles for our internal newsletter, I would point to the already declining numbers joining the missionary ranks in places such as Ireland and a fairly predictable future of a shrunken, ageing and marginalized missionary presence (which is exactly the case today). On a more positive note, though, I would suggest that the situation was also an opportunity to build on the work of engagement and empowerment we had started and encourage a genuinely local church led by the real leaders already in the community who could integrate the Christian message in ways that would truly reflect their world. I added that we, as representatives of the world church, could be channels and facilitators of a process of mutual enhancement. While it was clear that many of my colleagues agreed in principle with these ideas, it was also clear that they were unable or unwilling to confront a system as enormous and ancient as the church. Besides, it was their lives, their world; it was what they had committed themselves to. And who was I to question all this? In the end, I realized that what I was advocating would not happen: not here, not in the constrained world of Kenyan politics, not in the fearful, reactionary world of the Kenyan Catholic church, which looked to Rome for approval (and financial support).

So I finally left Kenya in 1984 and went to the US, where I wrote a PhD with Thomas Berry, whose cosmological framework of what he called 'the great work (mission?) of our time' as fostering the emergence of a new (geological) era went beyond the human-focused assumptions of even radical liberation theology to a more profound liberation and transformation for us all – what he called an 'ecozoic era', which would be characterized by mutually enhancing human – earth relations.[1] His ideas brought me to the United Nations Environment Programme, where I helped develop one example of this kind of expanded mission: the Environmental Sabbath project, whose purpose was to engage the religions of the world in a mission that transcended, though integrated, the focus of efforts such as TfT. Later, I founded a non-profit organization to elicit a 'spiritual Earth Charter' in preparation for the first UN-sponsored Earth Summit in Brazil in 1992 through a series of interfaith dialogues around the world. My colleagues and I saw this Earth Charter as the beginnings of a new and fuller foundation for the work of an expanded human development mission.

More specifically in terms of the TfT method, I developed programmes in what I called the 'art of dialogue', which I described as participation in the emergence of meaning, as a way of – in my view – enhancing the Freire-based approach. Dialogue, I felt, was the underpinning skill set that is essential if the process of transformation is to get beyond simply structural reform. I saw dialogue as interacting in a way that allowed new shared insights – shared meaning – to emerge, by treating differences in a way that would allow new meaning to be created or discovered (understanding, that is, without necessarily agreeing).[2]

I also developed dialogue-based programmes for leadership training and community-building with the Centers for Disease Control and Prevention, which, for a number of rich years throughout the 1990s and the post-9/11 era, I offered to state and local health departments around the US. This work with community health leaders emphasized the critical nature of going deeper than the TfT process seemed to allow. For example, exploring the roots of a situation in the TfT way would result in a critique of systems and structures (including laws and policies) and decisions to find ways to change these. Dialogue would have the same goal of changing unjust systems but would include in its process the exploration of assumptions, both individual and collective, that were at the root of these systems and structures, and that lived in all of us. This awareness could lead to expanded thinking and insights that would go beyond typical social justice efforts. In a similar and related way, the dialogue approach's focus on exploring assumptions could also expand thinking beyond simply the human perspective to include the larger ecosystems that humans are simply part of without being superior to. The result could be insights and ideas that would be more comprehensive, that would go beyond a 'distributive' justice to a radically 're-formed' justice. The word 'justice' has at its root the sense of 'right relations' (the Hebrew *tzedakah*). Berry would sometimes criticize many justice efforts as too narrow, comparing them to rescuing drowning people by taking them onto a lifeboat that was already sinking.

In a sense, dialogue was, for me, a further stage in my developing understanding of a missionary approach: an understanding that had begun with the theory of liberation inspired by exciting new church thinking; grown through the TfT approach, which offered a way to implement this liberation-mission; then expanded through Tom Berry's framework of participating in 'the great work' of helping to bring about a new era founded on mutually enhancing human–earth relations; and finally enriched with a dialogue method that offered ways and skills to break out of what D.H. Lawrence called 'the glass bottles of our ego'.

Comment

My initial 'missionary work', inspired by Anne and Sally, served as both an important foundation and a touchstone for subsequent efforts in the field of human development. The ecological perspective of Thomas Berry expanded the context and thereby also the definitions of human development, while the art of dialogue enhanced the process of interaction by heightening self-awareness and listening capacities that lead to more comprehensive outcomes. On a more personal note, TfT was also an invaluable part of my own (constant, continuing) transformation process. Today, the process has brought me full circle in a way, back to my original calling, though with a deeper sense of what that calling is. Today, I am perhaps more a missionary than ever, although now the mission is related to Berry's 'great work' of fostering the advent of an 'ecozoic era', while my missionary method is simply an enhanced form of 'Wow, is that the way you do it?' – a TfT empowerment that is enriched by the art of dialogue.

Notes

1   See Thomas Berry's *The Dream of the Earth* (1988) and *The Great Work* (2000), and others.

2   Dialogue – from the Greek words *logos* (meaning) and *dia* (through) – can be defined as participating in the emergence of meaning. It is to be distinguished from 'debate', which means 'to beat down, defeat, etc.' *(debattere)*, and 'discussion', which means to analyse and decide among options (the Latin *discutere* means to 'break down' or 'shake apart'). In its modern usage, 'dialogue' was developed initially by the quantum physicist David Bohm, whose work with lasers as effective and incisive instruments formed out of photons coming together and focusing in the same direction inspired him to explore the possibilities of human beings thinking together in order to become instruments of creativity. His essential ideas are found in a small book called *On Dialogue* (1990). Bohm's ideas were further developed by others, including William Isaacs (1999) and Daniel Yankelovich (2001). I developed training programmes in the art of dialogue for leaders and teams in many organizations and also explored its potential as a spiritual practice for fostering the emergence of an expanded awareness and identity ('Dialogue and spirituality: the art of being human in a changing world' in Banathy and Jenlink, 2005).

References

Banathy, B.H. and Jenlink, P.M. (eds) (2005) *Dialogue as a Means of Collective Communication*, New York, NY: Kluwer Academic/Plenum Publishers.

Berry, T. (1986) *The New Story: Life from a Planetary Perspective*, Langley, WA: Context Institute.

Berry, T. (1988) *The Dream of the Earth*, San Francisco, CA: Sierra Club Books.

Berry, T. (2000) *The Great Work: Our Way into the Future*, New York, NY: Bell Tower.

Bohm, D. (1990) *On Dialogue*, Ojai, CA: David Bohm Seminars.

Isaacs, W. (1999) *Dialogue and the Art of Thinking Together: A Pioneering Approach to Communicating in Business and in Life*, New York, NY: Currency.

Yankelovich, D. (2001) *The Magic of Dialogue: Transforming Conflict into Cooperation*, New York, NY: Simon and Schuster.

CHAPTER 13

The heart of the matter: deep listening and connecting across cultures as human beings in Australia

Ruth Crowe

Dr Ruth Crowe *was on the International Leadership Team of the Grail for eight years. Now she is the co-ordinator for Training for Transformation in Australia. She works with teams to provide TfT workshops in eastern Australia and the Pacific. They offer workshops around Freire's insights and methodologies to professionals in a variety of areas in society. Listening to the people is a major focus, as well as animation, codes, and Theatre of the Oppressed.*

This chapter presents a reflection on the importance of 'deep listening'. All TfT practitioners need to take time to experience this occasionally, as it is fundamental to the work of transformation.

Your smile is an open window which tells people you are inside the house.   *Nigerian proverb*

I joined the Grail, an international women's movement, in the early 1960s. It was international and that's what I wanted to do with my life – to be with people of other cultures outside Australia. Young, open, wanting adventure and challenge, I was glad to be living at a time when Christians (and others) went overseas, not as missionaries, but with the wider vision of getting to know people of other cultures, sharing their daily lives, trying to understand their world views, life issues, and concerns. Surely this was a way for people to really connect with one another, to engage in making the 'kingdom of God' visible in our world. This vision directed my life then as it does now. As I interact more with people of other faiths, I realize that we are united in this common vision, to build a better world so that all can enjoy peace, harmony, and equity.

In 1980 and 1982 the chance came to fulfil my dream: I was invited to go to Tanzania. I could teach English and help young women, some over 20 years old, to pass exams, so they could obtain scholarships and go to high school. That would certainly contribute to making life richer for some of these young women, giving them opportunities and choices they may not otherwise have had. I was also delighted to be in Tanzania under Julius Nyerere to experience how his vision of *ujamaa*[1] worked in practice.

I did teach English. I did get to see the advantages and disadvantages of a socialist system. There was very little food available in the country that year. There was drought, few supplies of grain, beans, or vegetables, no soap, no toothpaste, no sugar, no cooking oil, very few medicines. When I reflect on this time, I realize I never thought of going home. I never thought of running away. I was there and I wanted to share the experience with my sisters and brothers. Intuitively I knew that here was a 'gift'. Here was a chance to share life in the reality of being deprived of the most basic human needs. Sharing this experience transformed my life. Tanzanian Grail women told me: 'We are very sorry for you; we are used to this, but you are not. *Pole*' – a beautiful word in

Kiswahili that means 'take heart' or 'have strength'. This loving and supportive wish was offered constantly throughout the day, for the work you did, for a journey, for the discomfitures you might feel, and in any of life's difficult situations.

There was also the matter of my being the only one at the centre who could drive the Grail's Land Rover. This vehicle was used not only for the needs of the centre, but to take women from the surrounding villages to hospital for the birth of a baby, to take sick children and others to the dispensary at any time, night or day, or to bring home the bodies of the dead. When I drove a family to the dispensary at night, with a child dying of measles, through the pain and suffering I felt a bond grow between us.

In our whispered conversation in the lamp light of the dispensary, I came a little closer to understanding the impact of poverty and deprivation, the grief that follows the death of a child – anywhere, anytime. These shared human experiences brought me very close to people of another culture, living in another part of the world.

'Being with' and living among the people of Tanzania was a great gift for me at that time of my life. Sharing with others from a different culture and recognizing that we humans have the same fundamental human needs helped me realize that sharing experiences of hunger and deprivation, grief and loss, laughter and song can result in the formation of deep relationships. The ones formed that year have lasted a lifetime. I began to understand solidarity and reciprocity. I saw that I received much more than I was ever able to give. I became much more aware of the inequities in our world, the dominance of rich western countries economically, culturally, politically. I saw the impacts of this and determined to make a commitment to work to change the systems that maintained these injustices and inequities.

During this extraordinary and privileged year in Tanzania, I discovered another 'treasure': Training for Transformation (TfT). Paolo Freire's philosophy was a 'fit' with my own philosophy of life. His methodology and processes would, I saw, enable me to give form and substance to my dream of making the world a better place for all, with the poor and marginalized front and centre of the process. It was all there! The 'prophetic' insights of Freire, his philosophy, and his work with basic communities remain an inspiration, a model. His writings are seminal for social activists.

One of the greatest challenges of being involved in working for the transformation of people's lives is learning to 'listen deeply' to individuals, groups, and communities – and taking the time to do so before jumping into action. 'Deep' listening, so people will and can speak, is at the heart of Freire's philosophy and methodology. It is a way of life we can adopt as practitioners of TfT. 'Deep' listening, and taking the time to do this, is truly about engaging with one another at a deeper level of consciousness, 'being to being'. As a friend put it: 'Listening is a deep work of the soul.' It is particularly rewarding for all concerned to experience listening in this way, especially in cross-cultural situations. Taking the opportunity to 'be' with rather than 'work' with people can support them to truly transform their lives. It just takes time!

Now that I have more time available to choose what to do with my life, I find myself coming back to a place of being with women of another culture, this time in my own country, and enjoying the time to listen. Over the past couple of years, a few non-aboriginal women have joined a group of young aboriginal mothers and their children who gather weekly in a community centre in Sydney. I am the 'co-ordinator of transformative education' in the NGO that began this initiative. There is sometimes distrust between aboriginal mothers and non-aboriginal people because of a history of government departments taking children away from their mothers if they are reported to be neglecting them or not coping with them well. Today this is still the practice, and it often results in the department taking children away from young, single aboriginal mothers and putting them in foster homes. I felt it was a privilege to be asked to be with this group of mothers and their children.

A friend asked me recently, 'Well, how's it all going after two years with the group?'

'I'm really enjoying it,' I responded.

'What do you actually do?'

'We are still very much at the "listening" stage,' I replied.

It is hard to explain the power of listening, of being heard and sharing stories and having fun together. This waiting for each other to trust, sharing a space together once a week, starting with superficial remarks about the weather, rather than starting to do something, is not really a valued way of doing things in our society. Before we came together as a group, I gave some thought to what we could offer these women. 'Life skills' was probably a good place to start, I thought, and gathered my materials on how to help other women grow in self-esteem, self-confidence, and a sense of self-worth.

At first I thought the young women were very shy; they didn't say much. Of course, I came to understand that they were waiting to see if they could trust us. Would I/we turn up each week to be with them? Could I/we be trusted to listen to their 'story' and understand their living situations and concerns without criticism? Would I/we love their children as they were or was there a possibility that I/we would be part of 'reporting' them to the Department of Community Services because we thought they were not coping well with their family? We did turn up each week. They kept coming, and slowly, as the weeks went by, we were able to talk to each other and hear each other's stories. A number of their partners were in jail; others just walked out on the women and the family. Only a couple had steady relationships.

During the early gatherings one of the non-aboriginal women offered to teach the mothers how to massage their children. As the weeks went on the women asked for a massage too and eventually were happy to massage each other.

One day, Mara said to anyone who wanted to listen, 'You know, I've never cooked in my life.' Mara has three children. Then she said she wanted to learn, so we began to cook and eat together each week. Then Jacinta, who was on maternity leave from her job, talked about going back to work, which prompted a conversation with all the women about the dream they had for themselves once the children all went off to school. Some also spoke about the cost of childcare facilities in Sydney and the fact that is was unaffordable for many single mothers, so their dreams were on hold. Another week, someone shared how tired she was. We did the exercise around 'If women went on strike for a month, what would be the result?' This led to much laughter and sharing in the group as well as bringing home to them the triple jeopardy for women – production, reproduction, and building the community.

The women now chat and share much more easily with each other and with us. They feel they have found a safe place to be together and to share about life. The children, too, have begun to play well together. We are all growing in trust and in our relationships. The materials about how to help people grow in self-esteem, self-confidence, and self-worth are still in a folder somewhere.

After two years we are still together and a few other mothers have joined us. In this cross-cultural situation, in a tiny corner of our country, we have broken down some of the barriers that often separate aboriginal people and non-aboriginal people. We have been able to talk to each other, sometimes heart to heart. As in Tanzania, we have shared experiences and are forming relationships. Generative themes will come as the weeks go by and we will follow the process to support these women to transform their lives in the way they want. That is and always has been the main aim of our working together, to help this small group of aboriginal women, so deeply wounded by the machinations of a world dominated by white society for so long, to transform their lives. They see they have the potential to move onwards to a better life for themselves and their families.

Notes

1   *Ujamaa* was a major feature of Nyerere's policy. It literally means 'family hood' and involved developing the spirit of close family relationships and caring in self-sufficient villages.

CHAPTER 14

Dialogue and nonviolence: a spiritual calling to renewal in Scotland

Vérène Nicolas

Vérène Nicolas[1] *supports teams and individuals working with local communities and people in poverty, in Scotland and abroad. Specifically, she facilitates individual, organizational, and community renewal by sharing the skills and principles of collaborative leadership. She is also a tutor on the Training for Transformation diploma course in Kleinmond, South Africa, and is actively involved in local projects in the Govan area of Glasgow, Scotland, where she lives.*

Kindness is the language deaf people can hear and blind people can see. *Ugandan proverb*

I discovered Training for Transformation (TfT) in 1996 when working in Ballymun, one of the poorest communities of Dublin, Ireland. Some people I worked with had attended workshops delivered by Partners, an organization delivering TfT with community development and faith-based initiatives. My colleagues had been touched by their experience and this aroused my curiosity. In August 1997, I took part in one of Partners' workshops. The practice of what I later learned is called 'critical dialogue' struck a chord with me. I loved the participatory and community aspect of the workshop: I was thirsty for meaning, friendship, and practical tools for action.

At the end of my university years in France, and although from a Protestant family, I went to Ireland and took part in a programme run by the Jesuits called Jesuit Volunteer Community, where young people live in a community for a year, work alongside marginalized people, and deepen their spirituality. It was in this context that I worked in Ballymun. As I had studied agriculture, I knew nothing about community development and very little about issues of poverty. I had never heard of Paulo Freire and popular education and had no familiarity with working-class culture. Yet something like a spiritual calling moved me and I continued on this path. With hindsight, I feel grateful to have started my work with local communities in Dublin, where people were familiar with Paulo Freire and TfT – mainly because of Partners' work, but also because of what I perceived as a vibrancy of soul in the Irish psyche. In my opinion, it isn't by chance that Partners was born and has been sustained in Ireland. I would have had a very different ideological and praxis-based introduction to community work had I started this journey anywhere else in Europe.

Being very new to community work, I encountered TfT with perhaps some naivety but also with a fresh and open heart. I enthusiastically embraced everything I got introduced to: articulation of the personal, interpersonal, and wider societal levels of transformation, group dynamics, tools for self-discovery, and so on. However, it was the praxis of dialogue that really struck a chord. I loved the depth of inquiry that the 'psycho-social method' offered (see Hope and Timmel, 1995). Despite my limited experience at the time, I had an innate sense of the power of dialogue to create meaning, healing, and liberation. The skills to facilitate it came with practice.

Immediately after taking part in the Partners workshop, I moved to Scotland and joined the Centre for Human Ecology (CHE), a small educational charity interested in the relevance of 'human ecology' to unearthing the roots of poverty and environmental destruction in Scotland and beyond, alongside teaching this academic discipline at a postgraduate level and undertaking research.

Human ecology can be broadly defined as the study of relationships between humans and nature. At the CHE, we are particularly interested in what causes the relationship between humans and nature (and, of course, between humans themselves) to break down. Why have we evolved as a species that so violates the earth's carrying capacity? What in our biology, psychology, or theologies creates violent economic and social responses to life? Why are we finding it so difficult, at both individual and collective levels, to recognize, empathize with, and protect the vibrancy of life?

However, it is not enough to study only the causes of a problem. CHE also focuses on practical, sustainable responses to our ecological, social, and spiritual crisis. What critical articulations need to be made between personal transformation and social change? What pedagogies, research paradigms, and organizational cultures are most aligned with our vision of a sustainable world? What does our personal life tell us about change agency and how do we resource our action?

These questions, alongside my own personal sensitivities, took me on a lifelong journey of inquiry into the practice of dialogue to facilitate an awakening of consciousness and to trigger committed action with regard to the earth and its peoples. The tools and principles of TfT, as I learned them with Partners and then in Kleinmond on the TfT diploma course, were my starting point. Although the CHE's raison d'être was essentially academic at the time – through its master's degree in human ecology – colleagues had a real interest in testing their models and assumptions in real-life situations. They opened up space to explore the relevance of TfT as an applied human ecology tool – for example, how to engage our ideas and vision with real people in real places, how to tap into the reality of their lives, develop critical consciousness, and provide them with tools for action. We worked with activists from some of the poorest communities of Glasgow and later with black and ethnic minority communities in Scotland, exploring issues of belonging and engagement in local democratic structures.

With hindsight, and although we actively engaged with local communities and tried to spread TfT in Scotland (as part of a network of Freirean practitioners), the most radical and exciting part of our work then was the master's degree.[2] Our course truly departed from mainstream academia. It was a vibrant experiment in radical learning with its 'head, heart, and hand' pedagogy – 'head' for the rigour of intellectual knowledge, writing, and research methodologies; 'heart' for the emotional and spiritual awakening necessary for individual and collective change; and 'hand' for the skills, methodologies, and practical initiatives for change. Despite having to use a certain amount of 'banking education', we facilitated a learning experience that students described as life changing. In my opinion, this was because they developed a systemic and rigorous understanding of the challenges we need to grapple with and they studied in an environment where not only their intellect was expanded, but also their heart and soul; where they learned practical tools to further their change agency and had a year-long experience of community that few had experienced before; where the sharing of food, insights, grief, walks, and music nourished deep friendships.

While this side of the CHE was innovative and impactful, the work with communities felt more experimental. As an organization, we were seen primarily as academic and our partners struggled to see how our mission matched what was required for grassroots action. In particular, some of us (myself included) had not yet grasped the subtlety of power dynamics in this area of work and how, despite unquestionable goodwill and commitment, our difficulty to address issues of privilege, class, education, and language might have created barriers to effective engagement and legitimacy. However, research projects inspired by our 'head, heart, hand' pedagogy received wide acknowledgement in the media at the time.[3] One example was *People & Parliament: Reshaping Scotland? The People Speak* (1999) at the time a new, devolved parliament was being established in Scotland. Another was called *Who's a Real Scot?* (2000), which engaged people from ethnic and minority backgrounds to explore issues of identity and belonging. Research that asks questions about things that matter (the 'generative themes') is also a form of dialogue. In both projects, participants enjoyed the opportunity to explore who they were as people (through the values they hold dear, or traditions that contribute to an inclusive sense of belonging) and what gave meaning to their lives (friendship, connection with the land, meaningful work, etc.).

One aspect of our educational practice that flourished in these years was our ability to facilitate powerful transformative learning events. An illustration of this happened through my inputs on the TfT diploma course in Kleinmond (in 2007, 2011, and 2013). I held workshops on climate change, ecology, and culture (with one of the CHE graduates), and most recently on truth, conflict, and nonviolence. After the week on ecology, participants reported being excited about a new sense of identification with nature and of the absolute importance of making environmental issues central to development education. After the latest course, they spoke of recognizing the fear and obedience that permeate most of our cultures and the importance of developing cultures of trust and care.

What are the key ingredients of this educational practice?

For each event (or week in the context of the diploma), a theoretical frame provides an overarching structure on which students can 'peg' their learning. Various activities on the learning journey allow them to navigate between personal situations (such as the signs and impact of climate change in their countries, personal grief about the loss of connection with tradition and land, or the painful reality of conflict in their families and workplaces) and a much bigger picture (for example the impact of so-called modernization on the deeply spiritual and earth-connected culture of Ladakh, or the meaning of nonviolence in the struggle for India's independence). They are also given some practices and principles to take home in order to deepen their connection with nature (for the week on ecology and culture) and their ability to speak truth with care (for the week on nonviolence).

It is also important to mention that this educational practice is rooted in what is called the 'needs (or needs-based) consciousness'. Everyone who is familiar with TfT knows about and is inspired by Manfred Max-Neef's model of fundamental human needs, especially as it led to the 'wheel of fundamental human needs'[4] widely used in communities across the world to discern generative themes and leverage for action. Other humanistic thinkers and practitioners have worked on the notion of needs: one of them is Marshall Rosenberg, founder of the practice of nonviolent communication (NVC) (Rosenberg, 2003), and there are other people following in his footsteps.[5] NVC is described as a spiritual path, a communication method, and a practical, learnable way to embody nonviolence in our actions, words, and thoughts. The practice of NVC gives us important resources as transformative learning facilitators. First of all, 'the needs consciousness' gives us a model of human nature packed with concrete practices and principles to help us resolve conflicts (inner and outer), facilitate healing and reconciliation in communities, and create conditions for trust and dialogue in organizations. Also, the light it sheds on human dynamics allows us to stay closely connected to the students' experience as their learning unfolds, to discern 'the question behind their questions' (i.e. what they truly care about), and to enable them to feel deeply heard. This creates trust, which in turn helps them relax and gives space to stretch them and broaden their consciousness.

I come back now to where TfT took me. For various reasons, the master's degree in human ecology was closed in 2009 and this shifted my praxis away from university to organizational and community settings. The focus of my work is now on facilitating individual, organizational, and community renewal through the lens of collaborative leadership. The practice of dialogue is a key component of this, always rooted in needs consciousness. Practically, the work takes the form of training and mentoring, practice groups, collaborative decision-making, and inquiry processes. Although this work is in its early stages of development, three areas are worth highlighting:

- Who is engaging?
- Why are they engaging?
- What is the scope of this approach?

People who engage with my work belong to teams or organizations working with local, grassroots communities both in Scotland and abroad. One example is a network of teams working in the poorest parishes of the Church of Scotland. Another is a team of senior staff from the local government's planning department in the Papua province of Indonesia that wants to understand how to develop partnership working with local communities. One of the initiators of this work is Maria Latumahina, a graduate of the 2013 Kleinmond diploma course.

Typically, within their organizations, people are confronted with structures that often get in the way of human flourishing and collaboration. At grassroots level, they usually encounter dynamics of poverty and vulnerability such as mental and physical ill health, substance abuse, unemployment, violence, apathy, lack of control over assets, and over-reliance on authority to determine the community's future. As individuals, they often lack the inner resources to face a web of complex human dynamics. The main reason why they engage with my work is that they realize how fundamental the gap is between their aspirations (what they care for and the vision they have of themselves and of their work) and what they can achieve. They therefore live what Quaker author Parker Palmer (2004) describes as 'divided lives': the inner is not in accord with the outer; the 'soul' does not meet the 'role'. This can have tragic consequences for individuals, organizations, and the people they serve: loss of motivation and self-esteem, illnesses, conflict, competition, and corruption in the most extreme cases.

Typically, when they engage with this work, people are taken on a learning journey that helps them understand human nature and themselves better, come to terms with actions they or others sometimes take against the common good, and work out practical strategies to address the impact of these actions. They also learn tools to transform conflict (intra- or inter-personal) and to foster trust within their teams by speaking truth with care, developing a culture of feedback, and creating simple structures to run effective meetings. Lastly, they explore how healing and reconciliation can help communities transform old wounds into opportunities for growth and effective engagement.

Key theoretical models focus on understanding what it takes to shift from cultures of fear to cultures of trust. As the former inhabit us in different ways – we carry them in ourselves, in our organizations, and in our nations – and as fear and violence have created deep wounds in our psyches, this work always involves a certain amount of grief and trauma-healing. When working with faith-based organizations or in cultures (such as Papua) where faith – whether animistic, Christian, or Muslim – is still a day-to-day experience for most people, it is also important to relate this work's philosophical and spiritual foundations to people's religious texts, stories, and aspirations. For example, when working on self-compassion, I might quote Isaiah 43:1 ('Before I was born the Lord called me; from my mother's womb he has spoken my name') to describe the sense of tenderness that we want to emulate when approaching ourselves and the life-denying judgements that we carry. When exploring nonviolence, the Holy Qur'an (5:30–35) has Abel saying to Cain: 'If you stretch out your hand to kill me, it is not for me to kill you, because I respect God, the Cherisher of the Worlds.' For secular audiences, poems that speak to the soul (for example, from David Whyte or Mary Oliver in a western context) can have similar inner traction, which is to say that this work is of a profound spiritual nature. It connects with our heart's deepest desires – connection, truth, meaning, peace, beauty, courage, mystery, and so on – and discussions on this need to be facilitated with great sensitivity, as in the process of discovering what is most important to us we also realize how disconnected we are from it.

Reflecting on the insights drawn from my praxis over the years, I am calling for a redefinition of what 'training for transformation' entails. While facilitating critical dialogue among local people is key to any process of transformation, I would argue that a grassroots consciousness will not stick (nor truly emerge in the first place) unless civil society organizations undergo a major cultural change – from fear and authoritarianism to trust and collaboration. It means, in practice, that in these organizations, individuals stand in their truth, are anchored in their 'true selves' (soul), act in integrity with their values, and are held by structures that reflect and sustain this culture of trust. So, while being well aware that this framing broadens and makes the skill set required to bring about transformation more complex, I am arguing for the philosophical foundations and the practice of TfT to be considerably reinforced in these areas.

Of course, this requires that facilitators of transformative learning also engage in psychological and spiritual work. To illustrate this, let me reflect on some of the challenges that I personally found in working with communities (namely the issues of legitimacy and power mentioned above). When engaging at a grassroots level, it came to me that one of the main obstacles for people to trust my intention has been my difficulty in sharing with authenticity. Because of the culture I grew up in, I have a tendency not to share my fears, doubts, truth, or vulnerability. As a result, sometimes people find it difficult to see my humanity, to relax in my presence, and to want to work with me. Added to this, as I have access to resources such as education, networks, language, and 'middle-class' skills, I can come across as 'cold' or 'directive' in the eyes of people who have less structural power. To address this, I regularly invite feedback on how my actions impact on others, I am slowly learning to speak my truth and show vulnerability, and I am letting life transform the rigidities that inhibit me from relating to others with heart, flow, and spontaneity.

To conclude, it might be important to say that, as I have almost exclusively engaged with individuals and teams so far, seeing the impact on communities and at a deep psycho-social level will take time. Over the years, the work has changed in scope (from nurturing personal development and leadership qualities to facilitating organizational change and community renewal) and in its content (tools, models, and processes). Transforming cultures of fear and unhelpful power dynamics requires a slow process of maturation within each of us and in our organizations. This will be a lifetime journey.

Notes

1   See www.verenenicolas.org.
2   See contributions from CHE colleagues to Williams et al., 2012.
3   See *People & Parliament: Reshaping Scotland? The People Speak* (1999), available at <http://goo.gl/MQMQad> and *Who is a Real Scot?* (2000), available at <http://goo.gl/qQriAc>.
4   See <http://goo.gl/116ctd>.
5   See the work of Miki Kashtan, one of the key theorists and facilitators of NVC, at <http://baynvc.blogspot.co.uk>.

References

Hope, A. and Timmel, S. (1995) *Training for Transformation: A Handbook for Community Workers*, Volume 1, Rugby, UK: Practical Action Publishing.

Palmer, P. J. (2004) *A Hidden Wholeness: The Journey Toward an Undivided Life*, San Francisco, CA: Jossey-Bass.

Rosenberg, M. (2003) *Nonviolent Communication: A Language of Life*, Encinitas, CA: Puddle Dancer Press.

Williams, L., Roberts, R. and McIntosh, A. (eds) (2012) *Radical Human Ecology: Intercultural and Indigenous Approaches*, Farnham: Ashgate.

PART FIVE
Freedom from patriarchy

Keywords: breaking the glass ceiling; building unity; flexible approaches; gender rights; human rights; linking systems; problem-posing; education; respecting learners' needs; songs for awareness; web of discrimination; women's power

http://dx.doi.org/10.3362/9781780448312.006

CHAPTER 15
Training for Transformation: rooting and branching in India

Mercy Kappen

Mercy Kappen *is a board and staff member of Visthar Ecumenical Training Centre in Bangalore, India. She has facilitated the gender module in the Training for Transformation diploma course in Kleinmond every year since 2004. The month-long TfT programme on gender, which she organizes at Visthar every year, is based on the TfT philosophy and methodology, and is also used in programmes held there for American students. She has used TfT in training in Afghanistan, Bangladesh, Sri Lanka, Nepal, Myanmar, Hong Kong, and Thailand.*

In this chapter, Mercy reminisces on the influence of Paulo Freire and TfT in her life and work, giving examples of good practice and adaptations in the context of South and South-east Asia. She also highlights the challenges arising from a mechanical application of the method and underlines the need for deeper rooting in a spirituality of transformation.

To appreciate the beauty of the valley, one must walk through it.   *Zambian proverb*

In retrospect

I was introduced to Paulo Freire and *Pedagogy of the Oppressed* in the late 1970s by my mentor and guru Sebastian Kappen. Subsequently, in 1981, I had the opportunity to participate in a one-month course on development and liberation offered by INODEP International in Paris, an institute founded by Paulo Freire. I used to be involved with community-based groups in South India called 'sanghas'; these focused on political mobilization of the poor and the marginalized around their issues of concern. They were very different from the state- or World Bank-promoted self-help groups of today.

The action groups in India in the late 1970s and the 1980s were greatly influenced by Paulo Freire and his philosophy and methods. *Pedagogy of the Oppressed* almost became a manifesto for their work with communities. Then came *Training for Transformation: A Handbook for Community Workers* by Anne Hope and Sally Timmel from the Training for Transformation (TfT) Institute in South Africa. These books served as a guide or manual for several people in their awareness-building programmes. I had developed great admiration for Sally and Anne, for their commitment to translating the philosophy and approaches of Paulo Freire into simple, manageable concepts, and methods and tools for training. But it was only in 2003 that I met them.

I have been with Visthar since its inception as a member of the board of trustees and as programme director. Visthar is an academy of justice and peace studies with strong community involvement in Karnataka, South India. My responsibilities included organizing and facilitating training and studies, and networking with civil society organizations in the country. I have also been part of the autonomous women's movement in India. Over the last 15 years, the focus of my work has been on capacity-building of civil society organizations in gender, diversity, and social transformation. A considerable amount of this work has been devoted to conceptualizing and enabling national and international NGOs and faith-based organizations (FBOs) to perceive gender as a cross-cutting perspective and in mainstreaming gender within organizations and programmes.

It was Sister Elsa, a participant on a TfT course at the Grail Centre in Kleinmond, who made the connection and paved the way for collaboration with TfT and Visthar. With Elsa, we organized a consultation that brought together people who had been applying Paulo Freire in community organizations and friends who had been part of DELTA and TfT with Sally and Anne. Several young activists and representatives of NGOs in Bangalore participated in that programme.

Following this, we had discussions on how Visthar and TfT could collaborate. Sally and Anne invited me to join the facilitation team for TfT in 2004. I spent two months on the first residential phase of TfT and gained immensely from the experience. Since then I have been there for all the TfT diploma courses, facilitating sessions on gender and feminism.

Although I had been exposed to the philosophy of Paulo Freire, it was my participation in TfT that helped me to root myself and relate concepts and theories to my life and work experiences. I used to read everything available on the topic with which I was dealing and still feel inadequate and nervous. TfT helped me with the deep insight that as a facilitator you don't need to know everything. You need to trust the participants and build on their experiences and knowledge base. You don't have to be an 'expert' with all the concepts and theories arranged in your head. What you need is a commitment to social justice and transformative processes. In order to achieve this, we need to create teaching – learning communities with a focus on the head, heart, and hand. I learned to challenge the dualities of the emotional and the cognitive and evolve integrated perspectives in my world views and practice.

With the perspectives and skills gained at TfT, the Visthar training became transformative. We brought in exercises such as the 'River of Life', which helped focus on participants as subjects of learning with their unique life journeys and ways of knowing. We became more conscious of the multi-directionality of learning and the links between the personal and the political, between self and society, the individual and the collective. We stopped talking of empowering others; we became more and more convinced that 'Nobody liberates anybody else, and nobody liberates themselves all alone. People liberate themselves in fellowship with each other' (Freire, 1970).

TfT in gender, diversity, and social transformation

Since 2006 we have been running a month-long certificate course called 'Gender, Diversity, and Social Transformation'. Although we have been following participatory methods in our training since our inception in 1989, it is in these courses that we have really applied TfT in its true sense. The course brings together participants from Africa and Asia working with human rights organizations, national and international NGOs, FBOs, women's groups, and students. This is basically a TfT in gender. Sharing and learning from the lived experiences of participants are woven into the process. Another integral part of the course is the teaching – learning events where participants apply the problem-posing method and facilitate sessions on issues identified by them. This was an outcome of my time on the TfT course in Kleinmond. According to the feedback from participants over the years, these practice sessions have been the most helpful in taking forward what they have learned to the constituencies in which they are involved. Teachers from mainstream schools who have participated in our courses have incorporated the problem-posing method in their classes and are excited to report how this shift has energized students and enriched their vocation.

We follow through the different stages of the problem-posing method in facilitating sessions on gender roles and relations, violence against women, reproductive health and rights, gender and food security, climate change, and so on. We have developed codes for each of the topics we deal with and follow the steps to problematize the issue, identify the root causes, and arrive at action plans to bring about changes at different levels. In the process, participants reflect upon and analyse the world in which they live or the institutions of which they are a part and the role they play in reinforcing or subverting the status quo based on social relations of, for example, gender, caste, and class. The daily or routine events that we take for granted, that are considered normal, are subjected to scrutiny from the perspective of the different actors involved in them. Women and men who have internalized gendered ways of living and relating, who have a naive consciousness that it is the fate of a woman that she is overburdened, beaten up, humiliated, and marginalized, begin to rethink and question the way things are. This 'inside out' change is what is most important. Some are aware of their reality and have a basic analysis but do not do anything to change it. They are afraid of the repercussions, afraid of tilting the balance. The course instils the courage to critique the status quo, think of alternatives, build solidarity, and take action to bring about change.

Figure 15.1 is an example of a code we use for sensitizing the participants on gender-based divisions of roles and work and their implications for women. We know that there is a division of roles between women and men in most societies, but the general society does not stop to think how this affects our lives, and particularly its impact on women, their identities, and their choices.

"Darling, if you just take care of them for the next few years,
I will take care of their ideological development when they grow up."

Figure 15.1 Illustrating gender-based divisions of roles and work
Source: Basin and Thapar, 2013

We begin the session with this code. Participants are asked to describe what they see in the picture, observing closely the expressions of the people in the picture, the articles on the floor symbolizing different forms of work, the positioning of the man, woman, and children, and so on. At the first level of analysis we stay with the code and ask the participants to analyse why what they see in the picture happens, why the woman is overburdened with multiple responsibilities while the man is sitting with the newspaper and reading. He looks happy and relaxed while the woman looks tired and harassed. They also read the text in the cartoon and discuss its meaning and implications. Then we move on to relating the code to real-life experiences by asking the participants whether this happens in real life. Invariably, across class, caste, ethnicity, and region, the answer will be yes. We then encourage both women and men in the group to share their experiences. We then look at the consequences of this division of work and roles on women, men, and children. They are encouraged to look at the problems this division can give rise to. They are immediately able to come up with issues of denial of rest and leisure, and opportunities and choices for women who are expected to play the roles of obedient and docile wife, caring and nurturing mother, and efficient employee at her workplace. Women are expected to play multiple roles. Men, on the other hand, are expected to be breadwinners and heads of households. The session then digs deeper into the root causes of this kind of division of labour. Why do we perceive women primarily in their reproductive role? Why is the reproductive role taken for granted, not valued or recognized as work? And we come to the root cause – the patriarchal ideology and practice that give primacy, power, privileges, and priority to men. Individuals and social institutions that consider man as the head of the household, the ruler, the priest, and all-powerful reinforce patriarchy. Participants reflect on attitudes and behaviours that deeply entrench patriarchy, resulting in the division of roles and spaces, discrimination, disparities, and the disempowerment of women. The next step is to work on an action plan to address the problem. How do we change mindsets and the cultures and structures that devalue women? Participants come up with possible action, including gender sensitization of both women and men, redesigning the curriculum and educational practices that reinforce gender bias, sensitization of religious leaders and decision-makers, and so on.

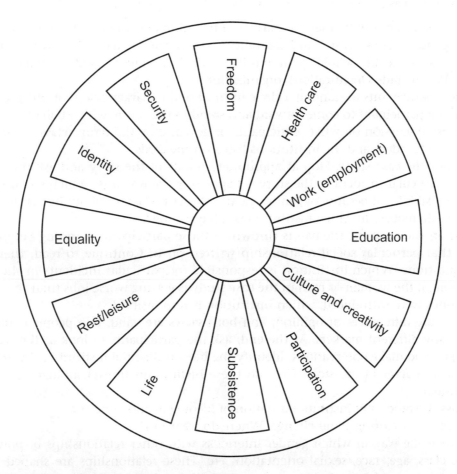

Figure 15.2 The wheel of fundamental human rights

Envisioning a gender-equitable society is another creative and reflective method we have drawn from TfT. This visualization exercise helps in giving expression to the kind of gender relations that the participants envisage. Each group is asked to interpret another group's depiction. The basic principles and behaviour patterns of a gender-just society are taken from these presentations and summarized, with additions from the whole group. We have also adapted the wheel of fundamental human needs to explore the topic of gender and rights (Figure 15.2). We redesigned it so that each spoke represents a right as enshrined in the Universal Declaration of Human Rights. This serves as an important tool for our sessions on gender and rights. We have also very effectively used team-building and leadership development methods specifically focusing on gender and leadership.

Acknowledging and going further

Although Paulo Freire never theorized on gender, he was aware of the complex web of social relations that influences and impacts the lives of women and men. In 1993, he wrote: 'Oppression must always be understood in its multiple and contradictory instances, just as liberation must be grounded in the particularity of suffering and struggle in concrete, historical experience.' TfT has brought in this perspective with Book 4. To take this forward, we have evolved methodologies to strengthen participants' understanding of the links between social relationships and institutions, especially of family, community, market, state, and supra-state institutions, in reinforcing or challenging power relations based on gender and other identities. The gender sessions I facilitate on the TfT courses follow an intersectional approach and highlight the complex weave of social relationships and institutions. The following is an illustration of the methods used.

A case study is used as a code in this session. The following steps are followed:

- Draw a circle. Put out two sets of markers of two different colours. On one set of cards write 'sex', 'gender', 'class', 'caste', and 'disability' – you can also add other identities. On the other set of cards write 'household', 'community' (including religion), 'state', 'market', and 'supra-state (World Trade Organization)' organizations.
- Request participants to stand in a circle in front of the marker placed on the ground.
- Request a participant to come forward and stand in the centre with a ball of twine.
- Facilitate discussion on what participants understand by the terms 'class', 'caste' or 'race', 'sex', and 'gender', and the institutions listed on the cards.
- Read out the case study. Stop at appropriate points of the story and ask the participants why a particular incident in the story is happening the way it is. Which social relationship is responsible? Is it because of gender, caste, ethnicity, class, or disability? Or is it related to sexual differences? In which institution is it happening?
- Based on the answers, the ball is thrown to those participants standing before the cards with that particular social relationship written on it. Continue to read, then stop and ask questions. Which institution is responsible for particular incidents in the story? For example, if the woman or man in the case study is getting worse jobs than they did before machines were introduced, which institution is responsible?
- If there are differences of opinion, and both views are valid, two people could be asked to occupy different markers. At the end, ask the participants to look at the web that has emerged and make observations. Identify the most influential institutions in the life of the central character in the story. How do these institutions impact, influence, or affect the individual?
- Discuss the process of institutionalization of ideologies and policies.
- Discuss how we bring about change. Where do we begin?
- Reinforce the way in which gender interlocks with other relationships of power such as caste, class, age, race, sexual orientation, etc. These relationships are shaped in turn by the institutions of households, markets (including private media), community (including religion), state, and supra-state organizations.

This exercise clearly brings home the point that we need to scrutinize the actual rules and practices of the institutions and pay attention to the interactions between institutions in order to bring about social change. Isolated interventions without analysis of the overall picture will not lead to systemic changes, but only sticking-plaster solutions. Institutions can be transformed only if those whose interests are at stake challenge the existing rules, practices, resource allocations, and authority and control structures.

Challenges and learning

One of the main challenges comes from participants who quickly pick up the concepts and methods without internalizing the values and goals of TfT. This does not lead to transformation but rather to a reversal of power relations. It is like moving from being the oppressed to the oppressor. For example, I had this experience with one batch of TfT participants: a core group representing the participants dictated terms to the facilitators, leaving no room for dialogue.

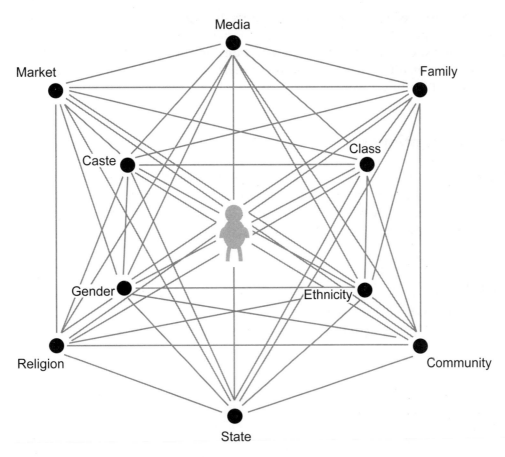

Figure 15.3 The complex web of relationships

They set boundaries and rules. While one can appreciate that the participants are challenging and questioning the authority traditionally vested in the facilitators, we need to be cautious about the power imbalances this gives rise to.

How do we address the question of power within TfT? A process that leaves one section powerless and at the mercy of the other cannot be transformative, whether that section is facilitators or participants. TfT needs to deal in depth with the concepts, sources, and types of power. 'Power within' is a deeply spiritual concept that comes from deep convictions, a consciousness of unjust social structures and systems, and a commitment to bring about change. If we do not achieve this, we will not have the 'power to' change. What is required is an overthrow or transformation of the status quo, not an internalization of oppression and the oppressor. We need to fight against the oppressor who dwells within us, not just outside us. 'Responsible non-conformism' is what we should encourage.

Another challenge relates to the internalization of the TfT process. TfT, as I understand it, is not about tools and techniques. It is not about manipulating the marginalized and the vulnerable to accept the facilitator's ideologies and world views. I have observed a tendency among TfT alumni to ritualistically follow the problem-posing method, with no grasp of the lived experiences or context of the people they work with or a vision of the alternative world. Participants are geared to come up with predetermined answers and solutions; this becomes very evident in the learning events facilitated by the participants, although it is understandable given the time constraints and the compulsion to perform. We need to move beyond this instrumentalist approach to a holistic paradigm that is truly dialogical.

Although TfT has incorporated gender in the fourth book, gender has not really become rooted in the diploma course. It remains an add-on, often brought in during the last phase of training. This does not help in weaving gender and other analytical frames from the start and into all aspects of the process. We also need to explore ways to address the mindsets of participants who uncritically follow religious scriptures and justify women's subordination in society or condemn women and men with different sexual orientations. How do we understand and celebrate diversity and learn to respect people who are different and advocate for their rights as well? I recommend we strengthen the components of feminist theology and spirituality in the course.

The journey continues

'Knowledge emerges only through invention and re-invention, through the restless, impatient, continuing, hopeful inquiry human beings pursue in the world, with the world, and with each other.' We need to keep these words of Paulo Freire in mind as we enter the next phase of TfT and continue our journey in hope.

Reference

Basin, K. and Thapar, B. (2013) *Laughing Matters*, Delhi: Jagori.
Freire, P. ([1970] 1973) *Pedagogy of the Oppressed*, London: Penguin Books.

CHAPTER 16

Ingenious indigenous: exploring transformations in health and well-being in Latin America

Bethann Witcher Cottrell

Dr Bethann Witcher Cottrell *has a doctorate in food and nutrition. She discovered TfT through Dr David Hilton, who worked at the World Council of Churches, and with him she wrote the* Transformation for Health *manual. She is currently working for Care International in Ghana where she is the director and global co-ordinator of food and nutrition security. In its 'Social Analysis and Action' programme, Care International uses this methodology widely as it seeks the underlying causes of food insecurity and malnutrition. With its country office staff, it explores the social norms around gender and reproductive health, and food and nutrition security, catalysing change at both the relational and the structural levels of the agency.*

This chapter includes an account of using Transformation for Health *with two different groups of indigenous women in Latin America, one in Ecuador and one in Mexico, around the themes of individual empowerment, health, and well-being.*

A zebra takes its stripes wherever it goes.   *Kenyan proverb*

I was in the library at Michigan State University looking for books on infant and young child feeding to prepare for my master's thesis on women's barriers to breastfeeding. I spotted a small book with a red title on a white cover, *Pedagogy of the Oppressed*. The title intrigued me. I picked it up. The author was Paulo Freire. He was a Brazilian. Having been raised in Brazil, I was excited to find this book by a Brazilian author and felt compelled to read it. One day. One book. One author. One connection. One life path redirected.

I changed my thesis to the use of the Freirean methodology among Mexican-American migrants picking truck crops in Michigan. Freire himself was in Michigan that summer and became an adviser on my thesis. Together we decided to use pictures of the population itself as codes. I spent a summer with the migrant families photographing every aspect of their lives with their permission. Finally, we projected the pictures from a generator on a truck onto a large white sheet hung up high in the middle of the camp. What a joyous evening. Everybody loved seeing themselves larger than life on the big white sheet. 'Look, there's Juanita! Can we see her again?' Great entertainment. No educational value, liberating or otherwise. The failure continued as my academic committee would not allow me to change my predicted generative theme to their actual generative theme. I moved on to 'So what!' And began to work on the women's generative theme of obesity. Finally, as I got going, the migrants packed up their trucks, gunned the engines, and headed back to Texas. Ah, failure! And lessons learned: pictures of the actual population with whom you are working cannot be used as codes for that population; external control inhibits the process; and the process cannot happen in a short period of time.

With failure and lessons learned in my pockets, I continued my studies and ended up in Ecuador to do my PhD dissertation. There, my popular education attempts garnered the attention of MAP International. As I joined the MAP International team in Ecuador, I was surprised to find that all their work in agriculture and health was implemented only with Quichua men. Strongly believing that development could not happen without the involvement of women, I began a process of listening to men. Sitting in long Quichua meetings, I asked one question: 'Who works the most, men or women?' Invariably, the answer that always came back was that the men worked the longest and hardest. As we made a list of women's chores that grew in length, lights began to flash in the eyes of the men. As if a match had been suddenly struck in the collective Quichua male consciousness, they began noisily to talk among themselves. I sat in silence, unable to understand a single word, but able to sense what was happening. Finally, stunned by the realization, they said that the quality of their families' lives could not improve without the involvement of women. One question opened a self-discovery process that led these men to request a women's programme.

By the time a group of women had been assembled, the relationship of trust was such that the men allowed me to meet alone with the women. We came together to explore what a 'women's programme' would look like. Every woman sitting on the cold dirt floor of a thatched roof adobe home had buried a child. With a shiny new PhD in international nutrition and enough knowledge of the Quichua not to know much about anything, my assumption was that their priority had to be maternal–child issues. My surprise came when they stated that what they wanted to learn was the word of God. Yes, they were interested in improving the lives of their children and families but not through maternal – child health education as I knew it. They wanted to learn the word of God, *la palabra de Dios*. And they repeated it over and over again.

If I truly believed in liberating education, it was critical to start where the women were, no matter how difficult it was for me. I knew nothing about the Bible beyond the fact that Jesus was the central character and he had a mother named Mary. I looked up Mary in the Bible, from which I gleaned that she had responsibilities, sacrifices, and blessings, and I developed the mother's day workshop with the Quichua women around these themes. I sent the women off to talk about how, like Mary, they had responsibilities in their lives. Off they went, and they wouldn't come back. Unfamiliar with the language, I was not unfamiliar with non-stop talking, deep emotions, and tears. Never before had they been given the opportunity to tell their own stories and join together to seek their own solutions. Together we built a programme of leadership development for Quichua women through exploring the lives of Biblical women. By beginning at their beginning, the women gained the self-esteem and confidence to build a women's programme that included health education and income generation.

Their concern for the well-being of their children surfaced as we explored the roles of women together. Two serious problems were malnutrition and death from diarrhoeal disease. We began to explore their food and nutrition reality. A brief input on nutrition was provided, from which they extracted messages and visuals based on their own understanding. They used these to teach women in their own villages. They learned how to teach other women to hydrate their babies using oral rehydration solution and 'diarrhoea dolls' made from gourds. As their confidence continued to grow, they planted home gardens and community gardens. Finally, they ventured into guinea pig-raising projects that provided extra protein for their children as well as extra income for the mothers. The women continued to grow and to identify other things that could improve their lives. They wanted literacy education and to learn how to sew. These new desires went beyond what MAP could provide. They were not deterred. With a new sense of self and new knowledge, the women had the self-confidence to identify other avenues to help them achieve their goals.

Years later, another opportunity surfaced to work with indigenous women, this time in Mexico. Dr Ann Digirolamo had conducted research on caregivers of young children and identified a high level of depression among these women. In response, she wanted to give something back to them that might help them cope with the harsh realities of their lives – poverty, low literacy, domestic violence, alcoholism, machismo. She had heard about the Transformation for Health work that Dr David Hilton and I were doing, adapting Training for Transformation to a health context.

She contacted me to work with the Mexican women in Xoxocotla, a semi-urban indigenous town outside Cuernavaca.

An adaptation of the five-day Transformation for Health workshop was held with 14 caregivers at the nutrition centre in Xoxocotla. The women went through a process of examining issues in their lives and their community. Codes such as the one below were shared and discussed to facilitate the women's critical thinking and reflection about their own lives, their own cages, and the open doors that were available to them. Their value and strength as women in the community were emphasized and we witnessed participants emerge from long-term depression, develop fewer health complaints, begin to lose weight, and have the confidence to return to school.

In a subsequent workshop, this same group of women identified those things in their lives that were barriers to their quality of life. They identified four topics: poverty, interfamily communication, environmental sanitation, and disconnection from God. Women were then given disposable cameras and six weeks to photograph these topics in any way that they saw them. The cameras were handed back and the photographs developed and returned to the women, who then selected one or two around which they wrote their story. In their story, they presented the issue they chose to address, their experience of the issue, and recommended solutions. We then assisted the women in converting the photographs, stories, and recommendations into slides and posters for display. With their posters and slides in tow, they travelled to Cuernavaca to present their work at the National Institute of Public Health to a packed auditorium. When one academic at the back of the room got up and asked, 'Did the women do this themselves or did the facilitators do this for them?', the women of Xoxocotla sitting at the front took hold of the microphone and told this audience of academics: 'All of you think that we can't do anything because we are poor, but we are here to tell you, yes we can, and we did, and we will!'

It did not end there. Returning to this group of women, we asked them what tools and methods from the workshops they had attended worked for them. What would they like to use to facilitate this workshop with other women in their community? They set their objectives, selected six sessions, how many and how long. A process of community-based curriculum development resulted that was then assembled by the facilitators and presented back to the women as their own toolbox. In pairs, the women went to their own family members and neighbours, formed small groups of women, and facilitated the process they had been through themselves.

Still not satisfied, the women wanted more. As they are short in stature and mostly overweight, they had a burning desire to learn how to manage their body weight. Back to the drawing board. A group of four Mexican and American facilitators put together a five-day nutrition curriculum and the process was repeated. The women identified their own barriers to a healthy weight, offered photo-voice presentations, and initiated advocacy in their community, schools, and churches. They developed their own community-based process for a healthy weight curriculum. They took this out into their communities to facilitate a workshop for other women based around simple messages that they themselves had selected from their learning.

Activities relating to true health, which isn't medical but addresses the physical, mental, social, and spiritual needs of people, liberate them and their communities from all that holds them back from well-being. This is done through listening carefully to people's own generative themes, which empowers them to reclaim responsibility for their lives and their health.

One woman from Xoxocotla shared that she had moved from being a woman of submission to being a woman who put a banner across her bedroom door stating: 'I, as a woman, am valuable.' Success lies in the indigenous women knowing that yes, they can – and in the heart of such a woman.

CHAPTER 17

When songs puncture power: rewriting lyrics to reflect gender realities in Kenya

Adelina Ndeto Mwau

Adelina Ndeto Mwau is the deputy governor of Makueni county in Kenya. She is responsible for the Department of Development, which gives her the opportunity to work with grassroots groups on land rights, gender-based violence, and violence against women and children. She has been involved in Training for Transformation since 1974, when, as a very young primary school teacher, she attended the first workshop of WINDOW (Women in the National Development of Women) and then one of the DELTA workshops in Kenya. After working on literacy for some years, she specialized in gender education and became an independent consultant running courses in many countries. She helped produce the Oxfam manual on gender education. She was of a member of the previous parliament in Kenya and Deputy Minister for Labour.

This chapter tells how TfT helped to unite women to challenge certain aspects of the new constitution in Kenya, and to break through the glass ceiling for women in government.

An elephant can do nothing to a tamarind tree except to shake it.   *Senegalese proverb*

I am now the deputy governor of Makueni county, one of the 47 counties we have in Kenya. There are only nine women elected as deputy governors in Kenya. My journey to where I have reached today started when I went to a Training for Transformation (TfT) programme that Anne Hope and Sally Timmel had organized. I was a young teacher then, teaching in a local school in Makueni county. I first worked in a small town in Machakos county in Kenya, teaching adult literacy classes using Paulo Freire's approach to education. This opportunity gave me a grounding in using education for critical thinking.

In the training, I was exposed to the TfT methodologies of critical analysis and thinking and I have never been the same again. After this training, I started to see the world and my community through a new lens, and started to question my position and condition as a woman. This experience started a fire in me, a fire that even today is burning, a fire that will continue to bring life to me and to the community where I live and work.

The approach of TfT gave me a new view of the world and helped me develop an analytical mind through asking questions and not accepting that situations are the way they are because it is the will of God. Since then, my analytical mind has been constantly sharpened and has helped me to become the person I am today: a woman leader in my community, a woman leader in Kenya, and a woman leader in my family. I have worked and adapted the TfT methodologies in different programmes and organizations in different parts of the world with a lot of success. In my growth, I have come to appreciate and discover both culture and God's creation.

I worked as a national adult education co-ordinator: my role was to support Kenyan Catholic development offices to adapt Paulo Freire's philosophy and approach to adult literacy. I worked among many Kenyan tribes – including the Maasai, Samburu, Gabbra, Rendille, Borana, and Turkana, among many others – developing reading materials, training teachers, and organizing writers' workshops for the new literates. The materials developed helped learners to 'read and write their reality', to read and write their history and culture, and to come up with strategies for change.

I later worked with Oxfam (Kenya) as gender programme officer, where my role was to engender Oxfam programmes in Kenya. I adapted TfT in my work of gender training for Oxfam. In 1994, with two other gender trainers from England, I co-authored the Oxfam gender training manual. I also worked in Zimbabwe with a women's organization working throughout Africa to help women use law in their development work. I was the East Africa programme officer for Kenya, Uganda, and Tanzania. I have adapted TfT in all my work, including as a politician.

Engaging with grassroots groups to eradicate gender-based violence

I mentioned that I have adapted TfT in the many programmes with which I have worked. The Women's Research Centre and Development Institute is one of the organizations I founded. We work on a programme where animators are trained to deal with issues of gender-based violence. As part of this process I have looked at popular songs and analysed them to see what messages they carry about men and women. We found that they often demean and abuse women and give men power over women. We were concerned that women dance to these songs, internalizing the messages without even questioning them.

We decided to organize a training workshop with the most popular songwriters and musicians in Makueni county, where I work. The key objective was to create awareness as to how their songs continue to perpetuate women's invisibility and oppression in society. The musicians who were invited did not all turn up, and the 16 who did came reluctantly. At the beginning they were indifferent and did not even want to stay for the whole workshop. We started by building a common understanding of what gender is and how gender is constructed, maintained, and reinforced. We looked at the socialization processes of both men and women. We did this by looking at songs, sayings, proverbs, and also how religion and education reinforce the traditional position of men and women. We analysed some songs and proverbs and looked at who has power and who has none in the songs. We also explored the impact these songs and proverbs have on both women and men, and on the way they perceive themselves and each other. Participants were touched. A light went on in them.

We used the analysis tool called 'the 24 hours of men and of women'. This looks at what men and women do in a whole day. We used this tool with the objective of helping the musicians become aware of the workload women have on any given day. This '24-hour day' code of the activities of both men and women was an eye-opener, enabling people to see that women are often overworked and that men often spend most of their time in leisure, and that men do not honour their responsibilities concerning reproductive issues in their families. With this new awareness, we were able to ask them to look at their own songs and at how they portray women. They were shocked to realize the messages in their songs: almost all the songs portrayed women negatively or in powerless situations.

In the workshop, they tried to rewrite their songs with the new awareness. We were surprised at the songs they came up with. The workshop took place just a few days before the 16 days of activism on gender-based violence, a campaign that takes place throughout the world from 24 November to 10 December each year. We invited the same musicians to come and create new songs for the campaign activities. They came to the activities and entertained large groups of people who turned out to hear their music. People were surprised to hear their new messages. Women and men were dancing to the new messages that were giving women and men positive images.

The songs described women doing well in their homes and encouraged men to come out and join women in the merry-go-round of their many different roles and start taking responsibility in the family. Some songs portrayed women in positions of professional or political leadership.

The songs challenged the traditional sexual division of labour and called on young girls to aim for professions that are male dominated.

The musicians wrote songs to challenge injustices perpetuated by government officers, clan leaders, and political leaders. They wrote songs about how the police and courts treat women who come to report cases to them. They challenged men to stop gender-based violence. They sang songs celebrating the importance of the woman's role in the family and community, and advised men to support their wives in the reproductive issues of the family. People who came to the celebration noticed the change in the songs and recognized themselves in them.

Kasiva is a single mother who has never married. For several years she had been trying to get access to and control of her father's land but her family, clan, and community did not see the need for her to have land on her father's farm. As an organization, we had tried for more than three years to help her get justice; finally, we managed to get her a title deed after a long battle with her family. We had to go to court and involve the police, but eventually Kasiva won the battle. However, the journey was quite surprising ...

The day of 10 December is set aside to celebrate international human rights day. It also marks the end of the 16 days of activism against gender-based violence. On this day, our organization chose to celebrate Kasiva's right to share ownership of her father's land, and to have the same and equal rights as her brothers. We had asked the group of musicians to compose songs to celebrate the day, to challenge the injustices Kasiva was going through, and also to challenge the structures and systems that have been denying Kasiva her right to inherit land from her family. The song about Kasiva became famous; one could hear it on the radio. Bit by bit, the government officers, family members, and clan members started to feel uneasy with this information, and they decided to grant Kasiva her rights!

One of the songs that the musicians wrote is what Kasiva and her women friends danced to:

Ii aai aume Iai mbaitu
Syana sya aka ii aume
Nitwanoie II aume.

The song calls men and women to come out and work together to build their families and the country as one way of eradicating poverty.

Learning from this experience

Songs in many African communities have been created to share information in society. One can study development changes through songs; one can also analyse changes in society by listening to what popular musicians compose and sing at any given time. Songs of the 1960s in Kenya were about the changing roles of women and men. This was because, for the first time, women went to study in Europe and America and came back as professionals, getting jobs that were traditionally male. One of the songs composed and sung by the late Daudi Kabaka in the 1960s is an example: 'Msichana Mrembo kama wewe ni Kitu Ngani kimekufanya usiolewa. Elimu unayo ya kutosha hata gambo hukaenda ukarudi.' The song tells of a beautiful girl who has gone to Europe and has come back and has not got married. Her younger sisters are already married. Daudi Kabaka's songs are some of the songs we analysed in the workshop.

PART SIX
Crossing cultures, building bridges

Keywords: courage in resettlement; crossing cultures; expanding possibilities;
               identity and belonging; integrating immigrants and refugees, mediating
               cultures

http://dx.doi.org/10.3362/9781780448312.007

CHAPTER 18
Becoming a cultural mediator in Switzerland

Vero Schoeffel

Veronique (Vero) Schoeffel helped to start DELTA in South Africa. After five years she returned to Switzerland, where she works as a consultant and trainer running workshops for people preparing to work in a culture different from their own. She has also done much international work in places such as Madagascar, Bolivia, Zambia, Kyrgyzstan, and Ireland. She aims to empower people and teams by increasing their intercultural competence.

In this chapter she shows how the Training for Transformation methodology and philosophy were used in training the caretakers in large blocks of flats in Switzerland in intercultural competence. At the end of the programme the caretakers had expanded their conception of their role, from just caretakers responsible for the upkeep of the buildings to building understanding and acceptance among tenants from many countries and cultures living under the same roof. As one of them said: 'I did not understand people from other cultures. Now I am a cultural mediator.'

A feather alone is a delicate thing, yet it carries a bird all over the world.   *Sudanese proverb*

I am a French woman who studied translation and international development at the University of Geneva, Switzerland, in the 1980s. At that time, I was involved in the Young Christian Students (YCS) movement and this changed my way of thinking. Through YCS, I became sensitive to the struggle against apartheid and met courageous South Africans including Father Albert Nolan and Sibusiso Bengu, as well as a number of South African students and teachers. I decided to spend some time in South Africa as a volunteer, to learn and to give form to my ideal of a more just world.

I joined a Swiss organization that prepared volunteers for assignments overseas, and I started attending preparation workshops. One day a woman came to tell us about her experience in South Africa. She showed us a set of books called *Training for Transformation* (TfT). I looked into them and found them powerful. However, she immediately added that I would not be able to buy them in South Africa because they were banned by the government for being 'too dangerous'. I remembered the books and the names of the authors and went to Cape Town.

One year later, the news spread in the community of development practitioners that Anne Hope, one of the authors of TfT, was back from exile, and that she would settle in Cape Town. She offered a class at the University of Cape Town on adult education, based on TfT methodology. I registered, met Anne, and loved the programme. Anne and I became friends. She was about to start the DELTA programme in Cape Town. Our energies and skills were very complementary, and when she invited me to join her in this new adventure I accepted with joy. Working with Anne changed my way of training and influenced my life deeply. Together, we started DELTA in the Cape and the Grail movement in the Western Cape. We were soon joined by two wonderful South African women: Dikeledi Xorile and Nabawaya Wessels.

After five years living and working in Cape Town, I went back to Europe, specialized in intercultural communication, and continued working nationally and internationally, focusing on the interface between development, intercultural competence, and empowerment, using the philosophical foundation and the participatory methodology I learned through TfT.

My work today

Currently I work with multicultural groups or with professionals working across cultures. The aim is to expand our concept of culture, to discover some fundamental similarities and differences across cultures, and to develop the art of moving across cultures in culturally appropriate ways, in order to 'negotiate shared common meaning', as Stella Ting-Toomey says in her book *Communicating Across Cultures*. This shared common meaning is central for any common project to develop and be sustainable.

This chapter focuses on one of the groups I have worked with. It highlights how workshops on intercultural communication combined with a TfT approach can be deeply empowering.

I chose a group in Switzerland, to underline that empowerment processes need to happen in Europe as well. I was blessed to work with a group of caretakers in a large, multicultural town in Switzerland. These professionals look after blocks of flats that, under the same roof, host dozens of families from all over the world. The tenants behave in very different ways, which are often unintelligible to the caretakers, who hold many solid keys in their hands but sometimes lack the intercultural one. Caretakers are not the most prestigious professional group. They are often under-respected and under-acknowledged. People think of them only when the corridor needs cleaning, when the water does not run, or when the light does not switch on. Generally, the profession gets more criticism and harsh words than recognition and appreciation.

Caretakers as cultural mediators

Marta Pinto, a young woman in charge of integration programmes in the town, had a vision: in addition to being repairers of broken taps and cleaners of staircases and laundry spaces, these professionals could become key players enabling multicultural and multi-religious communication among those living together under one roof. I accepted her invitation to design a programme that aimed to develop intercultural competence for the caretakers whom she invited to attend the training. The group met four times over two months, and again a few months later in two additional workshops, in order to share experience and deepen knowledge. Between each session, participants were invited to apply their newly gained knowledge. The challenges and joys of this practice were shared at the beginning of the following training session.

Empowerment and participation were at the heart of our process. The need to talk and share their professional challenges was originally more acute than the wish to develop intercultural skills. In a true TfT spirit, the first session was thus largely dedicated to creating trust, sharing experiences, and giving each other appreciation and support. In a profession where appreciation is very scarce, deep listening and honest appreciation are empowering. Laughing or crying together about the terribly rude or disrespectful attitudes of some tenants is healing.

TfT practitioners know that community work is neither sustainable nor transforming unless it is based on trust, deep listening, and affirmation. Many processes and exercises have been developed over the years for this purpose, as included in the four TfT books by Anne Hope and Sally Timmel, and Partners' two books called *Partners Companion to Training for Transformation*.

As time went by and the hearts of the caretakers became lighter, we focused the work on culture, cultural differences, cultural identity, and intercultural competence. Theoretical inputs and new tools were woven into the process, offering new knowledge and new perspectives. We approached the complex concept of culture bit by bit, and explored its implications for our behaviour. We realized that our behaviour is determined both by our personality and by our culture.

Cultural differences and mutual understanding

Using stories, films, and our own personal experiences as codes, we discovered that verbal and non-verbal communication is very different from one culture to the next. This leads to misunderstanding among the tenants. Value differences are at the heart of this misunderstanding.

Non-verbal communication

In some cultures, we learn to look into the eyes of the person we talk to, as a sign of respect and interest. In other cultures, respect and interest is shown by not looking at the person, but by looking down. So if people with these two different cultural patterns greet each other, both may be offended. The first one's perception will be 'that person is so rude, they do not look at me when talking to me'. The second may well think 'this person is so rude, challenging me by looking straight at me, and showing no respect'.

We discovered that eye contact is not the only area in which we need to get new cultural knowledge. Touch, use of space, volume of voice, clothing, and silence are just a few other dimensions of communication that are expressed differently from one culture to the next.

We talked about the implications of these differences in a block of flats, and about the role caretakers could play in explaining non-verbal differences to tenants who feel uneasy about the behaviour of others, and how they could try to negotiate spaces where tenants feel respected in their ways while also respecting other tenants' ways. One major discussion was about respecting the different smells coming out of each kitchen, where different foods are prepared and cooked in different ways. How can each family be more careful about the strong smells they produce, while being more tolerant about smells they are not used to?

Another important step was realizing that shaking hands is not the only polite way of greeting; participants who had decided that 'these people are so rude' realized that there were other ways to greet each other. They became interested in learning more about greetings and their meaning. Some even decided to try to practise new ways of greeting where it seemed appropriate.

Verbal communication

The same discovery took place when we talked about verbal communication. The most striking example was around direct and indirect communication. Direct communication involves saying what I mean as I feel it, straight out. Indirect communication means saying the same thing in a different way, in order not to hurt the other person and not to lose face. The meaning is not in the words but in the context. This cultural difference is an issue when people using different styles talk about delicate issues such as solving conflicts, saying no, or talking about disagreements. The direct communicator will say 'I disagree with you'; the indirect communicator will offer statements such as 'this is an interesting proposal' or 'I'll think about it', which actually mean 'I disagree' in an indirect style.

Interculturally competent caretakers understand various communication styles and develop the skill of adapting their style to the style of their interlocutor. This is not just about being polite. It is about a paradigm shift: 'How can I say the same thing in a different way?'

Cultural values

Cultural values and beliefs are behind our cultural behaviour. The caretakers reflected on the cultural values guiding their life and their work before exploring other values they encountered among their tenants. We looked at films where cultural value differences led to dramatic or hilarious situations, and realized the relationship between values and behaviour. One film was *My Big Fat Greek Wedding* directed by Joel Zwick. It is a comedy showing how a multicultural couple (she is Greek, he is European-American) goes from one surprise to the next as their families mingle during the preparation for their marriage.

Whether a wedding is the affair of two people, two families, or two villages depends on the cultural values of those involved. How many people come to the block of flats to celebrate a wedding and how long for, and how loud the celebration will be, also vary.

Funerals raise similar questions. Do people grieve in the intimacy of the family, or do relatives and friends come to express their grief and support the family? When does one give a sign but stay distant, in order not to disturb the grieving family? When does one pay a visit in order to support them in their grief? How long does one stay? When does one offer to bring food?

One of the caretakers told the story of a tenant coming to her to report that in a neighbouring flat the woman had been crying a lot over the past few days. She was worried, and wondered if the husband was abusing her, and if there was anything she could do. The caretaker reassured her, telling her that actually the woman was weeping for her mother, who had died recently in a faraway country. As a refugee, she could not go back to mourn. In her culture, loud crying is appropriate in that situation. The tenant decided to pay that woman a visit and to support her in this lonely grieving.

When caretakers organize timetables for use of the common washing machine, what competence do they need in order to deal with the fact that people and cultures do not all relate to time in the same way? Some will consider a time commitment as sacred, and will always clear their laundry away before the deadline. Others will always consider this time as an indication, an attempt, but they may give priority to something else that seems more urgent or important to them than emptying the washing machine for the next tenant.

And now?

It was wonderful to watch people grow over the sessions, moving from being interculturally sceptical, sometimes racist, to being interculturally competent. When people understand the meaning behind the behaviour, they can depersonalize it. Through practising empathy, they can join the other in his or her experience, and share it.

Today, a number of caretakers have broadened their perception of their role and have started to function as cultural mediators between tenants of different cultures, making the people living together richer and less tense in their block of flats. The press and the radio reported on this pilot experience and other towns became interested in developing similar programmes for their caretakers. The programme is constantly adjusting to new contexts, and while it is transforming caretakers' intercultural competence, it is being transformed itself.

Success factors for intercultural empowerment

Over the past few years, I have worked with many multicultural groups in many countries in Africa, Asia, Latin America, and central and western Europe. Looking back on these experiences, common factors emerge that contribute to the empowering effect of intercultural training:

- Group processes are more meaningful than individual learning.
- It takes time and practice to walk the road to intercultural competence. Training over a few sessions and practice in between has proven to be the best way to move from knowledge to competence.
- Respectful listening and dialogue about generative themes are essential.
- The focus should not only be on sharing new knowledge, but on empowering people, on trusting in their potential.
- The learning is more powerful if participants have similar roles or functions.
- The learning is deeper if the theoretical inputs are directly connected to people's reality.

Transformation witnessed in participants

- Greater clarity about their own cultural identity.
- Acquisition of knowledge about other cultures and about intercultural communication.
- Greater self-confidence.
- Reduction in stereotypical or racist statements.
- Greater respect for difference.
- Expansion of their role.
- Growing interest in other cultures – and in their own.
- Transformation of the perception of cultural difference – from superiority to interest.
- More positive energy.
- More joy in their work and across cultures.
- Lower stress across cultures and the capacity to cope with uncertainty.
- Trying to understand before judging.
- Awareness of the difficulties and limits of intercultural competence.

What I learned and what I would do differently now

- I became realistic about what is achievable if the time available for the training is short: some new knowledge, but not new skills, and no change in world view.
- I became careful about using participatory exercises in multicultural groups as they may not be culturally appropriate for all participants.
- I learned to be aware of the language and the communication styles of the group. I had to identify where I needed to expand my competence in order to respect everyone's styles.
- People will not open up to intercultural communication if there is something more immediate on their plate. I realized I had to listen to people's central issues first if I wanted them to focus their attention on the topic of the workshop.
- Like any other competence, intercultural competence needs attention, knowledge, and practice in order to develop and become interiorized. It is not enough to 'be nice' nor to 'just be yourself' to be an interculturally competent (TfT) trainer!

References

Sheehy, M. (2001) *Partners Companion to Training for Transformation*, Dublin: Partners Training for Transformation.

Sheehy, M., Naughton, F. and O'Regan, C. (2007) *Partners Intercultural Companion to Training for Transformation*, Dublin: Partners Training for Transformation.

Ting-Toomey, S. (1999) *Communicating Across Cultures*, New York, NY: Guilford Press.

CHAPTER 19

Evolving a new community in the 'developed world': working with immigrants and citizens in the USA

Sumaya Karimi

Sumaya Karimi *was born in Afghanistan. In her childhood she spent a year in the mountains with her father, who had opposed the Russian and puppet regime. He was later assassinated when the Mujahedeen (freedom fighters) were in power before the civil war. Her family took refuge in the USA, where she became active in the Refugee Women's Network. As a member of their team, she attended the diploma course in Training for Transformation at Kleinmond in 2002–03. She now works with CDF: A Collective Action Initiative in Clarkston, Georgia (USA) as the Community Engagement Co-ordinator, building a spirit of unity and common response to problems with both immigrants and American citizens. Sumaya uses TfT processes in a transformation course for Clarkston residents and public health students at Emory University.*

Her chapter tells how she discovered the writings of Paulo Freire as a 16-year-old, finding how much they had in common with her father's vision. She describes how she experienced the TfT training and how she and other staff members use this and other participatory methods as they try to adapt their own version of popular education to their situation in the USA.

Follow the river and find the sea.   *Zambian proverb*

As a young girl I spent time with my father in Kabul and in the mountains of Bamyan, where we were always in community meetings and women's groups. At 16, I read the Farsi translation of Freire's *Pedagogy of the Oppressed*, which clarified for me the significance of participatory approaches and dialogue. I started using participatory approaches to facilitate gender training in Afghanistan, worked on gender policy for Afghan NGOs, and subsequently worked on human rights training, using a participatory approach in Pakistan. When I came to the Grail Centre and reflected back on my work and my father's work in Afghanistan, I connected the dots between our work and Training for Transformation. TfT became part of my life after the second round of the diploma course.

Here, I am writing about how I adapted the TfT principle and training in Afghanistan, in America and in my personal life.

Arriving in the USA with my family, I settled in Clarkston, Georgia, near metropolitan Atlanta, which is one of the most diverse, gifted, complex, resilient, and entrepreneurial cities in the country. Clarkston has been called a new, multicultural American South: African-American, White, Burmese, Bhutanese, Nepali, Somali, Iraqi, Sudanese, and others live in Clarkston and many languages are spoken there (CDF, A Collective Action Initiative, n.d.).

I was connected with TfT in 2000, during the first month after arriving in the USA, when I attended the Refugee Women's Network's (RWN's) leadership training. This was based on Freire methodology and facilitated by Bethann Cottrell and Thanh Xuan Nguyen. In 2002, I attended the first diploma course where I fully internalized the Freirean concepts and began to use and adapt them. People who live through and survive wars need this transformative experience and the environment of a place like the Grail Centre to heal their wounds. My healing began in Simpsonwood during RWN's leadership training and continued through the second round of the diploma course. My success is based on the path I then created for myself and others and the people whom I met along the way. Since being introduced to TfT in many forms, I use this approach in all my work.

Creating a safe space where we value and respect community members' contribution and objectives in order to make decisions or simply share a frustration about injustice is the core of the participatory approach. I learned since my childhood as a small Afghan girl to stand up and advocate, but I learned to be a good and active listener in everyday life only by facilitating TfT. I called the TfT approach in my work 'community transformation courses' (CTCs). I discovered that people who were wounded did not need to be given a solution to their problems; they needed a space in which to share and be listened to. We need to help them find the solution by themselves and strengthen their capacity.

From 2003 onwards, everywhere I go, I have taken TfT as part of my work and life. When I worked with the organization Tapestri Inc. as an Anti-Human Trafficking Co-ordinator, I used the TfT approach in my work. I worked with women who were survivors of human trafficking. I listened to their stories and created a safe space so that they could share their stories without being judged and without feeling guilty. In the process they felt empowered. I supported them in re-establishing their lives – finding a house and job or going to school. I used their stories as a code to train community members about human trafficking.

Between 2004 and 2007, I went back to Afghanistan, where I was responsible for raising money and writing proposals. I used the informal listening and survey of generative themes to support the proposals and create additional programmes to support women's lives. For instance, during the survey, I found out that widows were interested in bringing in an income for their families by running small businesses. I worked with various organizations and funding agencies to find money to support the aspirations of widows in Paktia, Afghanistan. Women created a self-help group and started their own businesses. In another case, listening to female inmates' feelings and needs in a Kabul prison enabled us to advocate and create programmes based on their needs. In Afghanistan, when women with small children are imprisoned, their children are kept in jail with them. Inmates' children did not have any access to education. The mothers asked if someone could come to the prison and teach their children. We converted a room in the jail into a school and built a playground for inmates' children. The fact that someone was going to jail on a regular basis to listen to them and their concerns was a huge support for those women. In the jails, we also pushed for accountability of the staff for their inmates' well-being.

In 2008, I came back to the USA and worked with the RWN and revised and revived their leadership training programme. I facilitated the CTC for refugee and immigrant women leaders, who came from all over the USA. Before each course, I organized a focus group or interviewed the participants by phone. In the focus group I listened for the generative themes by asking them what they were worried, sad, happy, angry, and hopeful about. Although people who were not facilitators sometimes asked those questions spontaneously, after doing TfT I realized that, while conducting the survey for generative themes, the questioning needs to be very systematic in order to clarify their meaning. Since then, before any training, I hold a focus group and ask the generative theme questions and come up with a common theme that participants have strong feelings about, and then I design the five days of training based on their generative themes.

In the focus group, participants or community members usually have an astonished look and express surprise. Why is she asking these questions about our feelings? However, by the end of the focus group they say that it was therapeutic, that no one before cared enough about their lives to ask how they felt. The same people even say, 'I wonder how you are going to pull together some common theme?' Once they attend the training, they learn how to listen to generative themes by asking the same questions, and then come up with common themes to develop exercises and facilitate sessions. The public health students and community members, refugee and immigrant women participants are so creative. They create the most inventive and effective codes and processes. I learn from the participants each time I train. I truly experience being a participant and a facilitator at the same time.

I also facilitate a CTC at the Rollins School of Public Health, Emory University, from where public health students head out to the 'developing' world to 'fix' their problems. This course challenges some of their ways of thinking. At the same time, the CTC gives them practical tools to start working with communities. I not only adapted TfT for the American context, but I also adapted the length of the course. Usually, the training for trainers of TfT is best completed in two weeks (the diploma course takes almost two years). However, we cannot get anyone to attend a two-week course in the busy USA. Therefore, the 'Training for Trainers' CTC is a five-day course. To give a clear picture of this course, I am going to explain how the days are divided.

On the first day, participants watch and experience a trust-building process and then a reflective exercise or problem-posing exercises using a code. This is facilitated to bring people together to bond and enter into a dialogue around social issues. On the second day, they learn how to listen for generative themes, analyse a generative theme, create a code, write learning objectives, and develop questions and processes. The second day is packed but it works. After five years of facilitating at Rollins, finally this year no one was confused because I covered all the techniques of the methodology. On the third day, participants work in groups of three or four, creating an exercise and getting ready to facilitate. On the fourth and fifth days they become facilitators themselves.

In 2011, I started working in Clarkston with CDF, a collective action initiative. I brought CTCs into CDF. Now, the CTC is adapted to meet the generative themes of a diverse urban community in Clarkston. With this approach, we strengthen the capacity of residents and create a space where new relationships, bonds, and trust evolve. On one occasion, three participants (a Muslim, a Christian, and a Hindu) were working together and they developed an exercise on lack of community cohesiveness. Their code showed how our religions divide our community in Clarkston. As a facilitator, I was afraid to bring up such a sensitive issue, but they were brave and they did a good job facilitating the dialogue on community cohesiveness. Most of the CTC participants stay involved in the community, and many of them are working on different projects together. As a result, community members value and celebrate diverse cultures and people. For example, an African and a white American Christian, an Afghan and a Somali Muslim go to a temple to celebrate a Bhutanese festival. Muslim, Hindu, Buddhist, Christian, and Jewish residents come together to share meals and watch films in the First Baptist Church. After attending a CTC, Angela Moore, the First Lady of the First Baptist Church in Clarkston, said: 'My eyes are open. I see and work in Clarkston differently.' Charisse Drakeford, an African-American who works in Clarkston, came to a planning meeting for the CTC and introduced her fellow participants in the CTC as her family members. These are the different ways of creating space and simply being together that reduce divisions between religion and culture, with the hope that these divisions will vanish over time and Clarkston will become a place where people play, dance, sing, and share stories together.

The CTC creates a safe space where we share our suffering, our survival, and our struggle for justice. Community members realize that we are suffering from the same pain, the pain of injustice. Each one of us was either forced to flee our country or was never able to meet our basic needs or fulfil our dreams because we happened to be born into poor families. In the process of self-discovery and personal transformation, we create a place where people feel valued, renewed, and empowered.

Using transformative or popular education varies from one place to another. Experience taught me that the methodology has to be adapted to each context. Refugee women, Clarkston residents, and university students require different approaches. For example, the distribution of income in the USA and in the world is a good code to discuss poverty with Emory public health students. However, the story of the refugee woman who struggles to keep her job and meet her family's basic needs is a good code to discuss poverty in refugee and immigrant communities. In addition, the impact of the methodology is powerful and leads to action in refugee, immigrant, and local communities, while for those involved in formal education it becomes a tool they can use in their work. The impact of the CTC on a student's personal life and work in the developing world is huge. The CTC gives them a new way of being on their journey, energized by their commitment and enthusiasm. Most of them stay connected and go on to help facilitate community dialogue in the USA and around the world.

In my first two years facilitating CTCs, participants asked whether they could use codes for topics that were not addressing a specific problem. I did not know the answer, but I started using codes for themes that are not necessarily a spoken problem but are a reality of life: for example, the making of life choices was not necessarily a problem-posing code but rather an exercise that helped participants to reflect on their choices. For this, I used the following mime.

The mime

Before the session, write the following words or phrases very large on plain paper and attach a piece of string (4 or 5 feet long) to each sign:

- money;
- happiness;
- values;
- family and friends;
- international versus domestic job.

Ask for five volunteers from the group before the session. Ask each person to tape one of the words onto their chest, with the string attached. Another person sits in the centre of the group and the five volunteers surround the seated individual. The person in the centre holds the ends of the five strings attached to the people with words on their chests.

In silence, the five different people pull the person in the centre towards their sign. The person in the centre may start to pull the string in another direction.

After the point is made about how many of us are pulled in different directions, the volunteers and the person in the centre go back to the main group. Some questions are then posed to the whole group, such as how does one experience these different choices in our own lives? How does this make us feel? Who do we go to for support and advice? How can we help each other when faced with difficult choices?

The discussions that follow are always lively and helpful in sorting out choices for many present.

Personal success or growth

I have learned to create, design, and facilitate training. The week on personal development and on planning the use of one's time in the diploma course helped me to be effective in my work. For example, using a calendar is part of everyday life in the western world but is something that has to be learned by most refugees from Afghanistan, who have a different perspective of time. In the diploma course, we were asked to write our personal goals and objectives; all these skills have had an impact on my success in American culture.

TfT healed my wounds. I want to share one of my war experiences to give a sense of how the war impacted on my life, so that the reader can understand when I say that the Grail Centre created a safe and sacred space for me and healed my war wounds. I was in the fifth year of medical school when war broke out and continued for 10 days. During those days and nights of the war, the fighters were shooting machine guns behind our house. No one could sleep. When the shooting stopped, I went back to school. I was happy that the war had finished and I could go back to school. On the first day back at school, I realized I could not write a word. I felt illiterate. I could do nothing but cry. I was forced to leave the school and go to Bamyan and spend a week in the village. I went back to school and I was able to write but the scars of the wound were there. But when I attended the TfT diploma course, I felt that my thousands of wounds were healing, one by one.

The impact of TfT seems to be primarily on an individual's life. In my own work, I have yet to see its systematic impact on communities' well-being. I realize that this second stage of organizing and building allies will take patience and time. We are beginning to see some fruits, and, after much work in Clarkston, I hope to see the beginning of a new era.

It is the beginning of a new era when people trust each other and start working with each other on the issues that they care about. Development is a long-term process and requires commitment, openness, feedback, risk-taking, acceptance that a different way is possible, and belief in people's capacity, creativity, and potential, as well as in their ability to respect and accept all cultures and religions. Through this work we see that community development principles, approaches, and methodologies function in the developed world. A new consciousness arises in which community bonds create a different reality, where people can live in peace and harmony.

Reference

CDF, A collective Action Initiative (n.d.) 'Where we work' [online] <http://cdfaction.org/what-we-do/#where-we-work> [accessed 3 October 2013].

CHAPTER 20
Rebuilding communities: the voices of refugee women in the USA

Thanh Xuan Nguyen

Thanh Xuan Nguyen *is a refugee from Vietnam now living in New York. She is the founder of the Refugee Women's Network, but having handed over this responsibility to younger women now works as a consultant on community organizing. She has applied and adapted Training for Transformation work with both refugee and immigrant women in the USA and with emerging community organizations in Vietnam.*

In this chapter she describes her work in the leadership development programme with refugee women, helping them to deal with culture shock, find a role, and rediscover their own voices in their new context.

Every partridge has its unique way of scratching the ground. *Kenyan proverb*

I arrived in the United States as a refugee from Vietnam. With some English, I found myself translating for other refugees but I was frustrated by my inability to serve the refugees better. They faced enormous challenges, had limited resources, and were not always understood by the host agencies. Where the women came from, they were the glue of the family and the community. During the refugee experience, they had managed to keep their families fed and alive, and some had experienced traumatic assaults. But once they arrived in their new country, these women became invisible. Service agencies helped to look for employment for their husbands. Their children were put in schools. The women weren't seen as having needs or skills. They fell through the cracks.

In collaboration with several refugee women, we created the Refugee Women's Network (RWN) with the mission to harness our existing knowledge, expand our understanding of the American system, and learn new skills to make our voices heard on behalf of our community.

While doing research for a training curriculum on leadership, we found materials with top-down instructions and technical steps to follow, regardless of the trainees' level of education, language skills, cultural background, or understanding of their new surroundings. In 1998, while representing the refugee community at a local community meeting, I met Dr Dave Hilton from Global Health Action. Dr Hilton and his colleague Dr Bethann Witcher Cottrell were doing Transformation for Health, an adaptation of Training for Transformation (TfT) to the health context. They had each worked in Africa and Latin America and were bringing TfT methodology to Atlanta, Georgia. I was introduced to Transformation for Health and graduated from their first 'Training for Trainers' class.

The training was quite different from other types of training I had attended. What struck me was the participatory approach. I discovered that I have something to contribute, that although this is a new environment for me, I am not an empty vessel. This approach enthused me and I realized that I could use it with other refugee women. I was hit by Paul Tillich's statement: 'The worst thing in education is to throw answers like rocks before the questions are asked.' I was converted. And I told Dr Hilton and Dr Witcher Cottrell, who had introduced me to TfT, 'This is what I want to do for the rest of my life.'

I started applying TfT methodology inside the RWN with eight refugee women and one man. We created a safe space for each one of us to call on our knowledge, learn from where we were, and express our opinions. We practised going out into the world and speaking on behalf of our community. We also allowed space and time to deal with our own trauma, not as patients needing treatment but as family members needing a listening ear, understanding, and support. We bonded as a community trusting ourselves; we were able to lean on one another and to move forward.

The critical element that shifted my work was the vision of a spiral moving upwards, describing the learning and transformation process, learning to trust people and the process. An African woman living on the west coast called me two years after she had participated in the training and said, 'Now I understand what we discussed and why! And my group is still talking about it.'

Another important element was the spiritual connection between life and work, which helped me return to my roots and Buddhist faith. It strengthened my confidence to move inside the changing world of the West. From a small group of nine refugees, we expanded our reach to refugee communities across the USA. We adapted Transformation for Health for women from war-torn countries in Africa, Asia, Eastern Europe, and the Middle East. Each year we trained 50 women in two sessions. We all lived for a week in a retreat centre away from the demands of daily life.

The 'Tree of Life' was always a moving experience. The women had an opportunity to think and talk about themselves, their beliefs, and their achievements. Some drew small bushes, scraggy trees with deep scars and few leaves or fruit. Sharing and conversation started revealing how bountiful their lives were, and throughout the training week many came back to this exercise to include successes that had been forgotten. Drawing the community was an opportunity for participants to show their knowledge of their community and discover the similarity of the challenges that faced all refugees and other marginalized groups. Then, depending on the generative themes, we used related codes to facilitate discussions leading to solutions. The issues raised varied from group to group, but the need to understand and access the complex American healthcare system, earning income to meet family needs, reproductive health, and domestic violence almost always came up.

Codes used were culturally respectful. Sitting in a circle on the floor was a comfortable style of gathering and did not intimidate participants. Discussion, drawing, skits, and materials with simple words were essential. Input was clear and concise. Each participant brought her own cultural, educational, and religious background as well as the refugee experience. We started where she was, and answers or resources were revealed only after questions had been asked and discussions facilitated. A Muslim woman offered religiously appropriate codes for use with her community.

Over time, as the ethnicities of the refugee women changed, depending on the refugees arriving in the USA, the generative themes and codes changed to meet their specific needs. With each group, the training took a different path but the principles stayed the same: trust the people, trust the process. The main requirement of this free training was that the participants should return home to organize women in their community and replicate the training. Technical support in facilitation was provided if needed. The goal was to reach as many women as possible.

Following the local training, several refugee women's organizations, associations, and networks were created with the mission of organizing and strengthening their voices. They began to support newly arrived women, organized English classes and income-generating activities, and helped with access to healthcare and problems of domestic violence.

After self-discovery, we learned the power of collaboration. A group of organizations assisted survivors of domestic violence to work together, creating Tapestri Inc. to serve refugee and immigrant families and to advocate with the police and the justice system. A project working with men was created to train refugee men to lead discussions on violence in the home, its impact on the family, and the legal repercussions. A public–private partnership emerged, bringing Tapestri Inc., a local American Women's League, and the police together to establish the International Women's House, a shelter for non-English-speaking survivors of domestic violence and their children. In addition to having a place to hide away from violence, survivors can stay for a longer period to learn English and other skills to help them become self-sufficient.

Transformation does not happen overnight. It requires flexibility, respect, and time. Each person needs time to discover her worth, expand her mind, learn new skills, and develop relationships. Each human being is unique and has to walk her own journey. TfT provides the space and tools to engage in this journey, but transformation needs a lot of respectful, tender support and mentoring. Transformation inside an organization requires the same flexibility and tender support. I let go of the organization and the network of refugee women too early, trusting that they could continue on the strong path. There was a period of faltering and doubt, and the possibility of collapse. But with death, or near death, can come a new beginning. Refusing to let an organization that has so strongly shaped their lives disappear, several refugee women stepped in to continue the leadership development work, and with the appointment of a young Hmong woman, who had trained 10 years earlier, as director, the organization is moving to new heights.

Refugee women in the USA now play an integral part in refugee resettlement programmes nationally and locally. They serve on planning committees and on advisory boards for education, health, housing, and employment. A few have been elected into the political positions of their city or state. Many have extended their TfT methodology to include other marginalized communities in the USA and back in their home countries. TfT has transformed their lives and they want to ensure that they continue to work to make a better world for all.

PART SEVEN
Long march through the institutions

Keywords: breaking dependency; building responsive institutions; changing government practices; changing structures; changing traditional methods of 'teaching'; critical reflection and innovation; finding allies in structures; harnessing local energy; participatory methods; partnering with government; power of emotions; power in numbers; self-reliance; touching the heart; using existing structures for transformation

http://dx.doi.org/10.3362/9781780448312.008

CHAPTER 21
Unveiling the dependency syndrome: working with rural marginalized groups in Zimbabwe

Adelaide Musekiwa

Adelaide Musekiwa is a programme officer at Silveira House, a Jesuit-run development training centre outside Harare, which has a proud history of work in civic education during the independence struggle in Zimbabwe. Silveira House uses the Freirean methodology in all its community development projects, working with rural and marginalized groups. It puts emphasis on self-reliance and self-initiated projects. Several of its staff members have attended the Training for Transformation diploma course in Kleinmond. This story is about how TfT has helped break the dependency of poor marginalized groups in two districts in Zimbabwe and has improved livelihoods at the local level during a time of great impoverishment.

Some people dream of great accomplishments while others stay awake to do them. *Liberian proverb*

Dependency is not just a problem for African countries but manifests itself in many other non-industrialized countries around the world. It is a phenomenon that afflicts a country like a cancer – slowly destroying its health while it remains unaware of the progress of the disease. When my organization first arrived in the Mbire and Muzarabani districts of Mashonaland Central in Zimbabwe, the communities relied on hand-outs – grain – from international NGOs and churches. We conducted a listening survey which revealed that the communities lacked the capacity to provide basic infrastructural development and lacked skills in managing projects. After identifying the gap, we took the communities through the action-oriented approach of Training for Transformation (TfT) using the River code in particular. This is the story of how TfT contributed to breaking dependency.

A councillor in Ward 6 in Mbire said:

> Silveira House came to our rescue when we needed help the most. 2008 was a difficult year and life was tough but the training we received opened our minds to bigger things. We realized we could do things on our own without waiting for external assistance. SH taught us to look within, outside, and behind, and to use the resources around us. Either as individual families or groups, we have initiated income-generating projects. These projects are in piggery, goat-keeping, poultry, and fishing. We managed to identify different stakeholders who invested capital to kick-start our projects. Our children do not have decent classrooms and with the knowledge received we lobbied a certain organization which has helped in building a classroom block. As a community, we also played our part by contributing labour in moulding bricks, and providing other materials such as pit sand, river sand, stones, and water.

This story is a reflection of how groups and individuals can shift their thinking once equipped with the right educational tools. The adaptation of TfT was initiated by SH in the mid-1970s, inspired by the philosophy of Paulo Freire and the social movement in Brazil. Since that time, SH has continued

The classroom before training in Ward 6, Mbire   The classroom block after training

to adapt the methodology in all its programming activities. There are many stories of change to share, which were a result of the training offered.

Here is my own story. I first came to know about TfT in the late 1990s during my employment with a certain women's organization. At the time, I was in administration, and the two-week training workshop was really fascinating. I acquired many tools for training groups that I had never thought possible. What was really fascinating was the use of codes such as posters, skits, poems, and songs to generate discussion. It was so easy to relate to communities with the codes, and to enable them to come up with resolutions and strategies. After leaving that organization, many years later, I had another opportunity. I attended the full diploma course at the Grail Centre in South Africa. During that period (2007–08) I had a life-changing experience because I met with 33 other women from all over the world and forged alliances and bonds. I became more confident, articulate, and assertive. I also built on my 'people skills' and learned to work with groups at various levels. On the personal level, I became more tolerant of people and my listening greatly improved. Now I am a programme officer where I interact with many people of diverse backgrounds with different intellectual competencies. But I can boast and say I handle all my discussions quite well and carry myself with dignity and have a different world view from before.

TfT at the Grail Centre opened many doors for me and I have not looked back since then. I feel I can achieve anything I set my mind on because I have the necessary tools to venture into uncharted territory. The sky is really the limit for me! My consciousness has evolved to another level since 2008.

Adaptation and effectiveness of Training for Transformation

Groups tend to sit back and wait for external players to come to their rescue and resolve all their problems. Problems include water and sanitation, primary healthcare issues, community conflicts, and infrastructural development such as the building of hospitals, schools, and roads. Various players in the NGO sector employ different strategies to alleviate poverty. Most of these approaches involve doing things for the community, such as construction of a school block, a rural health centre, or a community hall, and similar things. SH chose to do things differently and adapted the TfT methodology in its work with various groups in the community. In the beginning, SH targeted commercial farming and political figures. This was the time of the liberation struggle in Rhodesia (as it was then) and Africans did not have space to meet and discuss issues central to their lives. SH created this space for those excluded from the political and economic structures to meet and reflect. By providing training, SH helped the people find solutions.

The two target groups – commercial farmworkers and political figures – came from different social backgrounds. Both groups required training to shift their situations to another level. The Freirean approach proved effective in training these two groups to analyse their situation, name the problems, and find solutions. This was done using a number of tools, including codes. Some codes were story-telling and skits while others were pictures, music, or poetry. The use of questions helped the groups to dig deep into their issues until they got to the roots of the problem.

It was really different from what other institutions were doing. It was called 'popular education' because it worked with everybody, whatever their educational level. The idea of letting groups discover things for themselves was refreshing. People were used to having 'experts' come in and tell them what to do. They believed the experts had all the knowledge. I heard this story from a man from Muzarabani district, who had been on our training:

> Before SH training I lived a difficult life and many other people shared the same fate as me. We looked down on ourselves and thought our poverty was God-given. Therefore we could do nothing about it. However, SH taught us that nothing remains the same and we have the power to alter our situation. I started a family project in gardening where I grew tomatoes, green leafy vegetables, and okra. I have a number of cattle so I sold a couple and used the money to purchase a water pump to boost my production. In the process, my garden grew and now I have hired three other people because the work is too demanding for me and my family. In the process, my income has greatly improved – I am now able to send my children to school, contribute towards community activities, and have a surplus for my whole family. My living standards have improved tremendously and I am grateful to the trainers at SH who brought change in my life.

Achievements of the pre-independence era: civic education

Before 1980, Rhodesia was under colonial rule, which made it almost impossible to speak about civic rights, but SH forged ahead. This was possible due to the non-confrontational approach that aimed to equip citizens with analytical skills, enabling them to take action after identifying their problems. After a workshop at SH in the mid-1970s, one of the trainees wrote: 'These training programmes are very relevant to us and it is what we need. If only so many other people could be reached and benefit from the civic education, our country would be better.' Many other training programmes followed and saw numerous local residents passing through SH for education in civic rights. The outcome of the training was the opening of the minds, hearts, and eyes of those who enrolled.

The commercial farmworkers were equipped with advocacy skills to lobby their white 'bosses' to provide certain social amenities. Various tools of engagement were used, such as negotiation and action-oriented initiatives. During that time there were virtually no amenities; after the training, groups lobbied for childcare centres, recreational facilities, and even for better housing to be provided by the white farmers. As a way of supporting the farmworkers economically, SH provided inputs in the form of seeds, fencing, and chemicals for gardening projects.

After some time it was realized that providing inputs did not work because it created dependency and lack of ownership. After an evaluation of the farmworkers project, this was one of the key findings. Hand-outs created irresponsibility and made people lazy. Unless the community is involved in the decision-making process and contributes to the project (be it construction or animal husbandry or human rights), the sense of responsibility and ownership will be missing. This revelation made SH shift its approach and concentrate on providing capacity-building, with an emphasis on self-reliance. This shift was implemented with different groups in Zimbabwe: small-scale farmers, traditional leaders, elected leaders, women's groups, and youth. The farmers began to explore using other seed varieties rather than planting the same crop varieties year in, year out. They began to cultivate their own hybrid varieties using indigenous knowledge.

New millennium achievements

After the war ended and Zimbabwe gained its independence in 1980, the work of SH continued with a lot of capacity-building. It was around mid-2000 that another shift occurred: to concentrate on development workers from various organizations. These groups were given TfT training, using Books 1 to 4. Usually the training was in phases and lasted up to three weeks. Trainees came from

Zimbabwe Project Trust, Concern Worldwide, Plan International, religious congregations, and many other organizations. Testimonies were given during monitoring and evaluation on how participants' leadership skills improved and leaders were able to manage their groups differently. Some of the key outcomes were improved listening skills, a consultative management style, and enhanced conflict management skills. This helped to build team work and group cohesion and to increase work output.

In the mid-2000s, SH shifted yet again and adapted the TfT methodology to work with marginalized rural communities. This time the training was aimed at breaking the dependency syndrome, which meant introducing sustainable development models in many rural communities. The shift was in response to calls to improve the livelihood of poor marginalized communities. The Mbire and Muzarabani districts are impoverished and dry, with poor rainfall. Maize cannot survive drought so the communities rely on small grains. There is constant hunger. There are challenges such as malaria, man-eating wild animals, and elephants that destroy crops.

When we started working in these areas in 2008, there was little infrastructure development and the communities were poor – not just materially but also educationally. This is when SH introduced education programmes targeting the chiefs, headmen, and village heads. These are the village leaders and decision-makers. The training made a huge impact on their leadership and governance was greatly improved. Furthermore, the leaders were better placed to deal with community disputes as they had acquired mediation skills. Their training included governance, conflict resolution, communication, and community mobilization. The approach was participatory and interactive, drawing on various tools. Two of the most effective codes were the River code and Johari's Window, which were used to analyse dependency and to gain self-knowledge through constructive mutual criticism.

While TfT was the principal methodology, SH also integrated the social teachings of the church to speak to the spiritual aspect of communities. Given these two factors, the training became holistic and addressed pertinent issues including socio-cultural, economic, and political matters.

There are many stories told by beneficiaries who have started income-generating projects and have managed to purchase land for housing. These testimonies were shared by the participants during an impact assessment of the TfT workshops held in the Mbire and Muzarabani districts. People's lives were altered by an increase in disposable income and improved living standards. Women are not left out of this story of change. Their earlier exclusion from many development activities due to 'culture' and power relations made them feel inferior, thus affecting their participation in community activities. Since receiving training, their attitude towards community work has changed. They now participate actively in community meetings and speak their minds. Some occupy leadership positions. The role of women is being recognized and men in the community are now conscious that development cannot be complete without the inclusion of everyone.

Recommendations

The approach adapted in our training programmes is not without its shortcomings.

SH should have carried out a baseline survey in both districts and presented its findings to the local authorities before engaging with the communities. This would have ensured that the most needy communities reaped the benefits of the training programmes. In contrast, the local authorities selected certain wards as they saw fit. The neediest communities were left out and remained impoverished.

The mixing of women and men during training worked, but only to a certain extent. Women in these communities were just beginning to emerge as co-partners in development. It is essential to support them in their own space where they can air their views without the dominance of men. In retrospect, it would have been better to create separate spaces for women in specific activities and training programmes, in order to build their leadership and strengthen their courage.

There is also a need to develop new codes and make changes to the current codes to ensure their relevance to today and to our changed situation.

CHAPTER 22
Every picture tells a story: justice and traditional culture

Donal Dorr

Donal Dorr *is a missionary priest and theologian. He worked for years in Africa and for shorter periods in Brazil, and is now based in Ireland. Having taken part during the second half of the 1970s in the five-week DELTA Plus training and various other DELTA workshops in Kenya, he was involved in the 1980s in establishing and developing a similar model in Nigeria and in other West African Anglophone countries. In succeeding years he has been a facilitator in Training for Transformation workshops in several east, central, and southern African countries, and in the longer Kleinmond advanced training. He has therefore been using this psycho-social approach for nearly 40 years. He is the author of several books on issues of social justice and ecology, the most recent of which is* Option for the Poor and for the Earth *(Orbis Books, 2012).*

This chapter describes a simple process that uses a set of nine picture codes to enable workshop participants to: 1) appreciate the values of the economic, political, and cultural–religious pattern of traditional society; 2) reflect on how these values are being undermined by modern western-style 'development'; and 3) to explore alternatives that can promote real development which respects people's culture and traditions.

Don't set sail using someone else's star.   *Swahili proverb*

What I am presenting here is an approach to social or structural analysis that I used to draw on the immediate experience of people in African countries. I found that this approach was suitable for people who do not have a high level of western-style education and who are used to thinking in a concrete way about the world around them. These were either rural people or urban people who were still fairly closely in touch with the traditional rural background from which they had come. Our approach here was not intended to be an *alternative* to the 'Dynamic Model' as outlined in Book 3 of *Training for Transformation*, but it was used at a relatively early stage of the training to heighten the participants' awareness of the values of their own traditional culture and to help them look critically at some of the problems of modern, western-style development.

Context

I first came across the Training for Transformation (TfT) programme in 1975 in Turkana in northern Kenya. Prior to that I had been a lecturer in political philosophy and then in theology. I had become very disillusioned with the 'banking' style of lecturing to students. Participation in the Turkana workshop was an amazing 'aha!' moment for me. It brought about a radical conversion in my life and it has changed the way I work over the 38 years since that experience.

Having taken part in the five-week DELTA Plus training and various other DELTA workshops in Kenya during the second half of the 1970s, I got involved in the 1980s in establishing and developing a similar model (which we called DELES – Development Education and Leadership Ecumenical Services) in Nigeria and in other West African Anglophone countries. In succeeding years I was one of the facilitators in TfT workshops in several east, central, and southern African countries, and more recently in the longer Kleinmond advanced training. I have also used this experiential approach in workshops on spirituality, which I facilitate for the kind of people whom I call 'searchers'.

My practice

Based on my experience facilitating workshops 'on the ground', I had become convinced that one of the most effective ways of empowering African people was to find practical experiential ways of facilitating them in valuing, perhaps even rediscovering, the richness of their own cultures. This provided a background against which they could analyse and evaluate the advantages and disadvantages of the more western models of development that have been adopted in most African countries.

Book 3 of *Training for Transformation* proposes an approach to social analysis that calls for an examination of the *economic, political,* and *cultural* structures of society. It occurred to me that we might provide a set of pictures that would illustrate the traditional pattern of life under these three headings. My co-worker and friend, Steve Lani Adeleye, who is a gifted artist, prepared posters of the kind of scenes I had in mind, adding in all the details that made them true to life for the people of his own culture.

We ended up with a set of nine pictures – three to illustrate different aspects of the *economy* of a traditional society, another three to illustrate different aspects of *politics* and *community decision-making* in such a society, and the final three to cover different aspects of the traditional *culture* and *religion*. Taken together, the nine pictures gave people the opportunity to reflect on the overall pattern of traditional society. One of the most important effects was that they helped people to appreciate the strengths of their traditional cultures – and to take a very critical look at the way in which modern 'development' has undermined the pattern and left ordinary people at a gross disadvantage.

We knew that if the pictures were to be used simply as visual aids for a lecture by a resource person they would be far less effective, because the understanding would not be drawn out of the participants' own experience and so they would be far less likely to really 'own' or remember it. So our aim was to use the pictures as what Paulo Freire calls 'codes'. This meant using the pictures not to give *answers* but to evoke *questions* and discussion for the participants, about what they saw in the pictures and about how that related to the reality of their daily lives. It was, of course, essential that the pictures used should be culturally appropriate – and that is why I am not including here any of the pictures we used, so that anybody who might wish to adopt this approach has to commission pictures based on the culture of the local people.

Economic structures

The first picture was of farmers at work, producing food mainly for their own families and for the town or village market. The second picture showed traditional craft-workers, producing goods mainly for use in the local community. The third picture was of a traditional market. I discovered that it was best to display these three pictures at the same time, so that together they formed one code. This is because the traditional society formed a coherent whole where each aspect was linked to the others and supported by them.

Reflection on the pictures brought out the fact that in traditional societies each area was generally self-sufficient in the production of food. Not merely each area, but even most *families* could manage to meet their own needs as regards staple foods, although some local craftspeople served the local community by specializing in their own work. Housing, clothes, footwear, cooking utensils, pottery, soap, farming implements – all these were provided by local workers, who, in return, got food from other members of the community.

The usual questions were asked: for example, 'What do you see happening in each picture?' People were then asked: 'Is this still the situation where you are living?' 'If not, why not?' The facilitator needed to be flexible, asking such questions as: 'Are you wearing shoes or clothes that were made locally?' 'Is your family eating food that was grown locally?' 'If not, where did the food, the clothes, and the shoes come from and do you know who made them?' 'What did they cost and who decided the price?' 'Has the price of these goods increased recently?' I found that it was also helpful to see if some of the older people could remember how the traditional system worked. I could ask: 'If people needed to borrow money, how was this organized?' All through this reflection we needed to remember that the aim of this exploration was not just to gain new information, and not just to encourage people to reflect on their economic situation, but to *empower* the participants. For this reason, it was really important for the facilitator at this stage not to take on the extra role of being a resource person who could give the answers, because this would have the effect of disempowering the local people.

The value of reflection on the pictures was that it brought out the fact that the members of a traditional community did not depend for their basic needs on some outside agency or on people whom they did not know personally. This was a great strength, since it meant that the problem of 'dependency' seldom arose. Almost all the goods bought and sold were produced locally. Only a few luxury items came from outside. Consequently, the fluctuations in world trade had only a peripheral effect on this market and this community. Prices of foodstuffs fluctuated according to the season, but neither the sellers nor the buyers were vulnerable to the unpredictable collapses or escalations of price that occur once the local market is tied to a world market. So the local currency did not lose its value – as so frequently happens nowadays in poor countries, because they are the weak members in the international system of trade.

The reflection on these first three pictures brought out some key points about the economic life of traditional societies:

- For the most part, what was produced locally was consumed locally.
- Similarly, for the most part, what was consumed locally was produced locally.
- Consequently, production was on a small scale.
- Most of the materials and sources of energy used were renewable.

Our aim at this stage was to help participants realize that the fabric of the traditional society was strong and had endured for ages. It enabled a people to survive most natural calamities. It was also flexible enough to allow for changes and growth. However, it was also important not to approve of an uncritical idealization of the traditional economic pattern.

We used the pictures to promote understanding and appreciation of the traditional way of life, but this led on very quickly to critical reflection on the changes that have taken place – and, particularly, the ways in which structural injustice has increased. Reflection focused on the disadvantages of mass production and world markets. Undoubtedly they lower costs if the costing is done according to the current economic models. But once people began to take account of the full social and environmental costs, the answer became more doubtful.

We noted the *environmental* costs:

- Mass production generally uses large amounts of non-renewable energy sources (e.g. oil) and minerals, so, from an ecological point of view, it is far more costly.
- When goods are produced for a world market, there can be enormous waste due to overproduction, because the demand cannot easily be predicted.

We also saw that the *social* costs of mass production and world markets are significant:

- Millions of people are at the mercy of a world market controlled by countries, or individuals, or forces that have no care for the welfare of the primary producers, so they can easily be put out of business, even though they may have an excellent product and be working very hard.

- In traditional societies, unemployment was unknown. The change from craftwork to mass production led to chronic unemployment. The hidden economic costs, and the not-so-hidden social costs, of long-term unemployment were extremely high – for instance, a great increase in crime and vandalism, as well as the loss to the community of the productive capacity of so many people.
- Craftwork was personally fulfilling, and there was generally a certain variety in the work so boredom was avoided; mass production, on the other hand, causes workers to feel bored and unfulfilled.
- Finally, mass production causes the worker to be 'alienated' from the product and the consumer – it puts a wide gap between the worker and the person who uses the final product. This is in sharp contrast to the situation where a small farmer or craft-worker knew the person who was to eat or use what was being produced, so that the product created a personal link between the producer and the consumer.

Some hours or days later in the workshop we could return to the pictures, looking at them this time in the light of the ideal values that the participants believed ought to be embodied in society. This led on to an exploration of 'alternatives', that is, the kind of economic structures that would incorporate what is best in both the traditional and the 'modern' ways of life, and then be adapted to provide the basis for a society that is truly just and ecologically sensitive and sustainable.

Political or decision-making structures

In the second set of three pictures we moved on to the subject of how authority is exercised and enforced in a traditional village community in order to ensure the harmony and welfare of the local people. Here again we found that it was best to display the three pictures together as a code to evoke critical reflection. The first of this set of pictures was of a local council of elders who had immediate experience of the problems they were confronting and who took decisions on a consensus basis. The next picture was of the head of a whole clan or tribe, who had authority at a regional level, mainly through the respect people had for this person and his role. The final picture in this second set showed a traditional African way of rendering judgement – an oath administered by a 'diviner' or 'priest' to people who believed that the oath would reveal who was telling the truth.

Processed as a code, these three pictures led to a very critical evaluation of the way in which authority is exercised today. We found that participants could go on to produce follow-up codes, such as dramas about arrogant bureaucrats and corrupt politicians, police, and judges. Interesting questions also arose about how well the interests of women were represented in traditional and modern society. All this led on to sharing about how to challenge injustices. When working with participants who set a high value on the Bible, we could use suitable texts about injustice and the struggle for liberation (Moses, the prophets, Judith, Jesus) as further codes. Participants could plan ways of working for more acceptable political structures – and here again biblical texts could be used as powerful codes, for example the Jubilee Year (Leviticus 25: 13–28) and the sharing lifestyle of the early Christians (Acts 4: 32–5).

Beliefs, values, and celebrations

The third set of three pictures brought participants into the area of their deepest beliefs about the meaning of life. We learned that in this case it was better not to display all three picture codes together, but to take them one by one. One key issue for the people we were working with was their understanding of sickness and how to deal with it. So the first of these pictures showed a traditional healer at work. Used as a code, it led to important insights, such as that health is not merely a matter of getting a particular organ of the body in working order; it also has to do with the state of a person's spirit, and with how the person is relating to the family and the community – and even to those who have died, and to the spirit world. The issue of witchcraft also came up as a hot topic. My experience was that the topic of sickness and healing was truly generative. The dialogue was very empowering for people because it caused a shift in power relationships between the participants and us as facilitators, since this was an area where the local people saw themselves as the real experts. When facilitated sensitively, the dialogue could lead to a critical assessment of both traditional and modern responses to sickness and concrete proposals for bringing about change.

The eighth picture was of children listening to the stories of an elder. The processing of this code heightened awareness that the traditional form of education was not cut off from daily living, as school is in 'modern' society. Children learned farming or trade, crafts or childcare, by working alongside the adults. This knowledge was set in the context of a body of traditional wisdom – which included folklore and specialized education for new stages in life (adulthood, marriage, becoming an elder, etc.). Further reflection and dialogue led to a critical evaluation of the modern school system and plans to challenge its inadequacies and injustices.

The final picture was of a traditional celebration. The aim of the facilitation was to empower the participants by helping them to appreciate how in the traditional dances, processions, or other ceremonies a community re-enacted the story of its origins, and of the other great events in its history. In this way the community became stronger in spirit and the harmony of the members was restored and fostered. This gave participants a renewed sense of purpose, empowering them to look critically at the western forms of religious and secular celebration, which seldom strike the same deep chords in the hearts of the people. They could then go on to plan deeply meaningful religious celebrations that would inspire them in their struggle for justice and respect for the environment.

CHAPTER 23

Making people matter: Training for Transformation in practice in organizations in Kenya and the United Nations

Thelma Awori

Dr Thelma Awori *grew up in Liberia but now lives in Uganda. She is a strong activist in the women's movement in Africa and a practitioner and facilitator of transformative learning. She taught at both Makerere and Nairobi universities in adult education and was a leader in the United Nations, finishing her career as Assistant Secretary-General and director of the Africa Bureau of the UN Development Programme. Her degrees in adult education are from Teachers College, Columbia University in New York (EdD) and University of California, Berkeley (MA). She has honours cum laude in social relations and cultural anthropology from Harvard University.*

This chapter looks mainly at how Training for Transformation impacted on a dialogical approach to education in various organizations, including the Department of Adult Education in Nairobi and UN agencies with which Thelma worked. When asked why she still works with TfT, she says, 'It is TfT that gives meaning to all my work.'

One does not climb a tree from the top. *Kenyan proverb*

The development industry in the last two decades has been moving into policy work supported by the rationale that if we get the policy right, everything else will fall into place. The large multilateral organizations, despite their rhetoric and good intentions, find it difficult to reach the people they are meant to serve. Going to the people is now left to non-governmental organizations (NGOs) and community-based organizations (CBOs). Yet there is little direct link between what the NGOs and CBOs do and what the large development agencies do. Consequently, everywhere in Africa, the cry is that there is no implementation of good policies. How can large organizations, and even some of our larger NGOs, reach over their organizational walls and see people, hear people, listen to people, and have these experiences influence the core of their work?

Training for Transformation (TfT) is an approach to adult education that was developed out of the work and writings of Brazilian philosopher Paulo Freire. Freire believed that development initiatives must be built on the issues of the people. He called these generative themes. Freire also believed that people have the capacity to solve their problems, working together in a process of reflection, digging deep into the reasons (the 'why') of their condition and then taking action to address these issues. Listening, dialogue, and problem-posing are therefore key tenets of his work and of the TfT methodology. Such thinking is politically correct in the development industry but the unconscious thinking of most development practitioners wonders, 'Can we really allow ourselves to be led by the people?'

Can the university reach the people?

I had just returned from the US with my MA in adult education, specializing in educational psychology. The Institute of Adult Education at the University of Nairobi hired me as a lecturer. My dilemma was how to teach participatory methods in a highly structured environment.

My learner-centred approach was having a hard time fitting in with the importance of subjects and exams, and with the power of aspiring professors. Participatory methods were being taught as a subject, not as practice. Fortunately, another colleague had also just returned from abroad with a master's degree in curriculum and instruction. Together, we decided to change the system of conducting the diploma course in adult education and to begin with the needs of the learners, which meant restructuring the curriculum. We also introduced the concept of team teaching.

Opposition to our ideas was palpable from other colleagues – and, surprisingly, from the participants. Participants told us: 'You have the knowledge, go ahead and impart it, and stop wasting our time, asking us about our needs as if you do not know.' Some colleagues could not accept sharing their powerful position over their subject content and over the students with someone else. After all, this was the university where professors knew the truth, had authority over what students learned, administered examinations, and passed or failed students. 'International standards' of education had to be adhered to. The process of melting down all of this resistance was slow. We fortunately had the support of the director of the Institute, who gave us a free hand to introduce new ideas.

It was at this point that Sally Timmel and Anne Hope showed up at the Institute in search of partners to help with their TfT work in Catholic communities in Kenya. We traded our assistance in their workshops with practical experience for our students. And so began my long journey with TfT, and the journey of the students and the diploma course as well. A small team of like-minded staff from the Institute joined Sally and Anne in running the training workshops all over Kenya. In exchange, they came and facilitated workshops with our students using the TfT approach and supervised their fieldwork.

Before long, the diploma course in adult education began to change substantially. Staff were facilitating in multiple teams and facilitating according to the flow of subjects in consonance with the thinking of the participants. This was possible because, in the first place, the participants became empowered as learners and as practitioners of facilitated learning in a participatory approach using TfT as a basis for their work as adult educators. Having learned that they had the power to direct their own learning, and that the power of the teacher was only equal to what they give, it was not possible for anyone to make long, authoritarian presentations to them. They began questioning forms of hierarchy and power in the learning situation and in the society around them. The difference between facilitation and teaching were clear to them. They preferred facilitation.

Important shifts in consciousness were visible in the participants. Many who came as closed individuals opened themselves to feedback after they learned about Johari's Window. As staff we spent fun-filled time developing the River code found in TfT Book 1 to show dependency in the learning situation and in the practice of development activities. These tools became standard practice in the diploma course. Course materials for socioeconomic analysis depended heavily on materials developed through TfT's wide connections.

Many other adjustments had to be made in the structure and conduct of the course. The kitchen had to become more flexible with meal and tea times. Face-to-face engagement with the participants changed from one- to two-hour blocks, given the varying structure of the course.

The most dramatic change was in the lives of the participants and the work that they did after the course. Some of the participants who graduated joined the small movement in Kenya that had begun at that time to question the democratic space using theatre. Many of those involved fled the country. One moved to another country and made a significant contribution there using community theatre for consciousness-raising. Others became so empowered that they went off to do their doctorates or to become leaders in the women's movement in Kenya, contributing to other parts of Africa, or working as consultants for international organizations.

The entire Institute of Adult Education did not change as a result of the introduction of TfT, nor did the university. The diploma course did, as there was a nucleus of staff with the intention of effecting change. Fortunately, the director at that time was open to change. Through the work of the students in the communities, the diploma also focused on some of the issues that they brought in.

Given the pressure for Kenya to address the massive problem of absorbing high school graduates into the university, the entire institute became the School of Distance Learning. Everything on the campus had to be done through distance learning. This policy changed the diploma course, limiting students' access to the practice of working in communities.

Can the United Nations reach the people?

My career at the United Nations gave me several opportunities to practise TfT. I was Chief of Africa for UNIFEM (the UN Development Fund for Women), and later its deputy director. UNIFEM was established to respond to the women of the world, particularly those who are marginalized and deprived. Two things that we guarded fiercely in UNIFEM were: 1) to keep women as our focus; and 2) to safeguard a space to be creative and catalytic. This meant we had to work as if women mattered – not the organization, but women. In that respect we promoted the knowledge and technology that women had developed, we put women (not UNIFEM) at the discussion and decision-making tables, and we supported and gave visibility to their efforts to gain access to financial resources. UNIFEM was a space where I could practise and give shape to my use of TfT. We helped women, planners, policymakers, and donors to understand the deeper reasons for women's exclusion and oppression, and gave women the courage and support to combat these. UNIFEM has now changed into UN Women and has been pulled more into policy dialogue.

I moved on from UNIFEM to the UN Development Programme (UNDP), a much larger institution that has been pulled constantly into the policy realm. The intention of creating policies is to make life better for people, but this intention becomes arrested at the level of creation with no implementation. Without implementation of policies, people have no services.

The first part of my tenure with UNDP was as Resident Co-ordinator in Zimbabwe. I found that, true to the culture of the organization, the key actors were the government ministries. My effort therefore was to open UNDP in Zimbabwe to civil society, to learn from them, support them, and respect them, as we did the government, and to bring civil society and government together.

With the international emphasis on poverty eradication, each country had to prepare a poverty assessment. The national poverty report would be the basis for future economic planning. I opted to get a CBO, the Africa Community Publishing and Development Trust (ACPD), to do the poverty assessment. Normally the poverty assessment is produced by the government, assisted by the World Bank or other international institutions that focus on the study of poverty. Using a community-based group would give volume to the voices of the people who experience poverty most.

There were lots of questions raised in the office. What would be the integrity of such a report in the eyes of our peers? What would be the reaction of government to this initiative? What would be the reaction of our headquarters? Given the powers vested in me as a representative of UNDP, I conferred with the government and nudged my office into moving ahead with the project.

This initiative had the possibility of changing three organizations: UNDP, ACPD and the government. For both the government and the UN, it could have become a tradition to conduct poverty assessments with the express inputs of the people. This did not happen, since not every country had a CBO that could produce such a report. But the success of the poverty assessment emboldened UNDP Zimbabwe to bring more NGOs together to work on the issue of water in dry and remote areas of the country in a programme called 'Give a Dam'. Much of this changed when I left Zimbabwe. The strategic inclination of most large, international organizations is towards government or their peers, not to the people. Concern is more with systems and discourse in which the people are the objects and not the subjects. This is not to say that there are no good people-oriented programmes in these organizations, particularly UNDP, which has many. But the general tendency is to move away from the people to the policy.

The data that ACPD gathered was more deeply qualitative than any survey could have gathered. Its quality was acclaimed by many. The report was presented as a complementary report to the one produced by the government. The ACPD report, *The Suffering Are the Cornerstone in Building a Nation*, was used and quoted at two high-level international conferences on poverty (see Chapter 7).

This was followed by a book entitled *Uprooting Poverty* produced for UNDP and the Ministry of Labour and Social Welfare, which were responsible for preparing the Poverty Alleviation Action Plan. This book was very popular and used widely in community programmes. The contract for the research gave ACPD the funds to revive its organization, and it has continued publishing books written by communities so that voices at the grassroots level can be heard. Some of their newer books are now written by children. The process of writing the books includes community analysis of their reality as they see it and their suggestions for change, which they themselves carry out, or of which new policies could address their situation. In the end, the voices of the people were heard and their lived experiences informed the plan to eradicate poverty in Zimbabwe at the time.

Can large, civil society organizations reach the people?

In Uganda, the Institute for Social Transformation has a contract to help 10 civil society organizations focus on gender justice both in their own organizations and in their work. Oxfam Novib has realized that achieving gender justice is a long haul and will take the concerted effort of all organizations. Oxfam has developed tools and materials for helping its partners recognize gender injustice and address it in their work and organizational structures. It has contracted the Institute for Social Transformation, a practitioner of TfT, to support its partners in this process.

The partners have now been trained in the TfT methodology and approach, as well as in the use of some excellent Oxfam tools such as GALS (Gender Action Learning Systems). The aim of the training was to reinforce the importance of the people, using their generative themes as a starting point for their work. Special emphasis was placed on looking at gender differences and how communities can work on improving gender justice.

The partners have realized some changes that promote gender justice in their office structures and workplace facilities. The challenge comes in going out to the communities and imparting this same understanding and skill. Time and funds are two of the big issues that come up. Staff members are busy responding to the needs of donors for reports. Log frames do not allow for the flexibility of responding spontaneously to issues that arise in the community or that are hidden in a culture of silence. It is interesting that there is little time to participate in local action to counter some of the excesses of government with respect to the people. What we call 'chasing the work plan' to achieve the number of workshops or numbers of people reached becomes the important thing. Time demands from donors, and the perennial need for funds, both mean that listening is in the direction of donors and not in the direction of the people. Many organizations have to keep up with the latest flavour of the month from donors and see how they can adjust the problems of the people to fit the flavour. The funding scenario is too tight to allow for adjusting the priorities of the donors to the people's concerns rather than the other way round. Realizing this dilemma, some donors, such as the Global Fund for Women, are becoming more flexible with the use of their funds, but only a small number do this. We are on a journey with these partners and intend to accompany them through this process.

Conclusion

Putting people first, not as objects but as subjects of their own development, is a frightening thought but it is the embodiment of our values. DAWN (Development Alternatives with Women for a New Era) gave us an important formula in the 1980s: 'Link the micro to the macro'. The challenge is how to overcome systems and mechanisms, and the work culture that characterizes our organizations.

CHAPTER 24

A 25-year journey in the ethos, ethics, and pedagogy of Training for Transformation

Peter Westoby

Dr Peter Westoby *hails from the UK but now loves living in Highgate Hill, Brisbane, Australia. He is a senior lecturer in community development with the University of Queensland and a research fellow with the Centre for Development Support at the University of the Free State in South Africa. He is also a director/consultant with Community Praxis Co-op in Australia. His experience includes work in South Africa, Papua New Guinea, the Philippines, India, Vanuatu, and Australia. His interests are in refugee-related work, youth work practice, and community development.*

The chapter articulates Peter's story of using Training for Transformation resources around the world and gives three examples of intensive work using this methodology.

No matter how far the town, there is another beyond it.   *Malian proverb*

I encountered Training for Transformation (TfT) as a 20-year-old learning about community work in Australia. It was 1988 and I had just moved into the inner-city neighbourhood of West End, Brisbane, to involve myself in solidarity work with various marginalized communities. These included communities of refugees, aboriginal groups, and people living with mental illness. Along with several other young people, I had been invited by Dave and Angie Andrews, who had just returned from doing more than 20 years of community work in India, to join them in learning about solidarity and community work in the area. Dave became one of my community work mentors and very early on he showed me Books 1 to 3 of the TfT handbook and said something like, 'Peter, this is the bible of community work.' Twenty-five years later, having worked as a community worker, trainer, and engaged scholar/academic in diverse contexts such as India, Australia, South Africa, Papua New Guinea, Vanuatu, and the Philippines, I can say that Dave's statement has proven to be true. Over the years I have read hundreds of books on community work and community development, but I always return to TfT as a practical resource that is also theoretically sound.

At the time of discovering TfT, I was a young community worker being mentored into practice. However, many of the learning models I had previously observed and had been subjected to – in schools, university, and even community settings – were didactic, more oriented towards supporting learning processes through what Freire called 'banking' methods. There was an assumption about experts having knowledge that they could 'deposit' into the heads or hands of young students such as myself.

Discovering TfT also coincided with being introduced to the literature of significant author-activists such as Paulo Freire, Mahatma Gandhi, Frantz Fanon, Jacques Ellul, and Ivan Illich. Their theories, along with the practice embodied within TfT, struck a chord, resonating with my need to shift from 'banking' to dialogical forms of facilitating community-based learning and social change.

I started a journey that has continued until now, with my work consolidated into my most recent publications – *Theory and Practice of Dialogical Community Development: International Perspectives* (Westoby and Dowling, 2013) and *Learning and Mobilising for Community Development: A Radical Tradition of Community-based Education and Training* (Westoby and Shevellar, 2012) – both of which document my own practice and research around dialogue within community development and community-based education practices.

Reflecting back on my discovery of TfT, I can still remember the ideas that resonated. Firstly, there was the 'aha!' with regards to the power of dialogue as a crucial component of learning. It is an 'aha!' that has stuck with me for 25 years, and the focus of much of my academic and work life has been around the role and practices of dialogue within community development and community-based education and training. Secondly, what stood out was the tried-and-tested nature of particular techniques or methods to enable dialogue – such as the use of codes, how to identify community-level generative themes, how to deal with conflict, and how to analyse social issues.

Some of the critical elements that shifted or changed due to TfT included integrating technical processes, such as those mentioned above, into my life and work, reinforcing the kinds of ideological and spiritual commitments that had come to inhabit my life. I wanted to participate in change processes, but, following Paulo Freire's admonition, I wanted to do it with love and humility. He states: 'Dialogue cannot exist, however, in the absence of a profound love for the world and men. The naming of the world, which is an act of creation and re-creation, is not possible if it is not infused with love. Love is at the same time the foundation of dialogue and dialogue itself' (Freire, 1972: 62).

The combination of a spiritual and emotional commitment to love, and the technical ability to facilitate real dialogue and the generation of hope fuelled by concrete action, was powerful.

Practice

After 25 years of practice I could share so much, but let me share three stories – focused respectively on Australia, Vanuatu, and my global workshops on 'dialogical community development' enabled through using a code from Steinbeck's classic novel *Grapes of Wrath* (1939: 151–2).

Australia and Community Praxis Co-op

In 1998 I returned to Australia after four years of community work in South Africa. Along with some friends and colleagues, I established a non-profit co-operative called Community Praxis Co-op, committed to 'peace, justice, and sustainability' (see www.communitypraxis.org). One of the key initiatives of the organization was taking the lead with numerous other partners (mainly local government authorities) to develop what has become known as Building Better Communities, a community-based training programme that supports the learning and mobilization of residents in neighbourhoods across Queensland. The detailed story of this work has been told previously (see Buckley, 2012) but, in a nutshell, it is a programme that uses the principles and practices of TfT to support residents in marginalized neighbourhoods to:

- build a vision for community;
- analyse the issues and challenges the neighbourhood faces;
- learn attitudes and skills for building community, and initiating local-level projects;
- construct groups and/or, with others, actual activities or actions of change.

The programme is TfT-oriented in that some of the activities from Books 1 to 3 are used, but more pertinently the principles of learning and change are adopted within the design and process.

Vanuatu and the kastom governance partnership

In 2004 I was invited to support a team of engaged academics in an AusAID-funded, eight-year initiative in the Pacific nation of Vanuatu. The *kastom* (the local Bislama word for custom) governance partnership was developed by the then Australian Centre for Peace and Conflict Studies, the Vanuatu National Council of Chiefs, and AusAID. The partnership was designed to facilitate 'conversations' with chiefs, along with women, youth, and church leaders, around tough, complex community issues to do with conflict, governance, and development. I was tasked with designing and leading the facilitation of the regular five-day workshops with these four constituents. These workshops were at the heart and soul of the partnership.

I remember early in the design phase sitting with the paramount chief of Vanuatu and several leading national chiefs and having a conversation about what the word 'workshop' meant in the local context. The answer focused on the normative practices of workshops, whereby 'experts' would turn up in communities with PowerPoint slides to 'educate the people'. We reflected on these practices together and agreed that the project in no way wanted to mirror such approaches – we did not want experts, although there was plenty of expertise. The alternative hope was for mutual processes of education enabled through the creation of quality conversation. After many hours of consideration, we came upon the local Bislama word of *storian* to describe what we envisaged might happen – a process of story-telling and dialogue. The five-day workshops from then on became known as *storians* and they embodied the dialogical methods of TfT from day one. Sometimes particular codes or activities from the TfT handbooks were used, but mostly new codes or activities were created or designed (for example, the use of a DVD, or a local story about custom) in liaison with a *kastom* reference group, drawing on the kinds of examples learned within TfT. The work also drew on John Paul Lederach's adaptations of Freire's ideas for conflict transformation work and explicitly focused on what he named the *elicitive method*. I would say that adapting TfT into an elicitive cycle that foregrounds culture within the process of learning has been a crucial development in my practice.

The elicitive model begins with concrete experiences through a series of discovery-oriented activities (see Figure 24.1). Such activities are designed to act as catalysts for participants to discover what they do, and how they do it. Secondly, participants name and categorize the processes they use. Thirdly, participants engage in what Lederach (1995) refers to as 'contextualized evaluation'. In other words, once participants have a heightened awareness of what occurs in their situation, they can examine it more objectively and consider the strengths and weaknesses of the approaches utilized. Fourthly, participants recreate and adapt their approaches, based on their evaluation. Finally, through either simulations or real-life experiences, participants try out their adapted models through practical application. One of the key differences between this and other models is that the elicitive model explicitly privileges culture (ibid.). It is grounded in the view that culture and indigenous (or endogenous) knowledge are the 'seedbed' that gives rise to processes and models that better meet local needs.

This model offers a powerful process for people-centred and culture-centred learning work and is now firmly positioned within my array of practices.

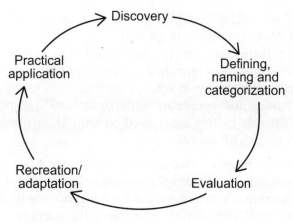

Figure 24.1 The elicitive model

Dialogical community development

Finally, I am often invited to facilitate workshops on what I have called and published as 'dialogical community development' (Westoby and Dowling, 2009, 2013). When I am invited, I usually become stuck because people expect me to arrive and be an expert on the topic, usually demonstrated within university settings by giving a lecture. Instead, I have drawn on the experience embodied within TfT and have structured the learning experience through introducing a code, a model, and some particular content. The code comes from a couple of pages of John Steinbeck's novel *The Grapes of Wrath* (1939: 151–2), and the model is known as the spiral method. This spiral model is an adaptation of Freire's work for community development and can be depicted in the following way (Figure 24.2).

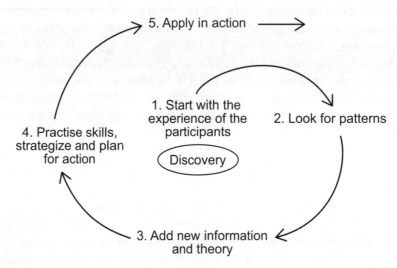

Figure 24.2 The spiral model

The spiral model initially draws on the experiential learning cycle of Kolb (1984) by inviting participants to reflect on their experiences. Like the elicitive model, it seeks categorizations and pattern formation. However, the third step within the spiral model is what differentiates it, through the inclusion or insertion of new theory and information. The fourth step in the spiral model is to connect with the new knowledge, practise skills, strategize, and plan for action. Finally, the fifth step calls for the strategies to be applied in action.

In terms of content, this workshop uses the code and the method to consider how dialogue and community development interact. In many ways, this can be summarized as how dialogical processes lead to:

- the movement from 'I' to ' we' (from individuals to the community) – how dialogue leads to the shift from individuals to participatory groups;
- the movement from 'private concerns' to 'public action' – how dialogue leads to those groups gaining an understanding of how their perceived private concerns are actually public issues requiring collective agreements to act;
- the movement from 'to' or 'for' people to 'with' or 'among' people – how facilitators of change (community workers in this case) need to shift their dialogue orientation from service delivery to solidarity with people.

Over time, my work has grown to be more eclectic, and I have learned two major lessons. Firstly, it is important, while being committed to dialogical methods of learning and social change, to have access to several models of learning. Each model guides the processes of dialogue. For example, I usually draw on the experiential, the elicitive, the spiral, the narrative, and the participatory learning and action models and have elsewhere articulated them in detail (see Westoby and

Shevellar, 2012). Secondly, I have learned that the art of facilitating social change through community-based education and training requires both the 'art of questioning' (Paulo Freire co-wrote a book with Antonio Faundez called *Learning to Question: A Pedagogy of Liberation* (1989)) and the 'embodiment of a craft'. With respect to the former, questioning is most certainly a crucial skill of training – knowing when to ask a question, being responsive to questions, creating platforms where people find their voice and question things themselves. With respect to the latter, the craft of TfT is something that you learn, like an apprentice, through practice, reflection on practice, and critical feedback from a mentor. However, as with learning any craft (Sennett, 2008), once practices become habitual, then those practices are inhabited or embodied – they become tacit (Schon, 1983: viii). The practices, methods, and theory of TfT then become part of who you are as a trainer and as a person.

Impact and learning

One of my main achievements, linked to the legacy of TfT within my life, includes my previously mentioned life-long practice and research work around dialogue, culminating in the books mentioned earlier. Second was the establishment of Community Praxis Co-op, a well-respected non-profit organization in Australia that facilitates many community-based training programmes within neighbourhoods using the TfT method. Finally, from 2011 to 2013, I have been the 'consultant' in designing a four-year bachelor's degree in community development in South Africa at the University of the Free State (one of only three universities planning to deliver this degree). The curriculum for the first year will explicitly draw on the TfT volumes, which will be used to establish the ethos, ethics, and pedagogy of both the degree and the tradition of community development that the students are taught.

The Australian-based Building Better Communities and the Vânuatu *storians* – two of the stories recounted above – have both been subject to thorough evaluations and have been shown to have had substantial impacts. For example, within Building Better Communities, two formal evaluations have been conducted and have demonstrated the profound impact of the course on participants, and also numerous community-based initiatives emerging from the programme (Community Praxis Co-op, 2003, 2006). The same can be said for the Vanuatu work, again with independent evaluators establishing the integrity and effectiveness of the programme (AusAID, 2012).

One of the challenges of using TfT is an assumption about it being a normative set of practices that can be thought of as universal, that is, as cutting across culture. This entails presumptions about being able to use the processes and exercises in any cultural–historical context. Through the 'school of hard knocks', I have learned that this is not always the case. For example, my work in contexts such as Vanuatu – where the cultural practices around group processes are so profoundly different to TfT participatory processes – has shown that sometimes I had to approach things differently. This often focuses on issues to do with gender and generation (women and youth) participation in group conversations oriented towards training.

Secondly, a 'failure' is to assume that co-facilitators are familiar with either TfT or at least the ethos, ethics, and pedagogy embodied within it. Often I find myself at odds with co-facilitators who 'like to talk', or to present a lecture. Despite their rhetorical commitment to participation and dialogical methods, their embodied practices often tend to go in the opposite direction. In hindsight, I wish I could have made more space to induct other facilitators into the methods of TfT without coming across as patronizing. I am still not sure how to do this without alienating other 'experienced' people, but grapple for a solution of how to do it.

I would love to see networks, or 'communities of practice', in different parts of the world, which would gather and reflect together on their TfT practice. For example, to be able to access such a network or community within Australia would be useful. The approach needs to include a more nuanced understanding of how culture and method interact, particularly when working in contexts where there is substantial cultural distance between participatory pedagogies and customary rules (recognizing that no custom or culture is static and that often customary rules are embedded within discourses and practices of dominating power). There could be more examples or narratives of how codes can be developed within a context, ensuring that facilitators are less inclined to simply reproduce the codes already existing within the TfT manuals, but instead develop new ones for specific situations.

Conclusion

TfT was given to me as a gift when I was young. I was lucky in accessing such a solid tool and methodology for my community work, one that continues to challenge my practice. TfT constantly challenges me to avoid drifting towards didactic methods – it invites the use of creativity and dialogue and facilitates concrete action. It is not an easy process, and I suggest that any new apprentices should find a mentor. My thanks go to Dave Andrews for introducing it and mentoring me – and, of course, to Sally and Anne for writing it.

References

AusAID (2012) *Vanuatu Kastom Governance Partnership: Case Study Report, September 2010*, Canberra: AusAID <www.ode.dfat.gov.au/publications/documents/vanuatu-kastom-governance-report.pdf> [accessed 19 February 2014].

Buckley, H. (2012) 'Building community leadership from the inside out: the story of the Building Better Communities training course in South East Queensland', in P. Westoby and L. Shevellar (eds), *Learning and Mobilising for Community Development: A Radical Tradition of Community-based Education and Training*, Farnham: Ashgate.

Community Praxis Co-op (2003) *The Delivery of the Community Praxis Co-op Local Community Builders' Training Course: A Guide to Good Practice*, Maleny, Queensland: Community Praxis Co-op.

Community Praxis Co-op (2006) *Building Community on the Sunshine Coast Project Evaluation DVD*, Maleny, Queensland: Community Praxis Co-op.

Community Praxis Co-op, DFAC, BCC and CSC (2003) *Reviving Local Communities: An Evaluation of the Community Leadership Training Project*, Maleny, Queensland: Community Praxis Co-op.

Freire, P. (1972) *Pedagogy of the Oppressed*, London: Penguin Books.

Freire, P. and Faundez, A. (1989) *Learning to Question: A Pedagogy of Liberation*, Geneva: World Council of Churches (WCC) Publications.

Kolb, D.A. (1984) *Experiential Learning: Experience as the Source of Learning and Development*, Englewood Cliffs, NJ: Prentice Hall.

Lederach, J.P. (1995) *Preparing for Peace: Conflict Transformation across Cultures*, New York, NY: Syracuse University Press.

Schon, D. (1983) *The Reflective Practitioner: How Professionals Think in Action*, Farnham: Ashgate.

Sennett, R. (2008) *The Craftsman*, London: Penguin Books.

Steinbeck, J. (1939) *The Grapes of Wrath*, London: Penguin Books.

Westoby, P. and Dowling, G. (2009) *Dialogical Community Development: With Depth, Solidarity and Hospitality*, London and Brisbane: Tafina Press.

Westoby, P. and Dowling, G. (2013) *Theory and Practice of Dialogical Community Development: International Perspectives*, Abingdon: Routledge.

Westoby, P. and Shevellar, L. (eds) (2012) *Learning and Mobilising for Community Development: A Radical Tradition of Community-based Education and Training*, Farnham: Ashgate.

CHAPTER 25

Shaking government officials emotionally: community facilitation in Papua New Guinea

Maria Latumahina

Maria Latumahina *is an independent consultant with a passion for and focus on the liberation of the Papuan people from socioeconomic oppression and environmental injustice. She is based in Sorong in the province of West Papua, and has been working on this issue since 1998. Her role has been mainly mobilizing resources, including technical assistance and financial resources to support emerging activists in the community, civil society, and local governments. After participating in the Training for Transformation diploma course in 2012–13, she started to work as a community facilitator.*

A bird that does not fly cannot discover the harvest. *Burundian proverb*

This chapter illustrates a stage in my life journey as I pursue my personal purpose in life, upholding principles of environmental justice and putting them into practice. It is the stage when I found Training for Transformation, and finding TfT brought me to a new way of living, a new way of working. I tell the story of how I was introduced to TfT, my diploma course, and how the course affected my being (intellectual, emotional, and spiritual) and my approach as I pursue my purpose in life. I also describe how I contextually adapted and applied the TfT method in my personal and working environment. Last but not least, I describe the impact that I have witnessed. This is probably the most powerful insight; it is almost indescribable, but I will try as I am truly willing to share it.

How I found Training for Transformation

I was introduced to TfT by Vérène Nicolas of the Centre for Human Ecology in Glasgow. I came to the TfT diploma course in 2012–13, at a time when I was searching for a new approach to inspiring individuals, groups, and wider communities to strengthen their inner capacity to walk the long path towards the vision of a sustainable Papua in 2100.

This is a vision that I shared with my colleagues, including the facilitating team and 15 selected bureaucrats from the development planning office (Bappeda) of the Papua province of Indonesia. As a person born and brought up in the remoteness of Papua, I see my dream and my whole being in this vision. In a nutshell, the vision says:

> By 2100, fair and equal access by all people in Papua province to happiness and a high quality of life, where the quality of the environment, including land, water, and air, is sustained and improved over time; where Papuans are capable of meeting all basic needs through the sustainable management of local resources and environmentally friendly technology; and where people in Papua province are able to sustain communal land ownership in ways that allow them to manage and share resources equitably.

We walked through the vision process over three years, from 2009 to 2011, under the auspices of a UK-funded project on climate change administered by the British Embassy in Jakarta.

When the project was finished, I was left with questions including the following:

- Do we truly have faith in the vision we set up and is the vision based on a strong spiritual ground? In other words, is this vision our reason for living?
- Does this vision reflect the reality, the pain, and the hope of the rest of our fellow Papuans, especially grassroots communities?

These two questions have been my guiding stars. TfT gives me a toolkit that equips and enables me in my further journey in search of an answer.

The underlying method of TfT involves the hand, the heart, and the head. This taught me two things.

Firstly, I have been working with my head and my hand, but less with my heart. I worked hard, but only promoting myself rather than promoting the work of God. Transformation is a work of love, and therefore the work of God. My belief system is Christian. Through the spirituality sessions on the course, I learned that Jesus promoted and died for the transformation of this world. Thus transformation is the work of love; it is the work that brings good news to the poor, liberty to the prisoners, freedom to the oppressed (Luke's Gospel, Chapter 4). This new consciousness has totally changed my approach: I have become more reflective and regularly ask myself if I am truly working for liberation of the Papuans.

Secondly, I had previously worked to improve knowledge through the education process, but I had been using the 'banking' education method. I told people about what a better world is, and how to create a better world according to world-class scientists, rather than helping people to discover the energy and potential within themselves, as individuals as well as a community, to define a better world for themselves and contribute in their own time and space. Hope and Timmel (1984, 1995: 16) say that everybody thinks the education they provide is relevant, but who decides what is relevant to a particular community? Initially I was struggling to make sense of this concept until I discovered for myself how the popular education that TfT promotes brought me to a new level of consciousness about education. My understanding about a workable education method shifted when I recognized how my emotions were shaken when I managed to see the link between emotion and motivation to act. On my second residential phase of the 2013 diploma course I was sitting in a session on popular education facilitated by Jude Clark. It was the session that shook me the most emotionally. The images used initially made me feel relaxed, my lungs were full of fresh air, then, as the slides changed and came to an image of a little girl holding a board on which was written 'My dad needs a job', I felt as if my lungs were full of black smoke. I could not breathe properly and my tears started to run down. I said to myself: 'This is the power of popular education.' My facilitation style changed totally as a result; the emotions of the people I facilitate became my starting point. I finally found the answer to the questions I had been asking myself, that had led me to the TfT diploma course. The vision of Sustainable Papua 2100 would be widely shared if and when it sparked the emotions of the people, when the Papuans were able to see that their pain would be released and they could reach for their 'star'. They will see their dreams matched by the dream of the 15 people from Bappeda.

My practical experience: a new consciousness in the community of Numfor and at provincial and district levels

'We are the ones we have been waiting for!' exclaimed one of the village leaders during the evaluation of the course.

I have been through so many real-life experiences in community awareness-raising programmes, but the one in Numfor speaks to me the most about the power of popular education. Numfor was selected as one of the Bappeda pilot sites mainly because of its socioeconomic dynamics and ecological challenges (Bappeda Papua's Sustainable Development Team, 2012). Numfor is located just north of Cenderawasih Bay (Geelvink Bay), between the island of Biak and the east coast of the Doberai Peninsula (Vogelkop or Bird's Head Peninsula) on mainland New Guinea.

According to the government census, the population of Numfor is 9,336 people. The people are a combination of indigenous and incomers from other parts of Papua as well as from the outer islands.

Popular education, applying the TfT method, was first brought to Numfor by the programme director of TfT, Ntombi Nyathi, and by Zunaid Moolla, an economist and one of the TfT facilitators. I called this training a process of liberating the soul. The training ran for 10 days, on 16–26 July 2013, and involved 25 community leaders and activists, 10 of whom were female. My role in that workshop was to provide simultaneous translation. I really enjoyed this role as it allowed me to observe and to practise facilitation skills at the same time. I had to talk and act just like the original facilitator.

In my observation, I was mostly struck by the level of trauma the community has been living with. One of the local leaders said, 'As local leaders we are under immense pressure from the system to function within the laws and regulations – even if they impact negatively on people' (Nyathi, 2013). The oppression that Numfor people have been facing reflects the oppression faced by all Papuans. Papua has been famous as an area where oppression and violence are part of our daily life. According to Chauvel and Bhakti (2004), the central government in particular relies on force to maintain its authority. Unfortunately, this reliance on force produces powerful counterproductive dynamics. It fuels the opposition, and hence the aspiration for independence and the continuous conflict with central government. The training managed to get the community to see the power of being with each other to help overcome the individual and societal fear they have been experiencing as a result of psychological pressure from the military and the authoritarian government for many generations.

Furthermore, the community also managed to see that the great challenge they are facing is their inability to focus on the common good rather than on differences. In one of the sessions on religious tolerance between Muslims and Christians, participants were emotionally shaken, and they became conscious of the root cause of social disintegration. There is no reason to think that the quality of life of Numfor people will be enhanced if only one religion is dominant.

The training was liberating not only for the island community, but also for the local government officials at both provincial and district levels. Six provincial and district bureaucrats attended the training. They witnessed how the community rose above their fear and became motivated to take responsibility for themselves. The result was a group of community facilitators and a plan to facilitate a set of actions around the issues of selling land, debt, waste management, and renewable energy, among other things. Further to this is a full commitment of the local government to support a three-year programme of Numfor community empowerment, working in collaboration with TfT.

Last but not least, the district government is planning to apply this method of facilitating village development planning across the district, and the provincial government is planning to introduce this method into two other districts.

Conclusion

I found TfT when I was desperately looking for new ways to work at engaging both community and government in pursuing our vision of sustainable development in Papua. TfT taught me about transformation as a spiritual journey as well as a cognitive and emotional one. We need to start where the emotion is strong.

My practical experience of bringing TfT to the island of Numfor in the Papua province of Indonesia enriched my 'self' as I witnessed spiritual and emotional liberation start to emerge. The people of Numfor began to see their own power as a community. The training was also a liberating experience for the local government, as they themselves were emotionally shaken and awakened to new consciousness. They also saw how the training sparked emotion and shifted the mindset of the people.

The commitment of local governments, both provincial and district, to apply this method across the district and in two other districts shows the impact of this method. I finally found a new way of working to enable people to work for the common good and for Papuan civilization. However, I immediately discovered that I am the only Papuan who has been on the course. How can I enable other Papuans to access the same resources so that we can expedite the multiplication of community facilitators? This question is another of my guiding stars, pointing towards a better future for Papua.

References

Bappeda Papua's Sustainable Development Team (2012) *Discuss Amongst Ourselves to Save Eden: A Study and Reflection of the Development Direction in Numfor Island, Papua*, unpublished.

Chauvel, R. and Bhakti, I.N. (2004) *The Papua Conflict: Jakarta's Perceptions and Policies*, Policy Studies 5, Washington, DC: East-West Center Washington.

Hope, A. and Timmel, S. (1995) *Training for Transformation: A Handbook for Community Workers*, Kleinmond, South Africa: Training for Transformation Institute.

Nyathi, N. (2013) *Training for Transformation: A Community Empowerment Initiative with Papua Provincial Development Planning Agency (Bappeda), Indonesia. A Report*, unpublished.

PART EIGHT
It doesn't need to be like this

Keywords: alternative economics; awareness of self; becoming; belonging; exponential injustice, food security; leadership; participatory methods for teaching economics; popular economics; search for simple and effective responses to injustice; seeking

http://dx.doi.org/10.3362/9781780448312.009

CHAPTER 26
Doing popular economics in South Africa

Zunaid Moolla

Zunaid Moolla *is a South African economist involved in economic research and analysis and economic literacy. For six years he has been facilitating the module in the Training for Transformation diploma course on critical approaches to economics, as well as an introduction to the political economy and alternative and new economics.*

In this chapter, Zunaid explains some of the simulations and experiential processes used to enable those new to economics to understand the causes of the growing gap between rich and poor and the devastating effects of globalization on employment and the well-being of both the middle class and marginalized communities.

Accomplishment of purpose is better than making a profit. *Nigerian proverb*

I have been associated with Training for Transformation (TfT) for about six years now. I got to know about TfT through Sally Timmel, with whom I worked on a few projects relating to economic literacy or popular economics shortly after South Africa's transition to democracy. My areas of focus in the TfT programme are political economy, critical approaches to economics, and alternative or new economics.

I started with TfT while I was running a consulting company that specialized in economic research and local economic development strategies. The main difference between my consulting work and TfT was that the former had no popular content. The target audience was comprised largely of local and provincial government officials. In 2010 I closed my consulting business and I now divide my time between TfT and Applied Development and Research Solutions (ADRS), a California-based company that specializes in the popular use of economic modelling techniques, and the Alternative Information Development Centre (AIDC), a research and policy-based organization in South Africa with links to trade unions and community organizations.

Through my work with TfT I became aware of the empowering potential of a teaching methodology in economics that reveals the power relations inherent in the functioning of economies on a national and global scale. This is something that is absent in the way conventional, mainstream economics is taught, discussed, or presented in the media. I then began to develop, together with Ntombi Nyathi, ways of presenting key economic concepts and their practical application in a country's economic life.

Explaining economic concepts (or jargon) and how an economy works can be daunting. How then to do this with groups who have no background in the subject at all? My work with TfT has been a wonderful opportunity to create teaching techniques that bring to life some of the fundamentals of economics. Take the circular flow of income and spending in the economy: economic textbooks generally describe this as factor and product markets – land, labour, and capital – supplied and demanded by businesses, households, or governments. The flaw in this, of course, is that it masks the relationships of ownership and control – in short, power relations – inherent in a market economy.

The TfT economics course usually starts with asking participants to give their views on what they know about economics, what they are curious about, and what they like and dislike about economics. This is usually done through buzz groups. They are then asked to form groups representing sectors of the economy – agriculture, mining, manufacturing – as well as government, a bank, retail operators, and landlords. Using stones as currency and cardboard boxes as commodities, the monies received as wages and as proceeds from sales are deposited with the bank or spent at the retail shop. A portion is paid to the government as taxes.

Participants are then asked to recall what took place and where they see themselves in the process. They easily describe the flow of money: from workers, businesses, and landowners to banks and government; from workers to shop owners; from banks to business owners and workers (loans). Not surprisingly, almost all of them see themselves as workers, albeit in the urban economy rather than as labourers in the agricultural, manufacturing, and mining sectors. When the 'trading game' ends, what strikes most participants is the huge disparity between the amount that workers end up with compared with that of the owners of businesses and the banks.

The next sequence in the trading game is to demonstrate the effects of a particular change in the economy, such as an increase in the interest rate or taxes. Business owners generally respond by reducing their work force, thereby causing a loss of jobs. The knock-on effect becomes evident as workers in other sectors lose their jobs. Here, participants see how the economic system is subject to shocks that can have dire consequences for thousands of workers and their families. The concepts of supply and demand take root as we go through the business cycle and show how connected one part of the economy is to every other part. The cumulative effect of boom and bust phases is a crisis, and when this happens in the largest economies it affects the world economy.

At this stage we introduce the concepts of growth and development, and gross domestic product (GDP) as a measure of an economy's health. By getting participants to place all the stones in the centre, we illustrate the purpose of GDP, which is to capture the total value added in an economy in a given time period. The importance of GDP is highlighted as a tool to provide useful insights into the performance of an economy from ratios of government expenditure to the largest and smallest sectors of the economy. What is a country's expenditure on education compared with that of other countries? How do household savings rates compare with, say, real increases in capital investment expressed as a percentage of GDP? Explaining GDP in this way, or the respective contributions made by each sector, shows its use in economic analysis and its importance in formulating policies.

GDP, however, is not a measure of well-being. In undertaking a critical examination of GDP, we highlight its shortcomings in that it does not measure national happiness, quality of life, damage to the environment, or the contribution that 'women's work' makes to the economy in the reproduction of society.

In their buzz groups, participants are asked to come up with what they think could be used in place of GDP or what could be used to supplement it. Their suggestions are then compared with some of the alternative measures that have been constructed over the past 30 years, such as genuine progress indicators, the quality of life index, and the human development index. A natural progression from here is an introduction to social indicators, which enable participants to identify issues in the living conditions of communities that have a strong bearing on social and economic development. Infant mortality rates, access to clean water, levels of safety and security, availability of transport, proximity to clinics and hospitals, and so on, are used to illustrate the importance of social indicators to assess the status of a community.

The sessions on economics usually conclude with a broad survey of economic alternatives that have been or are being tried in other countries. These include initiatives to set up alternative banking systems such as interest-free banking; the establishment of state banks; micro-lending organizations such as the Grameen Bank; the Tobin tax or taxes on financial transactions; complementary currencies; community-based trading systems that do not use currencies; and social entrepreneurship.

On the diploma course, participants are also given a short introduction to international political economy to make them familiar with some of the policies of advanced industrial countries and international financial institutions, which often have a decisive effect on the course of economic development in less industrialized countries. The content of this part of the course covers the stages of economic history from pastoralism to advanced capitalism, Johan Galtung's 'structural theory of imperialism', and the role played by the International Monetary Fund and the World Bank. The main learning tools used in this phase are 'Star Power' and the 'Dynamic Model' based on Gramsci. To convey Galtung's theory, participants are asked to form circles that represent a rich and a poor country with their respective centres and peripheries. The relationships between the centres are demonstrated as they form links with the aim of excluding both the peripheries. The Dynamic Model and Star Power also illustrate the relationships between the different institutions of society, the structures of power, and the degree of coercion and control they exercise through ownership of financial and other resources.

These teaching techniques often result in heightened awareness of the forces that drive economic relations and maintain the status quo. When combined with documentary films and videos, they provoke many participants to comment on their own positions in their respective societies and their consumption patterns. They often recall the simplicity of their parents' and grandparents' lifestyles and the harmony they enjoyed with nature. There is a realization that they need to distinguish between their real and perceived needs and wants. In the discussions that follow, many relate stories of local government officials who are ineffectual in providing even the most basic infrastructure despite the glaring poverty of people. There are also questions about ways to bring about political and economic change when people already live in a climate of fear of persecution if they oppose the status quo. Others also draw on the connection between economic systems and environmental degradation as something that is all too evident in the areas where they live and work. On purely economic issues, participants want to know what causes interest rates to rise or exchange rates to fluctuate, why the dollar is such a widely used currency, and why most African countries have so many poor people when they are endowed with large mineral deposits and other resources.

In Indonesia, where Ntombi Nyathi and I conducted a training workshop over a two-week period on the island of Numfor, the trading game proved to be a huge success. Our participants were residents from several villages on a remote island where modern means of mass communication are relatively absent. There is thus little knowledge of the outside world, and the lack of higher learning institutions also means that few have had the opportunity to be exposed to academic disciplines such as economics. Indigenous knowledge systems about nature and the immediate environment are what inform their world view. Despite this 'disadvantage', the island residents easily grasped the essentials of the trading game and were acutely aware of who benefited and who lost in the process of exchange of goods and money. It became quite clear what they needed to do if they were to control the development of their local economy.

Many of the teaching techniques that we currently use in the economics component of TfT have been used since the early days of DELTA in the 1970s, and are modified and adapted each year to take into account major changes. These experiential techniques provide those without a background in economics with an appreciation of its centrality in our lives. A variety of visual materials depicting some of the concepts or facts covered have been developed over the years, and these have been greatly added to recently. The display of such materials can reinforce the central points in the discussions or simplify some of the concepts introduced in the plenary sessions.

Conclusion

There is a veritable dearth of economic literacy in most countries, including those with relatively well educated populations. This is ironic in an age when economics determines such a large part of our lives – from unemployment to inequality to price increases and the permanent shortage of money for most households to afford basic necessities despite greater accumulation of wealth for the elite. This underscores the need to expand economic literacy in several countries around the world through the presence of TfT and also to use more creative and effective methodologies to explain and describe the workings of national and international economic processes. It seems less and less likely that radical change in economic conditions will emerge from the usual policy processes that are the domain of a few government departments, powerful interest groups, and consultants. There is a case then to be made for community-based organizations to undertake alternative economic growth and development initiatives of the kind advocated in the TfT programmes.

In arguing this, we must acknowledge that decisions regarding major macro-economic policy levers could never devolve to communities. I refer here to the interest rate, the exchange rate, taxation, import tariffs, and the money supply, among others. Communities can, however, introduce complementary currencies, run village banks on an interest-free basis, open community exchange trading systems, and provide a range of goods and services to minimize the leakage of money from their communities. These initiatives have been ably undertaken by many communities in countries around the world. They may not generate wealth as conceived in conventional economic terms, but they have the potential to at least ameliorate the desperate circumstances in which the poorest communities find themselves.

The module on economics can be said to have three aims:

- to make participants familiar with basic terms and concepts in economics;
- to make them aware of the forces that influence (or determine) local, national, and international economic situations;
- to present alternative economic solutions that provide a range of choices that they could make in order to change their community's conditions of life.

The third point captures, to some extent, TfT's expectation that, upon completing the course, participants would have an adequate level of understanding of who holds economic power and how that power is exercised in their respective communities or countries. This should enable them to identify areas of potential development around which they could mobilize their communities to improve those communities' conditions. While the expectation is not grandiose, it raises issues about possible outcomes that can be achieved by TfT programmes. The realm of possibilities can run from income-generating activities, the formation of co-ops, skills development, and social entrepreneurship to alternative energy production. These potentially transformative development initiatives should, however, be embedded in a much broader theory of change that is at the core of the work that TfT does. This entails understanding the impact of TfT programmes on both the agents of change and the objects of change.

CHAPTER 27
The global economy: 'a drunken ship disconnected from production'

Filip Fanchette

Filip Fanchette *is a Mauritian Catholic priest and an economist. After 12 years working at INODEP in France (Ecumenical Institute for the Development of Peoples), he took Paulo Freire's place at the World Council of Churches as the director of adult education for eight years, and is now back in his own country, where he is chairman of the Nelson Mandela Foundation. He has been working with DELTA and Training for Transformation since 1977 and introduced many of the most important elements of the training programme, including the wheel of fundamental human needs (an adaptation of the work of Manfred Max-Neef) and the Dynamic Model of Society (a diagrammatic presentation of the work of Antonio Gramsci). He continues to keep the programme up to date with a constant stream of new thinking and relevant articles that he has found on the internet. He often illustrates his thinking with quirky new maps and diagrams, which provoke an 'aha!' as a group experiences a new insight.*

In this chapter he looks at the exponential growth of the gap between rich and poor countries and the difficulty of deciding how to act effectively in the current situation, and focuses on the way the Indian government has recently passed legislation seeking to ensure food security for the very poor, which includes 67 per cent of the country's citizens.

> **If you keep your head and heart going in the right direction,
> you won't have to worry about your feet.** *Nigerian proverb*

> The simplest approach will prove to be the most effective. *Martin Luther King*

In the early 1970s when development education programmes began, things were clear. Equip people so that they would understand their situation and take their destiny in their own hands. Equity was the goal of development: equal access to and control over resources for everybody. Nobody would have imagined that 40 years later we would see such a concentration of wealth and its consequences.

In the 1960s, rich countries were 30 times richer than poor countries; now they are 80 times richer. Every year, rich countries give US$130 billion in aid to poor countries, but $2 trillion flows back to them from those same countries. The richest 300 people in the world are wealthier than the poorest 3 billion. According to *Forbes* (2013), 1,426 billionaires have 'an aggregate net worth of $5.4 trillion, up from $4.6 trillion'. Some 1.21 billion Indians had a combined gross domestic product (GDP) of only $4.7 trillion in 2012.

That concentration of wealth is only one indicator of the mess we are in today. It is a cause and a consequence of the economic crisis. On 15 September 2008, Lehman Brothers filed for bankruptcy. The crisis that had been slowly building since the late 1970s burst like a ripe abscess on the world scene. In the USA and Europe, $14.5 trillion went up in smoke. This was more than the whole US GDP in 2007.

And yet we had been warned – not only by a wide array of so-called heterodox economists, but by some who see themselves as orthodox.

In 2005, the housing bubble in the USA had burst and federal interest rates had climbed. On 7 September 2006, Nouriel Roubini, economics professor at New York University, in a meeting of economists at the International Monetary Fund (IMF), warned of an impending crisis. He was not taken seriously. In his response, Anirvan Banerji accused Roubini of not using mathematical models and of being 'a career naysayer'. In 2007, Roubini again diagnosed that the economy was heading towards a recession. At about the same time, the IMF put potential losses in the USA at about $945 billion. That same year, Alan Greenspan, in his *The Age of Turbulence: Adventures in a New World*, called the financial system 'a drunken ship disconnected from production'. Nassim Nicholas Taleb, who had questioned the value of economic predictions in *Fooled by Randomness*, came back that year with *The Black Swan*. This story of the takeover of the world by a small group of economists and financiers is fascinating. They are the ones – not Marx – who saw the economy as the be-all and end-all of human life.

The political class was knocked out by the crisis of the late 1970s. In the ensuing desert of political thinking, they fell back on polls, statistics, and reports by 'experts'. Instead of governing, they handed our future on a platter to mathematicians – economists who posed as scientists. In October 2008, after the crash, *The New York Times* ran an article entitled 'Government Sachs' to show how many of those who were handling the crisis worked with Goldman Sachs or were former alumni of the firm. 'Setting thieves to catch thieves'!

We see the same revolving door between financial institutions and governments all over the world. In 2008, economics students denounced 'toxic textbooks' used to 'indoctrinate millions of students in a quaint ideology (the perfect rationality of economic agents, market efficiency, the invisible hand, etc.) cunningly disguised as science' (Toxic Textbooks, n.d.). These economists used their ill-gotten political and intellectual power to further the interests of the most powerful by imposing all over the planet their partial truth as TINA – 'There Is No Alternative'. Economics (originally the study of the well-being of the household) was reduced to mathematical models. Bankers today still use those mathematical models to trade derivatives worth more than the GDP of the entire world. George Soros aptly called those derivatives 'weapons of mass destruction'. We all know how the financial crisis engulfed the whole world. The dozen or so bankers at its source were bailed out with taxpayers' money. Four years later, they go on sinning in their 'world casino'. They are content with paying fines to be absolved, and then start all over again.

Margaret Mead was right: 'Never doubt that a small group of thoughtful, committed, citizens can change the world. Indeed, it is the only thing that ever has.'

We are in such a mess that Raimundo Panikkar asked whether the human project, which has been developing these last 6,000 years, was the only one possible, and whether we should not be doing something else. At the core of the mess is the crisis of knowledge split into compartmentalized disciplines. This allowed technical-economic globalization to impose its rationality over human reason. It reinforces the false understanding of science as 'secure knowledge'. Scientists themselves value what they don't know. For them, an answer to a question always generates another question. Knowledge generates awareness of ignorance. As James Clerk Maxwell, the mathematical physicist, said: 'Thoroughly conscious ignorance is the prelude to every real advance in science.' Scientists would agree with George Bernard Shaw's 'Science is always wrong. It never solves a problem without creating 10 more.' Things are not 'either this or that'. Light can be both a quantum and a wave. Nicolas de Cues in the fifteenth century called it 'learned ignorance' and the 'coincidence of opposites'. A new study by two scientists who examined 6,000 published papers found that scientists are unduly influenced by the prestige of the journal in which a paper is published. One of the authors of the study, Adam Eyre-Walker, a biologist at the University of Sussex, admitted: 'It's very difficult to assess merit. We're all sort of stumbling around in a fog' (Diep, 2013).

In 1991, the collapse of the Soviet Union contributed to the unfettered expansion of financial capitalism. Ethno-religious fundamentalism was added to the world scene. Western civilization has, as Weber says, replaced the 'economy of salvation' with 'salvation by the economy', and it is in deep crisis. Fortunately, the homogenization provoked by globalization has provoked strong reactions against westernization and a rediscovery of identities. We have lost our faith in progress, in development. We all agree that development cannot be reduced to growth. But just adding 'sustainable' to development should not deter us from questioning our deepest assumptions. We need to do this in order to build stronger foundations for another world.

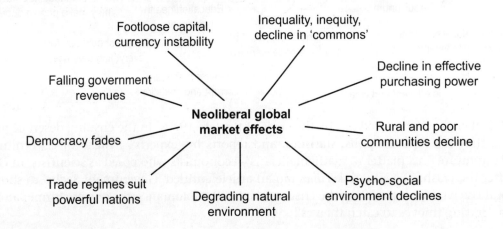

In times of insecurity we all seek to find meaning. The temptation is to look for security in theories that sometimes trivialize human suffering. As Michel Foucault wrote: 'Knowledge does not automatically lead to action.' Those of us involved in working with people must be aware of this; we cannot wait until we know everything we need to know ... and so we often oversimplify complex problems. At the core of Training for Transformation there is Freire's intuition that it is emotion that leads to action, and that there must be reflection on the action before further action. Yes, we are responsible. Hope comes from putting our ears to the ground, and both globalizing and de-globalizing.

Again and again, we need to re-evaluate, reconceptualize, restructure, relocalize, redistribute, reuse, recycle, recuperate, reintroduce. We must break from the economic and cultural dependency on the North, and re-link with other visions. Amartya Sen stresses that we must claim the 'freedom to choose'.

The objectives of 'the good life' are defined in many different ways according to the context. In other words, it is necessary to reconstruct and rediscover them in developing new cultures. It is necessary to give them a name. Perhaps it should be *umran* (or *épanouissement humain*), as it is for Ibn Khaldun, or 'the easing of the social conditions of all', as for Gandhi, or 'being well together' or 'the radiance of a well-nourished person free from all worries', as it is for the Boran of Ethiopia.

In 1995, the international community in Copenhagen declared that elimination of poverty was an ethical imperative.

It is for these people that the Indian government recently announced an ambitious $19.5 billion national food security bill. Passed by the legislature in the first week of September, the bill promises heavily subsidized wheat and rice for those who live below the poverty line – about 67 per cent of the population. As reported in the legislation, a total of 5 kilograms of food grains per month will be provided at a fixed price of 1–3 rupees (2–5 US cents) per kilogram through ration shops across the country. If the food security bill works as planned, it will become one of the world's largest welfare schemes and will make the right to food a law. The right to food is protected under international human rights and humanitarian law and the correlative state obligations are well established under international law. The right to food is recognized in Article 25 of the Universal Declaration of Human Rights and in Article 11 of the International Covenant on Economic, Social and Cultural Rights (ICESCR), as well as in many other agreements. The right to food is also recognized in numerous national constitutions.

Other relevant international instruments include the *Voluntary Guidelines to Support the Progressive Realization of the Right to Adequate Food in the Context of National Food Security* (Right to Food Guidelines), 2004; and *Voluntary Guidelines on the Responsible Governance of Tenure of Land, Fisheries and Forests in the Context of National Food Security*, 2012.

The right to food is authoritatively defined by the United Nations Committee on Economic, Social and Cultural Rights: 'the right to adequate food is realized when every man, woman and child, alone and in community with others, has physical and economic access at all times to adequate food or means for its procurement' (paragraph 6).

The UN Special Rapporteur, Jean Ziegler, has concluded that the right to food entails:

> the right to have regular, permanent and unrestricted access, either directly or by means of financial purchases, to quantitatively and qualitatively adequate and sufficient food corresponding to the cultural traditions of the people to which the consumer belongs, and which ensures a physical and mental, individual and collective, fulfilling and dignified life free of fear. (Ziegler, 2008: paragraph 17)

The Committee on Economic, Social and Cultural Rights also defined the obligations that states have to fulfil in order to implement the right to adequate food at the national level. These are as follows:

- The obligation to *respect* existing access to adequate food requires states not to take any measures that result in preventing such access.
- The obligation to *protect* requires measures by the state to ensure that enterprises or individuals do not deprive individuals of their access to adequate food.
- The obligation means the state must proactively engage in activities intended to strengthen people's access to and utilization of resources and means to ensure their livelihood, including food security.
- Whenever an individual or group is unable, for reasons beyond their control, to enjoy the right to adequate food by the means at their disposal, states have the obligation to provide for that right directly. This obligation extends to persons who are victims of natural or other disasters.

In his final book, *Where Do We Go from Here: Chaos or Community?* (1967), Martin Luther King Jr wrote: 'I am now convinced that the simplest approach will prove to be the most effective – the solution to poverty is to abolish it directly by a now widely discussed measure: the guaranteed income.'

References

Creswell, J. and White, B. (2008) 'The guys from "Government Sachs"', *The New York Times*, 17 October [online] <www.nytimes.com/2008/10/19/business/19gold.html?pagewanted=all&_r=0> [accessed 20 January 2014].

Diep, F. (2013) 'Scientists are bad at identifying important science, study finds', *Popular Science*, 10 August [online], <www.popsci.com/article/science/scientists-are-bad-identifying-important-science-study-finds> [accessed 20 January 2014].

Forbes (2013) 'Inside the 2013 Billionaires List: facts and figures', *Forbes*, 3 April [online] <www.forbes.com/sites/luisakroll/2013/03/04/inside-the-2013-billionaires-list-facts-and-figures/> [accessed 20 January 2014].

Greenspan, A. (2007) *The Age of Turbulence: Adventures in a New World*, New York, NY: The Penguin Press.

King Jr, M.L. (1967) *Where Do We Go from Here: Chaos or Community?*, Boston, MA: Beacon Press.

Taleb, N.N. (2007) *Fooled by Randomness: The Hidden Role of Chance in Life and in the Markets*, 2nd edn, New York, NY: Penguin Books.

Taleb, N.N. (2007) *The Black Swan: The Impact of the Highly Improbable*, New York, NY: Random House.

Toxic Textbooks (no date) [website archive] <http://archive.is/QAdXL> [accessed 21 January 2014].

Ziegler, J. (2008) 'Report of the Special Rapporteur on the right to food, Jean Ziegler', A/HRC/7/5, Geneva: United Nations Human Rights Council <www.righttofood.org/wp-content/uploads/2012/09/AHRC75.pdf> [accessed 20 January 2014].

CHAPTER 28

Flying on the wings of my soul: self-discovery journeys

Talent Ntombi Nyathi

Talent Ntombizanele Nyathi *is a Grail woman and the current director of the Training for Transformation course in South Africa. She co-founded Africa Community Publishing and Development Trust (ACPDT), an organization that focuses on using research and writing as tools for development, and was its National Director for nine years. Ntombi founded Africa Book Development Trust, an organization that focuses on setting up rural libraries in Zimbabwe. She is an experienced international participatory development facilitator who worked with the World Bank and European Union projects in Zimbabwe.*

Birds will flock to a fruitful tree.   *Senegalese proverb*

Who am I? When am I? How am I? Why is it so difficult to talk about myself?

These are the questions that I struggled with when I was asked to contribute a chapter to this book. I experienced contention within myself. As I try to connect with the 'self', I feel like I am running a race from within. As I run, I realize that I am seeking my voice. The dramas of life and the fatigue of the race are too noisy for me to hear this voice. It is only when I stop running, in those moments of stillness, that I connect with the voice. Then, I not only feel a bond with the voice, I also realize that in this space I can hear my heart beating. I could dance to its sounds as I would to music. I have found myself. I now have an identity. I am aware of my purpose. I am injected with new energy to actualize my potential. I feel I am becoming something new. I could stretch my wings and my soul could fly.

Exploring my journey to 'self'-awareness, my discussion is clustered in three sections:

- First, the 'seeker': in this segment, I explore personal experiences that have been spiritual and transformative.
- Second, 'belonging': in this, I share the values and principles that shaped the transformation within me.
- Third, 'becoming': a cluster in which I weave the 'seeker' and 'belonging' with the practical being.

Even though self-awareness journeys are interior, it is important to recognize that other people with whom we engage can impart life-changing experiences that help us to seek purposefully. My discussions will highlight the experiences and conversations that I have had with other people.

The seeker

I recall the first time I engaged with Training for Transformation (TfT). I was angry with the world around me. I felt I was uprooted from my purpose. The anger within me was projected towards others with whom I interacted. One of my mentors pointed out, three years later, that the first day I walked into the hall I was fat, dark, angry, and ugly. This was all true then. I felt as if events were claws, ready to dig deep into my skin, causing unbearable pain. For this reason I needed to defend myself, to make my voice the loudest. I wanted the facilitators to listen to 'me', to share my pain, even if I did not disclose the details. I set conditions for staying on the course. If the conditions were not met, I wanted to leave. I was not sure of what I was seeking at the Grail Centre.

One of the facilitators invited me to her room. She shared with me her stories of pain, seeking and finding meaning on her journey. 'When one door closes before you, turn around. You will be surprised to see that another door has opened. Have the courage to take that first step, and get out of caging your self. This is the myth caging our lives as women in the struggle.' Thelma Awori was not aware that this conversation changed my life. I left the room smiling within. The first people whom I met on my way out asked me what the good news was, because I was vibrating. I learned from this conversation that I had the responsibility to name and shape the future that I wanted. I designed long- and short-term goals. When I wrote my 'eulogy' during the course, I learned to name the things that I wanted to achieve. Stephen Covey's suggestion that 'beginning with the end in mind would make us better achievers' resonates with me.

One of the TfT participants, Sasha, tried writing eulogies with people in her community. More than half of the young people she was interacting with were HIV positive. The group broke down, and that ended the exercise. When she phoned to explain the situation, I realized that a process that might be deeply meaningful to people in some situations might be totally inappropriate in others. Self-awareness cannot be packaged and passed on to people. It is a journey that can be encouraged externally. However, each individual takes the responsibility to walk the rest of the journey. In Sasha's experience, even those who were HIV negative could not complete the exercise. The challenge is to live in constant awareness of when to say 'yes' or 'no'. If we do not become aware of our response, we may live a life where we say 'yes' to others and 'no' to ourselves.

I grew up in a village where girls were referred to as 'nobodies'. When a woman succeeds in life, they refer to her as a female 'male'. I am not sure if I yet comprehend the full meaning of this. These were some of the cages out of which I had already walked. I believed then that I had soared above the storms and had set up ways of demonstrating that girl children are worthy of respect. I love my traditional name, 'Ntombizanele', translated as 'a woman of worth'. I am a mature woman, but as I journey I recognize that horizons are never reached. They always stretch out further. I journey towards new horizons all through my life. I constantly seek to connect with my calling, and I am prepared to die for it should circumstances demand that. This is the inspiration that I got from Nelson Mandela, Mahatma Gandhi, and many others. To get to this level of awareness, I believe that humans need to search for deeper meaning linked to our belief in providence.

As a child, I prayed because I feared the punishment that awaited me in hell. As I matured through the experiences of life, I became aware that spending time exploring the 'self' took me to higher levels of consciousness and closer to God. The God experience significantly shaped some of the transformative journeys of my life. A friend of mine was perplexed by my commitment to holding conversations with God. He confronted me: 'What is challenging you in life that makes you so passionate about this "God thing" of yours?' I responded that I was seeking to understand my 'self'. Deepak Chopra could not have been more right when he suggested that to know God is to know oneself. Transformation takes place when the 'self' is brought into harmony with its purpose in life. When we connect with our purpose, we identify with the values it demands.

We move from the individual to the collective. 'I am because we are.' It would be wrong to assume that the journeys from the individual to the collective are always harmonious. I struggle inwardly when I share my 'River of Life' with TfT groups. The groups struggle with that too. I recall an experience when TfT participants declined to do the 'River of Life' exercise. One said, 'I know myself. Why should I draw a river to tell my story?'

I understood later that these participants had a painful past that they were not ready to share. As we seek self-knowledge, we confront our fears, we name them, we create space to turn the fears into opportunities that bond us to our calling. I do believe that my life is measured by the quest I choose. I create landmarks that guide my journey by paying attention to the following insights:

- The seeker may project anger and frustration onto the people with whom they interact, because it is easier to blame others than to face one's own limitations. The challenge for the seeker is to identify and name not only moments of awakening, but also individuals who can inspire her to find her own voice.

When seekers become visible to their own 'self', each knowing 'I am', then they also become visible to others: 'we are'. They identify and develop value-based relationships, make connections, and journey towards new horizons.

I dedicate the previous section, investigating relationships, to those who influenced my spiritual transformation.

Belonging – I am because we are

TfT brings together participants of diverse religious beliefs. The first two weeks are designed to harmonize relationships among participants. The first day uses processes that help people to embrace, appreciate, and celebrate religious diversity. During one of the opening rituals, a Christian young woman reached out for the Koran placed in the centre of the room. This was the first time she had seen the Koran. A Muslim young woman felt the need to protect the Holy Book. 'Do not touch the Holy Book! You are dirty and you will die,' she screamed. The Christian woman exploded: 'In the name of Jesus, I will touch it, and cleanse it!'

Adelina Mwau and I were confronted with this situation. We tried our best to keep the peace. For three weeks the two young women kept their distance from each other. In the fourth week of the TfT diploma course, the module is on spirituality. I had asked Donal Dorr to come and facilitate the sessions. Donal could not come. He sent us his latest publication, *Spirituality: Our Deepest Heart's Desire*. I approached Father Xavier, who was also a participant on the course. Our conversations with him assisted participants to understand spirituality as the highest level of understanding of the 'self' and its purpose.

After the session, the young women joined mass celebrations. When we evaluated the course, the spirituality module scored highest. 'I felt the need to defend my religion. Now I realize that I practise Islam because that is the way I connect with God. I am challenged to respect the different ways other people connect with God too.' This young woman went back to her community, in which she was a local councillor, and started going with people to their places of worship.

How do we know if we are in communion with God? I believe that life is a process of finding answers. It is imperative to explore the values that attract us to God.

When God is defined for us by others, we lose meaning. We connect neither with ourselves nor with God. One day I visited a place of worship with two friends. I was shocked when I learned that in this place the service would not commence until they had 10 men. I watched these women counting men as they walked in. What are the people in this place seeking? What keeps these women coming to this place? Change begins the moment we ask questions; only then can we live meaningfully.

Our journeys should not be clouded by fundamentalist religious beliefs that may be detrimental to our spiritual growth. We should connect with people who share our moral values. It is for this reason that I joined the Grail Women's Movement. The Grail connects and celebrates the divine through service. 'What ails you, the king, the society?' This the key question in the Grail legend.

My first encounter with the Grail was with a woman named Kathy Bond-Stewart. I loved her heart. She was simple and the most genuine so-called 'white' person that I had met. We visited one of the remotest parts of the country. The women sat quietly and would not talk in meetings. We followed them to the river. Women started swimming in the river. Kathy undressed and jumped into the water. So did I. The laughter and shouting were beyond imagination. The river opened up the women, and they started to tell their stories. What did the women see in us that they connected with? This experience showed me that values expressed in the simplest possible manner can be life-changing. Connections can be offered and received through small but significant interactions.

After our spiritual discussions in TfT, one of the participants, Rehema, a Muslim woman, went back to her country and initiated joint prayers between Christians and Muslims for a school that she believed was haunted. This initiative led to peaceful co-existence between formerly rival groups of Christians and Muslims in the community. Personal transformation can be meaningless unless it is shared to create communities based on principled practice.

The most significant learning about 'belonging' could be summarized as follows:

- Self-awakening happens when we identify with intentional communities that complement the core values that shape our lives.
- We identify with a range of diverse values-based religious practices that have the potential to nurture life and bond us with the divine within, around, and beyond us.
- We are called to live in constant awareness that God transcends all religions, and religion should be based not only on the search for God but also on the moral values of the common good.
- Writing a journal is a significant way of holding transformative conversations with God.
- Retreats are spaces that allow contemplative reflection that enhances both the individual's and the community's capacity to harmonize relationships and inform spiritually guided actions in the future.

Becoming – paths are made by walking

Actions are the means through which we translate our values into practical service for others and enhance our own experiences. I worked with rural communities in Zimbabwe for more than 15 years. The first time I visited the villages I was warned that the old women from the other villages were witches. I was not supposed to eat any food that they offered. We engaged an artist to work with the old women 'witches' to write folk stories from their culture. After the books were published, the old women took turns to tell the stories and play games with children in schools. They assumed a new identity as teachers. They introduced themselves as writers too. Five years later, the witch stories were heard no more. There is something that happens from inside us that is so strong that once we discover the 'self', nothing can defeat us. Labi Siffre was right when he sang that there is something inside so strong that it enables the 'self' to rise above all barriers. The experience of awakening brings understanding that the 'self' needs to be expressed in action. These women were transformed by responding to the challenge to 'read their reality' and rewrite their own history. Freire was prophetic in pointing out that when people 'read their reality' they begin to take transformative actions that lead to rewriting their histories. The process enables people to become 'subjects and not objects of their destiny'.

I experienced claiming my destiny when I got into a disagreement with two of my mentors, Sally Timmel and Carol Webb. Sally came up with new thoughts all the time. My first reaction was resistance. 'I do not want her to define my life.' As time passed, I realized that she was pushing me towards new horizons. I wanted to work with community development only, but she insisted that I do TfT too. I was angry. I wanted to leave again. She took us through the Myers-Briggs typology of personality. I learned through this exercise that I could do many things if I committed myself to taking action. Carol Webb used the word 'multitasking'. We planned our activities down to the smallest detail and got everything done within the agreed timeframe. The two mentors helped transform me into an independent person in my work. I do not leave things to chance. I plan and am innovative. I acknowledge the role of mentors and coaches in my life. The manner in which mentorship is practised should enhance the mentee's ability to take independent decisions.

I assumed TfT leadership in 2009. In previous years, one diploma course was run over a year and a half, training 36 people. By 2013, TfT was offering three different levels of training – introductory, certificate, and diploma courses – that involve more than 200 people annually. New relationships are formed with funding partners and civil society organizations from around the world. The essential point here is that transformation, becoming what one is destined to be, is born out of the challenges that take us out of old routines. Moving out of our comfort zones makes us scared and confused because we fear making mistakes. I feel I need other people to support me. Anne Hope and Ina Conradie accompanied me on my intellectual and spiritual journey into the Grail. Discussions with these two women helped me to rise above my fears. When I use the 'River of Life' with groups, I note that fear can be a block. I always have to tell my story first. Thereafter, the group feels comfortable to share their stories. Sharing my vulnerability with people builds trusts and creates relationships. The more I share my story, the closer I remain to the 'self'. In fact, I find love for myself and in the process I find love for God.

The first conscious and transformative 'God experience' happened during a retreat facilitated by Father Roger with the Grail. We discussed the female characters in the Bible. Among these were the widow who gave her last mite, and Mary and Martha. I started writing down my conversations with God in a journal after this retreat. These conversations constitute powerful prayers for me. I create space to be in communion with God on my own. Creating spaces is important. The Grail creates spaces that enable people to express the insights and principles that influence their lives, their search, and their service.

I celebrate the new person that I have become. I recognize that 'becoming' will always be part of my journey, right till the end. I continue to ask questions, and I live in such a way that the answers will come. Through this practice I find my calling, I connect with my maker, give life, and serve the common good. These practices and questions are the wings of my soul upon which I fly towards self-actualization.

Afterword

Anne Hope and Sally Timmel

Worrying is like a rocking chair: it swings you back and forth and takes you nowhere. *Kenyan proverb*

How effective is Training for Transformation? This is the question we have been asking ourselves for years.

As we listened to all the stories of the TfT practitioners who gathered at the Grail Centre in Kleinmond during September, and as we read the chapters they wrote during those days about their work, the answer came across loud and clear. It all depends on the quality of leadership and commitment of those running the programmes.

Growth in leadership takes time. Many of the skills people learn in TfT are valuable. They enable them to hold and sustain the interest of groups of people. Skills can be picked up on short courses, but that deep change of heart that lies at the core of a long-term commitment, especially a commitment to the well-being of those who have been discriminated against and marginalized, those who have been made to feel they simply don't matter – that type of leadership takes longer to acquire.

That kind of commitment requires not only skills but also deep personal self-knowledge. It needs the support of a safe community with other people who honour the same values, who are looking in the same direction, people who can both challenge and support you. It needs openness to both giving and receiving gentle but honest feedback. It needs a process, a cycle of action and reflection, daring to take action, to reflect critically on one's action, and to make changes where necessary before acting again. It needs the curiosity to search for deeper understanding of a community's needs and alternative ways in which others have solved similar problems. Such commitment needs the willingness to stick with the group even during failures, learning from these failures and helping others to do so too. It needs a deep sense of personal value, and the occasional recognition and celebration of your achievements, in order to persevere. It takes time and longer training, especially for young people, to grow in such leadership.

http://dx.doi.org/10.3362/9781780448312.010

More and more, we are convinced that TfT can be a superb way of fostering such leadership, especially on the longer courses. Where a really committed person has used the approach, in a particular context, and in a sustained way over many years, it has really brought about profound changes in the quality of life of a community, sometimes even in the culture as a whole, and in the laws. This is true of the Dalits and the Adivasis in Gujarat, the rural farmers in the Eastern Cape, some of the poor Irish communities around Dublin, the Maasai through the Neighbourhoods Initiative Alliance in Kenya, and in many village people and some government officials in Zimbabwe, to name but a few examples.

Another insight affirmed by these stories was that 'outsiders' and 'insiders' play very different roles in this education process. Both are essential. The outsiders tend to be 'catalysts', stirring a community out of old habits and routines. They enable the community to see new possibilities. Their role is primarily to find and foster leadership within the community. The 'insiders', those who are working with their own people, hopefully for long periods of time in the same area, with the same community, these are the people who can really bring about deep cultural change, important legal changes, practical economic opportunities, and a more fulfilling quality of life. Of course, to some extent, at different times, we are all both 'insiders' and 'outsiders'.

As Shakespeare says in *Twelfth Night*, 'Some are born great; some achieve greatness; and some have greatness thrust upon them.' Many of the leaders in these programmes would certainly not believe that they were born great, but they have had great demands thrust upon them as they began to feel responsibility for the well-being of their people. The TfT process has helped them to grow in leadership, and has enabled them to assist in the transformation of other people and to build happier communities.

APPENDIX
Tools to assess the impact of Training for Transformation work

An impact assessment is a tool that is useful for reflection, learning, and re-planning developmental activity. The impact assessment tools presented here are useful for Training for Transformation philosophy and practice with regard to its work with individuals, organizations, and communities. The process was developed by teams that focused on those three areas. We recognize and acknowledge that these tools have to be adapted for each user and for the environment in which they operate. The use of these tools will nevertheless mirror the TfT methodology embedded in the Freirean practice of social and structural analysis. This includes the process of listening surveys and group discussions, and the host of techniques, including plays, pictures, stories, music, and dance, as articulated in the TfT books and other sources.

Assessing the impact of TfT on individuals

Objective: to develop and to trigger critical consciousness in individuals through a process of reflection and action. The planned output is 'self-realization', engaging in a process of self-discovery.

The core objective of TfT programmes is to stimulate or provoke participants to interpret and deepen their understanding of their realities. To this end, TfT uses a range of methodologies to engage participants in a process of self-discovery to question various facets of their lives, with a view to effecting the renewal of their being and becoming. The tools aim to evoke consciousness of one's 'self' and surroundings – family, community, workplace, the natural environment, nation, and the divine order of the universe. By provoking deep thinking on these spheres of life, participants are called on to create a space conducive to reflection and action. It is envisaged that this tool will be used for personal reflection and face-to-face discussions and in organizations.

To tap into their life journeys, the tools engage participants in seeking answers to the following questions:

- Who are you?
- Who were you?
- Who are you now?
- Where are you now?
- How do you make sense of all this to move forward?
- In what ways has TfT changed the way you work?
- In what ways has TfT changed the way you relate/connect with others/the earth?
- What are the evolving traditions of change in you since you got involved in TfT?
- What are the challenges that you now see that you were not previously aware of?
- Where do you feel you have added value in your own life, your community, or your organization?
- What new knowledge, learning, or insights have you gained through TfT?
- What have you discovered about transformational change?

Inputs

- River of Life (also called the Journey of My Life; see Training for Transformation Book 2: 22)
- Tree of Life (see Book 2: 38)

- Handprint (author unknown)
- Johari's Window (see Book 2: 65)
- Personality traits (Myers-Briggs typology of personalities)
- 'Aha!' moments (author unknown)
- Potato Exercise (see Book 2: 41)
- Spirituality (see Book 1: Chapter 1)
- Healing Woundedness (narrative therapy)

Outcomes

- The power of the voice/assertiveness
- Creating and claiming spaces
- Taking a stand in favour of the poor (TfT philosophy)
- Identifying our core human values
- Approaching issues and challenges in our society with an analytical mind
- Being grounded and anchored in a set of values that encompasses the central ideas in TfT
- Cultivating an ethic of mentorship
- Opening minds

Impact on leadership

- Capacity to mobilize human and material resources
- Introduction of initiatives and innovations
- Creation of role models and mentors
- Establishment and expansion of networks of co-operation and actions on more specific social, economic, and political issues
- Establishing the credibility of acting according to ethical norms
- Good communication skills

Assessing the impact of TfT on organizations

Objective: to assess the impact of TfT on our organizations.

Bearing in mind that organizations play a vital role in extending the TfT philosophy and approach to local communities and other groups, it is important that the core values of TfT are present in the life of these organizations. While the unique character of each organization is respected with its specific aims and range of activities, there are certain essential aspects that need to be taken into account for a healthy and productive working culture to be developed and sustained in the organization.

The tool for measuring the impact of TfT on organizations proposes three major dimensions that a TfT-focused organization needs to reflect on and to review on a regular basis. These are people and relationships, approaches, and operational structure (Figure 29.1). These three aspects are rooted in the core TfT values of justice, participation, and wellness, which are to be seen from a holistic perspective. Depending on the organization's size and scope, the tool can be used both at and between different levels in the organization.

It is acknowledged that organizations are made up of individuals, each of whom will have their own level of commitment to TfT. The purposes of this tool should be seen not only as a measuring stick for TfT impact in the life of the organization, but also as a process of deepening commitment to TfT core values at the levels of both the organization and the staff members engaged in promoting their use in the life of communities and other groups.

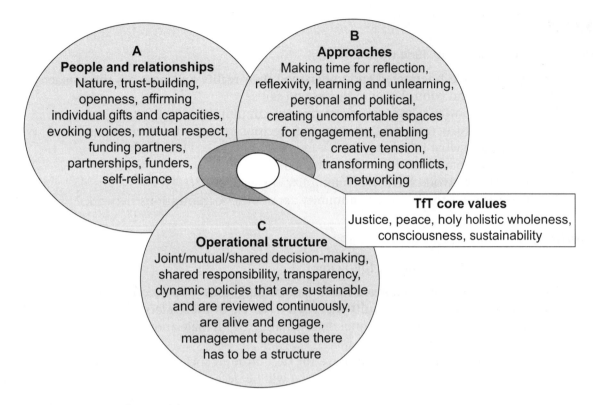

The assessment tool framework

It is envisaged that sufficient time will be set aside during the work programme to do justice to the importance of these internal aspects of an organization's or department's life. It is suggested that 5 per cent of work time or one day per month could be devoted to this.

The tool includes questions about the ways in which TfT affects the internal organizational culture and practices with regard to: people and relationships; approaches; internal operational structure; and any other dimensions that are not captured under these three headings.

Assessing the impact of TfT at community level

TfT is meant to help communities realize, reaffirm, and expand their potential to start questioning systems and choosing alternatives, and to interact with each other for the better good of the community.

TfT is based on a commitment to the value of participation and inclusion in the social, political, economic, environmental, and cultural aspects of life.

It is envisaged that the tools and processes selected from those listed below will be used creatively to measure the impact of TfT on groups and communities in suggested generic categories. Some or all of the following tools and processes could be applied according to the circumstances of the group: case study, interviews, listening surveys, focus group discussions, questionnaires, role plays, observations, statistics gathering, and research.

In all the categories listed below, the following question applies: 'In what ways have particular elements of TfT methodology been significant in the change that has occurred?' An open question is affirming and empowering and often uses the words 'what' and 'how', while asking for multiple examples stretches imagination and creativity.

Social

Helpful questions might include the following:

- How have women interpreted and understood their reality and how has this impacted on their access to and control over resources and skills?
- What shifts in power/roles have occurred in the community?
- What are the structures and practices of decision-making in your community? Who participates and what has changed?
- What networks have been built and sustained?
- What existing networks have the community engaged with?
- What awareness is there in the community about other organizations/networks?

Political

Helpful questions might include the following:

- How has the community changed its ways of holding leadership accountable?
- To what extent has the community increased its access to the leadership?
- To what extent has intergenerational representation (both male and female) been taken care of in the community?
- What vision does the community have for the future of society and how does it view its participation in influencing the changes that will be necessary?

Environmental

Helpful questions might include the following:

- How well has the community been aware of the value of its environment?
- What new initiatives have been undertaken by the community to protect the environment?
- What concrete benefits have community members enjoyed as a result of the new initiatives?
- To what extent has the community influenced other surrounding communities/institutions?

Economic

Helpful questions might include the following:

- To what extent has the community influenced local budget allocations?
- How have community members participated in the budgeting process?
- How have community members been using livelihood opportunities that exist in their area?
- To what extent have corporations been involved in community welfare?

Cultural

Helpful questions might include the following:

- How has the process helped the group to claim its identity and dignity?
- How has the community validated the diversity of cultures in its groups (recognizing that expressions of culture relating to intergeneration, ability, gender, etc. need to be validated).

Spiritual (questions around fears and hopes)

Helpful questions might include the following:

- How does the community celebrate the spiritualities present within it?
- How is the emotional intelligence of both individuals and the group nurtured in its expressions?
- What are the fears that surround the experience and expression of emotional situations?

- What are the things that community members hope TfT can help them to have or achieve? Which group is most concerned by these things?
- What are the concerns that community members have regarding TfT in their community? Which group is most concerned by these things?

These tools were devised by:

Annika Schabbauer

Rebecca Macugay

Bunmi Ekundayo

Evernice Munando

Gihad Adam Eissa

Gildo Nhapuala

Kenny Matampash

Lean Heng

Loretta Joseph

Matrine M. Mazyondo

Paul Bushayija

Richard Walsh

Rita Stukwasa

Shula Mafokoane

Three poems

Maasai blessing

To all of you – people of good spirits.

May our ancestors and the spirit of our Mother Earth strengthen your commitment to this noble initiative of Training for Transformation.

Naai ... may all of us be connected with nature ...

Naai ... may the struggle continue with a lot of compassion and humility ...

Naai ... may the founders be blessed always and forever ...

Naai.

We met as strangers, but we departed as true friends!!

Given by Kenny Matampash, September 2013

The sparks and flame of Training for Transformation

The Sparks

The flame circled,
    by countries,
      cultures,
        backgrounds,
          depth. ...
    accepting ... supporting ... respecting
No matter whence, the same path.

Small candles lit: symbols spread round:
    fire and water,
      hands joined, people connected,
        bridges, birds, spirals, waterfalls.

The sparks expressed ...
    ~ openness, zest for life ...
      ~ love of self and human kind ...
    ~ commitment to the marginalized ...
      ~ passion for change ...
    ~ courage and perseverance ...
      ~ vision ...
    ~ silence, reflection ...
      ~ deep listening, empathy ...
    ~ power from within ...
      ~ relation-creating power ...
    ~ fullness of life.
Creating with people
    ~ the common force in all life
      ~ eco-spirituality
    ~ life connections
      ~ energy in movement.

A hundred candles ... all lit from one flame.

The Flame

Training for transformation
    ~ gathered around the cherished flame,
        giving … receiving … sharing light
    ~ friendships, mentoring,
        self and others transforming
    ~ suffering caused by people,
        yet positively-changed people
    ~ the voiceless and powerless
        discovering new ideas
            learning to make a difference
                through this powerful wholistic methodology.

A guiding compass
    ~ to bring light to every dark place
        ~and healing
    ~ creating the space
        for people, pulsating potential, to dream
    ~ evolving consciousness
        trust in the divine
    ~ striving together for justice, equality and peace
        providing the blank page
            on which 'to make all things new'
    The spreading light of love.

Created by Kathy Bond-Stewart and Brother Richard Walsh at the Think Well called Training for Transformation in Practice, September 2013.

Where the mind is without fear

Where the mind is without fear and the head is held high;

Where knowledge is free;

Where the world has not been broken up into fragments by narrow domestic walls;

Where words come out from the depth of truth;

Where tireless striving stretches its arms towards perfection;

Where the clear stream of reason has not lost its way into the dreary desert sand of dead habit;

Where the mind is led forward by thee into ever-widening thought and action;

Into that heaven of freedom, my Father, let my country awake.

from Gitanjali *by Rabindranath Tagore*